# COLLISION COURSE

# COLLISION COURSE

## Economic Change, Criminal Justice Reform, and Work in America

KATHLEEN AUERHAHN

RUTGERS UNIVERSITY PRESS

New Brunswick, Camden, and Newark, New Jersey, and London

Library of Congress Cataloging-in-Publication Data
Names: Auerhahn, Kathleen, 1970- author.
Title: Collision course: economic change, criminal justice reform, and work in
    America / Kathleen Auerhahn.
Description: New Brunswick: Rutgers University Press, [2022] | Includes
    bibliographical references and index.
Identifiers: LCCN 2021011645 | ISBN 9781978817968 (paperback) |
    ISBN 9781978817975 (cloth) | ISBN 9781978817982 (epub) |
    ISBN 9781978817999 (mobi) | ISBN 9781978818002 (pdf)
Subjects: LCSH: Labor supply—United States. | Criminal justice, Administration
    of—United States. | United States—Economic conditions.
Classification: LCC HD5724 .A92 2022 | DDC 330.973—dc23
LC record available at https://lccn.loc.gov/2021011645

A British Cataloging-in-Publication record for this book is available from the British
Library.

References to internet websites (URLs) were accurate at the time of writing. Neither
the author nor Rutgers University Press is responsible for URLs that may have expired
or changed since the manuscript was prepared.

♾ The paper used in this publication meets the requirements of the American
National Standard for Information Sciences—Permanence of Paper for Printed
Library Materials, ANSI Z39.48-1992.

www.rutgersuniversitypress.org

Manufactured in the United States of America

For Alex

# CONTENTS

# CONTENTS

# COLLISION COURSE

# 1 · THE CONTOURS
## OF THE PROBLEM

This book is about the trajectories of two societal institutions that are converging in such a way that if this collision course is left unchecked, severe consequences for American society will result. These two institutions are the economy and the criminal justice system. The United States economy has changed in profound and permanent ways that are inconsistent with the outmoded yet still dominantly orthodox beliefs about the nature and place of work in contemporary American life. Simply put, the U.S. economy is increasingly unable to fulfill one of its primary functions—utilizing the labor of all able-bodied, working-age Americans. The analyses of labor market conditions presented in this book will show the following: the labor market has undergone severe polarization in the past several decades, resulting in increasing inequality; that job openings in all sectors of the economy are exceeded by the number of job seekers; that the labor force participation rate has declined significantly in the past two decades, most dramatically among prime working-age men; and that the reasons for these conditions derive from technological change and fundamental changes in developed economies that have profound implications for the future of employment dynamics in the United States.

Despite the feel-good political capital generated in some quarters by the rallying cry to "bring jobs back," the jobs that have been lost to automation and outsourcing will *not* return. All of these facts, taken together, demonstrate that we have entered a new era—one where increasing numbers of "working-age" adults simply cannot find employment—or cannot find employment that provides a sufficient income. In purely functional economic terms, the transformation of the American economy has resulted in increased productivity and wealth that is not dependent on human labor—rendering increasing numbers of would-be workers economically superfluous.

In the past forty years, the American criminal justice system has also undergone radical transformation. The United States is frequently characterized as unique among developed nations. One area in which this is unquestionably true is in the size and scope of our criminal justice system, in particular our use of incarceration. We imprison a larger proportion of our population than any nation in the world. Despite being home to less than 5 percent of the world's population, the United States houses 25 percent of the world's prisoners. In just four decades— following a century of stability in the size of the prison population—the United States has amassed the largest prison population in the developed world, at the time of this writing housing approximately 1.4 million adults in state and federal correctional facilities (Figure 1.1; Kang-Brown et al., 2020).

The reach and scope of American criminal justice is perhaps unfathomable for those in other countries. The exponential growth of the American criminal justice system that took place between the late 1970s and the end of the first decade of the twenty-first century is unprecedented. This expansion has been profoundly shaped by the American experience with respect to race, by the nature of the focus of American criminal justice on street crime, and by the geographically focused nature of urban policing; this confluence of historically specific circumstances has manifested profound impacts in many other areas of American society. The unique problems created by the confluence of criminal justice reform and economic transformation in the United States—given the character of the social welfare safety net (punitive and ungenerous) and the criminal justice system (prominent and extremely influential in other societal domains)—place the United States in an exceptional position with respect to the consequences of the intersection of these two institutional trajectories.

While mass incarceration grabs the headlines, it is important to recognize that all forms of criminal justice intervention have swelled in the last half century. There are now nearly five times as many American adults under restrictive community supervision as there are in prisons. In 2009, a widely publicized analysis from the Pew Charitable Trusts reported that one in thirty-one U.S. adults, or approximately seven million individuals, were under some form of criminal justice system supervision. This state of affairs has prompted some observers to describe the contemporary situation as "mass supervision" (Phelps, 2016, 2018; Miller & Stuart, 2017; McNeill, 2018).

Recently, the American criminal justice system has been evolving in ways that are likely to halt or reverse the spectacular growth of the prison population seen over the past four decades. A number of current reform movements in criminal justice have among their goals reducing the prison population; these include the proliferation of diversion programs and specialized courts, increased attention and resources devoted toward improving reentry outcomes, and drug policy reform. Changes in criminal justice policy and practice in each of these reform domains are currently working to facilitate the movement of the justice-involved from prisons to communities and to keep these individuals from returning once released— resulting in more and more of the justice-involved living outside of prison walls. Recent developments in criminal justice policy and practice strongly suggest that the flow of justice-involved individuals from carceral institutions to communities will further strain a labor market that is already unable to productively use the labor of all who seek employment. This book describes some of the consequences that will accompany the accelerated production of such "extra people" if nothing is done to address it.

After decades of public indifference to rising prison populations and swelling correctional expenditures, critical awareness of the criminal justice system now seems to be at an all-time high. The reasons for this deserve a separate analysis, which is beyond the scope of this work. Certainly, the events widely broadcasted on social media in Ferguson, Missouri in the summer of 2014 elevated concerns about policing in minority communities to the forefront of the national discourse—much as the filmed assault of Rodney King by the Los Angeles police did in 1991 (see Cobbina, 2019; Lowery, 2016). The events in Ferguson, as well as many recent controversial incidents involving the police, have fostered a growing awareness of problems *throughout* the system—policing, the courts, and prisons. Popular books such as *The New Jim Crow* (Alexander, 2012) and television programs such as *The Wire, Making a Murderer*, and *Orange Is the New Black* further press these issues onto the national consciousness.

The warehousing of surplus population in prisons over the past four decades has served to insulate against the effects of contemporaneous changes in the labor market. The falling demand for labor has been partially offset by the removal of a substantial segment of the labor force through incarceration. Situated in the context of economic debates about the effects of labor market regulation on employment dynamics in the 1980s and 1990s, sociologists Bruce Western and Katherine Beckett present an analysis that directly addresses claims made by free-market proponents that attribute low U.S. unemployment to the lack of government regulation in the labor market, in comparison to the higher rates of unemployment seen in more highly regulated European economies. They demonstrate that high rates of incarceration have masked the true extent of economic dislocation in the short term by removing large numbers of able-bodied men of prime working age from the labor force. However, over the long term, mass incarceration serves to *increase* unemployment as a result of the barriers faced by former prisoners in obtaining employment post-release. These authors characterize the expansion of the U.S. criminal justice system as a "large and coercive intervention into the labor market" and conclude that "strong US employment in the 1980s and 1990s has thus depended in part on a high and increasing incarceration rate … sustained low unemployment will depend on continuing expansion of the penal system" (Western & Beckett, 1999, pp. 1030–1031). With waning popular support for what is increasingly seen as a broken system, coupled with the fiscal constraints facing state and federal governments, this avenue no longer appears the viable release valve it once was. If current trends in criminal justice reform continue apace, we will have more and more members of society living *outside* the confines of prison walls. Even more working-age adults will be in the labor force, competing for the same dwindling pool of available jobs. This can't end well.

## CRISIS, OPPORTUNITY, AND CHOICES

This book grew out of a simple thought experiment. Having spent more than two decades engaged in criminal justice policy research, I am well aware that a proportion of our population cycles in and out of correctional institutions over the course of their lives. This population contains many individuals who suffer from multiple social and economic deficits that severely limit their chances of successful and full participation in American society. This population goes by a variety of names. Depending on the context, we call them career criminals, frequent fliers, and heavy cross-system users. Criminologist John Irwin described this segment of the population as "the rabble" in his seminal 1985 book *The Jail: Managing the Underclass in American Society*, observing that the individuals who come to be locked up "share two essential characteristics: detachment and disrepute. They are detached because they are not well integrated into conventional society, they are not members of conventional social organizations, they have few ties to conventional social networks, and they are carriers of unconventional values and beliefs. They are disreputable because they are perceived as irksome, offensive, threatening . . . the 'lowest class of people'" (p. 2). We shall return to this later.

I also know from my experience working as a criminal justice policy researcher that estimates of the average yearly cost of housing a prisoner range between $30,000 and $60,000 per year. My long-standing interests in poverty, inequality, welfare, and social control—and the relationships among all of these things—led me to the question, *might it be less expensive for governments to simply provide economically for a hypothetical individual over the course of his life than it would be to house him in prison several times over that lifetime?* From this followed other questions such as, where is the break-even point? How many episodes of incarceration does it take to make it less expensive to simply give the money directly to the individual, bypassing the criminal justice system altogether? Might doing so actually reduce the incidence of crime? Could this crisis be the opportunity to reverse the trend of growing inequality, and for Americans to think seriously about citizenship rights? How can we pay for it? The book you are presently reading came about in an effort to learn the answers to these questions.

As I delved into my research on the economy and the criminal justice system, what I learned fostered a growing sense of alarm. The collateral consequences of incarceration (and criminal justice contact more generally), among them barriers to employment, have been documented extensively by many researchers (e.g., Clear, 2007; Mauer & Chesney-Lind, 2002; Pager, 2007; Petersilia, 2009; Wakefield & Wildeman, 2014). As a result of the massive expansion of the criminal justice system over the last forty years, it is estimated that there are now approximately twenty million Americans with felony records; more than three times that—approximately one-third of the adult population—have a criminal record on file with a local, state, or federal agency (Council of Economic Advisers, 2016a; Eberstadt, 2016; Rodriguez & Emsellem, 2011). But as I learned more about labor market dynamics and economic trends in the past four decades, it became clear that it is not only former prisoners and other justice-involved individuals who will struggle to find work in today's and, more importantly, *tomorrow's* economy. The transformation of the American economy has displaced at least 20 percent of the adult working-age population (a conservative estimate, arrived at by summing the total officially reported unemployed and those involuntarily underemployed). Given the importance we attribute to work as the measure of an adult's worthiness in our culture, this forebodes serious trouble.

At the time of this writing, the world is facing the coronavirus (COVID-19) pandemic. The present is characterized by civil unrest and cultural conflicts, and the future direction of a great many American institutions, customs, and practices is uncertain. The pandemic has led to the most rapid and severe economic downturn ever experienced in the United States; millions of Americans are facing profound economic insecurity. The Coronavirus Aid, Relief, and Economic Security (CARES) Act, the largest package of economic relief in U.S. history, was passed by the 116th Congress in March 2020. Totaling $2.2 trillion, the CARES Act allocated $560 billion for economic assistance to individuals. While the allocations for business-oriented relief amounted to twice the amount provided to individuals in the form of extended unemployment benefits and direct economic stimulus payments, the inclusion of these provisions seems to acknowledge that sometimes governments simply need to *give people money*. The long-term consequences of the COVID-19 pandemic to the American economy remain to be seen, but it is likely that the economic contraction taking place at the time of this writing will be felt for a long time, transforming the relationship even more Americans have with the formal labor market. Advances in automation are likely to supplant human labor at an increased pace in light of the dangers and inefficiencies of the socially distanced workplace, leaving more and more Americans without work.

There seems no better time to view the crisis we now face as a result of the convergence of trends in the American economy and the American criminal justice system as an opportunity to rethink outmoded ideas about the economy, human nature, and the causes of criminal behavior, as well as antiquated and frankly harmful ideals of industry, masculinity, and the basis of social worth and deservedness of the rights of citizenship. If we are willing to let go of some of our less useful ideas about work itself, as well as similarly unhelpful (and false) ideas about welfare and assistance, and allow for the consideration of some new ideas, real societal transformation is within our grasp.

## THE COSTS OF HEGEMONIC VIEWS ABOUT
## WORK AND WELFARE

Stemming from customs and beliefs retained by the British colonialists, work is seen as the "price of admission" to full participation in American society, and indeed, defining of an individual's value. This is particularly true for men, who are ideologically tasked with the role of provider, worker, breadwinner. The history of welfare policy in the United States illustrates these values quite clearly. These notions are evident in the colonialists' rejection of "outdoor relief" (direct cash transfers to the needy), in favor of almshouses and workhouses (of which the modern prison is a direct descendant), and in the categorization of relief recipients as "deserving" (women, children) or "undeserving" (able-bodied men), a practice that persists to this day. The degrading nature of welfare arrangements, embodied in the infamous "midnight raids" undertaken by caseworkers in the 1960s designed to ferret out violations of "man in the house" rules, the dismantling of the social welfare safety net in the 1990s and the linking of work requirements to the receipt of the limited economic relief that remains after these reforms also reflect these ideas. Economic assistance for "able-bodied, working-age" men is—and has always been—virtually nonexistent. In the twenty-first century, work is becoming increasingly scarce as well, particularly at the low end of the income distribution. In chapter 5, I consider the relationships among masculinity, work, poverty, and crime and come to some fairly obvious conclusions. When young men in urban communities need work and are unable to find it through legitimate means, the bustling illicit economies found in the same communities in which justice-involved individuals are overrepresented will provide it. The justice-involved face enormous difficulties in the labor market—difficulties that extend even beyond the plight of nonjustice-involved job seekers involved in the Sisyphean task of finding steady employment at a wage sufficient to support themselves and their families. Introducing greater numbers of such individuals into a labor market that is *already* unable to provide work to all job seekers will have predictable consequences.

## IMPLICATIONS OF THE SOCIAL STRUCTURE OF
## CRIMINAL JUSTICE

One of the most distinctive features of American criminal justice is its *concentration*. The expansion of the carceral state is concentrated within individuals, in families, and in communities. This is addressed in greater detail throughout this book; different dimensions of this concentration have different implications for the issues considered in this book.

The concentration of criminal justice at the community level shapes community-level responses to these impacts. One way this is manifested is in the sustained presence of thriving illicit economies, which serve to fill the gap for individuals who cannot support themselves with legal employment. The societal consequences of this are considered in greater depth in chapter 5.

The concentration of American criminal justice also has significant implications for the proposal I offer in chapter 6. The concentration of the collateral consequences of criminal justice involvement within individuals—whether we call them high-rate offenders, frequent fliers, or high-frequency cross-system users—means that a solution that addresses the extreme right-hand tail of the distribution could have much greater benefits relative to expenditures than might be assumed at first glance. This right-hand tail contains the small proportion of offenders who account for a large proportion of criminal justice expenditures. With respect to the subset of the population who suffer multiple and severe deficits—the "Million-Dollar Murrays" that Malcolm Gladwell wrote about in the *New Yorker* in 2006—the exposure liability associated with mental illness and substance abuse, combined with the very nature of the reform movements that characterize the present moment mean that a reorientation of intervention strategies could offer returns far in excess of what might be expected by thinking in terms of "average" or central tendency.

## THE CONSEQUENCES OF DENIAL

The consequences that can be expected if we continue to deny or ignore the colliding trajectories of the economy and the criminal justice system are far greater than increases in crime or increases in recorded unemployment figures. At least sixteen million Americans report being unemployed or involuntarily underemployed. Add to this the number of discouraged and marginally attached workers (1.3 million as of June 2020) and it is apparent that it is not only the justice-involved who struggle to survive in the "new economy." These individuals are thwarted by an economy that fails to provide a place for them to thrive and succeed. At the same time, they are subject to the judgment of a society that tells them they lack worth because of their inability to find a job—a society that also fails to provide any reasonable alternatives for these individuals to meet the basic necessities of living. Some of these individuals are becoming increasingly divorced from mainstream social institutions; many of these people support themselves and their families exclusively through illegal activities.

Places characterized by high rates of joblessness are also those with high rates of crime and thriving illicit economies that provide opportunities to generate income (e.g., Fader, 2013; Hagedorn, 1998; Venkatesh, 2006). Declining rates of labor force participation over successive cohorts—particularly for young men of color—speak to an entrenchment of these arrangements, manifested in the emergence of a *permanent criminal class*, increasingly divorced from mainstream social institutions, reproducing itself over successive generations.

Economist Glenn Loury (2008, pp. 20–21) identifies the production of what he calls a "nether caste of untouchables" as a result of the buildup of the carceral state:

Consider the nearly 60 percent of black male high school dropouts born in the late 1960s who are imprisoned before their fortieth year. While locked up, these felons are stigmatized—they are regarded as fit subjects for shaming. Their links to family are disrupted; their opportunities for work are diminished; their voting rights may be permanently revoked. They suffer civic excommunication. Our zeal for social discipline consigns these men to a permanent nether caste. And yet, since these men—whatever their shortcomings—have emotional and sexual and family needs, including the need to be fathers and loving husbands, we are creating a situation where the children of this nether caste are likely to join a new generation of untouchables. This cycle will continue so long as incarceration is viewed as the primary path to social hygiene.

For the past forty years, we have warehoused these "untouchables" in prison facilities as the carceral state expanded. However, current trends in criminal justice forebode a great many more of these individuals in our communities, searching for work to support themselves and their families. Criminal justice reform strategies currently under way that are designed to curtail or reverse the growth of prison populations, such as diversion, increased attention to the successful reentry of formerly incarcerated individuals, drug policy reform, and changes to sentencing and community supervision revocation procedures will simply add more people to compete for the dwindling pool of jobs at the bottom of the income distribution—jobs that even when they can be had, frequently only provide a below-poverty wage. If steps are not taken to respond to contemporary social and economic realities, which in large part resolve to the fact that there is no longer enough work to utilize the labor capacity of all working-age adults, and a lack of legitimate means to provide for their well-being and survival, what do we *expect* to happen?

For a growing segment of our population, "criminal justice has become a key way that citizens and communities interact with their state" (Weaver et al., 2014, p. 7). For some, it is virtually the *only* form of intercourse with governmental institutions. Sociologist Sarah Brayne's (2014, p. 383) work on *system avoidance* finds "a strong, robust, negative relationship between criminal justice contact and involvement with surveilling institutions such as hospitals, banks, employment, and school." Brayne's study reveals one of the formative mechanisms for the perpetuation of a permanent criminal class: "System avoidance and subsequent unequal institutional involvement may have real consequences for inequality. Given that involvement with the criminal justice system is highly stratified by race and class, the negative consequences of system avoidance will be similarly disproportionately distributed, thus exacerbating preexisting inequalities for an expanding group of already disadvantaged individuals. Furthermore, lack of attachment to important institutions leads to marginalization and impedes opportunities for financial security and upward mobility" (p. 385).

Research examining trends in *social exclusion* in the United States leads to a similar conclusion. Social exclusion is more than mere poverty or material insecurity; it is a multidimensional concept that encompasses a lack of access to basic necessities such as housing and food, access to health- and safety-related resources and institutions, and participation and engagement with political and social institutions. "Social exclusion precludes full participation in the normatively prescribed activities of a given society and denies access to information, resources, sociability, recognition, and identity, eroding self-respect and reducing capabilities to achieve personal goals" (Silver, 2007, p. 1).

Sociologists Holly Foster and John Hagan (2007, p. 401) report that "when defined as youth aged 18 to 24 who are neither employed nor in school, administrative data indicate that about 15 percent, or 3.8 million young adults, are institutionally disconnected in America" (see also Aguiar et al., 2017; Zelenev, 2011). Mass incarceration perpetuates and intensifies intergenerational social exclusion through processes of cumulative disadvantage (Pew Charitable Trusts, 2010; Wakefield & Wildeman, 2014).

Brayne's (2014, p. 386) analysis of system avoidance provides empirical evidence of the erosion of trust with mainstream social institutions in general and the ways in which these responses perpetuate social exclusion: "Involvement with the criminal justice system in young adulthood, therefore, can have a powerful effect on life trajectories; paternalistic contact with the state may lead people to avoid institutions that promote prosocial adult activity. Finally, institutional avoidance has yet another unanticipated consequence. . . . Attempts at social control through surveillance may actually fuel the very behaviors it is trying to suppress. When people go off the books, their attachment to institutions key to desistance from crime, such as formal employment, is undermined."

When the formal economy cannot provide a place for these individuals, crime is a logical consequence for some.

This is by no means a recent phenomenon. William Julius Wilson has documented the phenomenon and consequences of *social isolation* in communities characterized by concentrated poverty for more than thirty years. Writing in 1987, Wilson explains:

In such neighborhoods the chances are overwhelming that children will seldom interact in a sustained basis with people who are employed or with families that have a steady breadwinner. The net effect is that joblessness, as a way of life, takes on a different social meaning; the relationship between schooling and post-school employment takes on a different meaning. . . . A vicious cycle is perpetuated through the family, through the community, and through the schools. . . . In short, the communities of the underclass are plagued by massive joblessness, flagrant and open lawlessness, and low-achieving schools, and therefore tend to be avoided by outsiders. Consequently, the residents of these areas . . . have become increasingly socially isolated from mainstream patterns of behavior. (pp. 57–58)

As I worked on this project, I discussed it with friends and colleagues and presented on the work at academic conferences and other venues. I encountered many people who found the notion of a *permanent criminal class* in America problematic, disturbing. The notion seemed to make people uncomfortable. Time and again, it was suggested to me that the language was perhaps "too extreme." I disagree. I, too, would like to live in a country where it would be ludicrous to propose that such a thing was possible, but a deep examination of the dynamics, evolution, and collateral consequences of mass incarceration belies the premise of those who would dismiss the idea entirely. Considering the nature of the transformation of the American economy and the future economic prospects of a significant number of people in America, it seems difficult to deny that a permanent criminal class already exists in the United States, and not an incipient form. Ethnographers have been documenting the lives of the urban poor for decades. While this literature is diverse in terms of the focus and insights produced by each, it paints a picture of little social mobility, reliance on thriving illicit economies and sometimes predatory crime for the necessities of living. My point is that whether it causes us discomfort to admit it, a *permanent criminal class already exists in the United States.*

The concentrated nature of criminal justice means that these individuals and communities are easily identifiable and relatively few in number. These features can be seen as *opportunities* to effectively target interventions (Kennedy, 1997). While my proposal—a means-tested guaranteed basic income (GBI) for individuals unable to support themselves through legitimate employment—may seem radical, the concentrated nature of the population to whom this intervention is targeted means that the costs and scope are likely to be much smaller than might be anticipated, while at the same time potentially having a much larger ameliorative impact than might be expected. We shall examine the implications of this concentration in greater detail in later chapters.

One thing is clear: our discomfort with the notion of a permanent criminal class does nothing to negate its existence. Continued denial of these realities threatens to do the opposite—to increase rather than decrease their numbers. The question we now face is this: what can we do about it?

## A WAY FORWARD

In light of these converging structural realities, I offer what may at first glance seem a radical proposal—the institution of a means-tested GBI for all Americans who fall below a certain income threshold—for whom the labor market does not and cannot in future offer a place to earn a living wage. It is my hope that the analyses I present will sway those who would reject such an idea as impossible or too costly. My intent is to demonstrate that the transformation of modern economic systems creates "extra people" who cannot be absorbed by the economy and that these individuals, driven as we all are by hegemonic belief systems, also experience the pressures deriving from these beliefs. Some of these individuals engage in crime, which not only damages *their* life chances but also has significant disruptive impacts on society. For the past forty years, we have been housing more and more of them in state and federal prisons—an untenable strategy for the future.

The analyses I present in this book focus on the costs of a basic income relative to the costs of incarceration in order to draw attention to the convergence of trends in these two institutional arenas. However, I advocate for a means-tested GBI benefit that would be available to all who are unable to achieve sufficient income in the formal labor market to meet the basic needs of living. It would hardly be a defensible position, and one even more politically untenable than the one I am proposing, to suggest that only justice-involved individuals should receive this benefit. I propose a means-tested GBI for all adults who meet the eligibility requirements.

Numerous arguments have been marshalled in opposition to the idea of GBI. The first of these is that we cannot afford it; it is too expensive to provide a basic income to *everyone*. Policies that do so are correctly called universal (or unconditional) basic income (UBI). The Alaska Permanent Fund Dividend, a sum paid to all permanent residents of Alaska annually, is an example of a universal benefit. (The stipend provided to all Alaska residents does not provide sufficient income on its own, so it is better characterized as a universal or unconditional *benefit* rather than a basic income.) Another example of a universal benefit is the Finnish baby box, which contains basic supplies for a newborn and also provides a sleeping vessel for the baby (in accordance with current recommendations for preventing crib death) to all expectant mothers in Finland regardless of income (Lee, 2013). I am not proposing a universal or unconditional basic income benefit. The GBI I envision is means-tested; those who *are* able to find employment that affords a reasonable standard of living would not be eligible to receive it.

Another frequently raised objection to GBI—one that is strongly reflective of prevailing attitudes toward the poor—is this: if we just give people money, they will become layabouts and refuse to work. This argument is easily rebutted on two extremely solid grounds. The first is a wealth of empirical evidence, from *research designed to investigate precisely this question,* that the premise is simply untrue. The second is even more fundamental. If the economy does not have the capacity to use the labor of potential recipients, what does it matter if it does reduce their (hypothetical) labor output? Who is harmed by providing these individuals an income that supports their existence?

Between 1968 and 1980, five large-scale experiments on negative income tax (NIT) were undertaken in the United States and Canada. NIT is similar in concept to a means-tested GBI in that both are based on the idea of an income "floor"—a threshold below which members of society should not be allowed to fall. The NIT experiments were just that—experiments in the classic sense. Guided less by theoretical or social justice–based concerns about inequality, the *primary* focus of these demonstration projects was to ascertain the effects of NIT on labor supply (Hum & Simpson, 1993; Levine et al., 2004). These experiments and their findings will be discussed at greater length in chapter 4, but for the moment, the results of dozens of studies can be easily summarized: there was virtually no impact on work effort in any of the five locations, which represented a wide variety of contexts and household types (urban, rural, two-parent families, single parents, childless families). The reductions in work effort that *were* observed were very small—less than 15 percent reduction in hours worked across all types of workers—and were mainly observed among secondary and tertiary earners in the studied households.

All of the NIT experiments were undertaken with the *express* purpose of evaluating labor supply effects. *The whole point was to find work disincentives.* None, or virtually none, were found. It bears mentioning that numerous positive effects were found, although these were in no way the focus of the experiments. These included the following: enhanced educational performance on the part of young children in recipient households, decreased incidence of low birth weight among the highest risk recipients, decreased high school dropout rates, and increased incidence of homeownership (Levine et al., 2004). So, not only did the NIT income guarantee fail to instill—or reveal—some sleeping drive for sloth, but it actually seemed to improve the lives of poor people in a multitude of ways.

The second rebuttal is simpler: *there are not enough jobs to go around anyway!* Leaving aside for the moment the ideological and cultural baggage that surrounds work, whether a means-tested GBI would induce poor recipients to work less is an increasingly moot question and has been for quite some time now. The U.S. economy cannot productively utilize the labor power of these individuals. Even if the provision of a means-tested GBI *did* spur recipients to a state of morally objectionable indolence, *so what?*

Some will argue that governments simply cannot ameliorate societal problems of this magnitude. My response to this is to remind readers of the role the Johnson administration's Great Society programs played in severing the connection between old age and poverty in the United States. In 1959, 40 percent of Americans aged sixty-five and older were classified as living in poverty. In 2012, this rate was 9.1 percent, substantially lower than the rate for children and nonelderly adults (House Budget Committee, 2014). Programs and reforms associated with the War on Poverty have unequivocally been credited with accomplishing this sea change

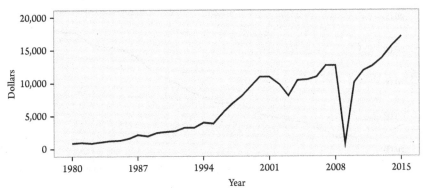

FIGURE 1.1. Dow Jones industrial average 1980–2015
SOURCE: Macrotrends.net

in the standard of living for the elderly in the United States (Council of Economic Advisers, 2014; McGarry, 2013).

I hope to make the case that the arguments in favor of a means-tested GBI are more compelling than those against it. First and most importantly, *we can afford it*. An honest assessment of the aftermath of the "jobless recovery" following the Great Recession reveals that the American economy is strong and productive. Gross domestic product (GDP) exhibits a steady rate of growth in the postrecessionary period. Corporate profits are booming. Figure 1.1 shows the closing values for the Dow Jones Industrial Average from 1980 through 2015.[1] It is clear that the Dow has healthily rebounded postrecession, reaching historic high values in 2015. However, not only do these profits fail to "trickle down" or create new jobs, but these unchecked "surplus profits" actually work to destabilize the economy over the long term. This is a direct result of what might be characterized as the collision course of technological progress and the logic and nature of capitalism. The growth imperative of capitalism demands that profits be reinvested. However, when the limits of production are reached as a result of technological advancement, further capital investment in the profit-generating enterprise is both unnecessary and unprofitable; holders of these excess profits seek investments that offer the greatest possible return. This leads to the creation of speculative, increasingly risky capital markets, which in turn leads to economic "bubbles" and subsequent crashes (Cassidy, 2010; Livingston, 2011).

James Livingston (2011) offers a cogent and well-supported analysis of the history of economic growth and contraction in the twentieth-century United States that demonstrates that since the second decade of the twentieth century, the driver of economic growth has been *consumption*, not production. Consumer spending comprises approximately 80 percent of total GDP. Therefore, increasing inequality hinders economic growth by limiting the amount of available consumption income.

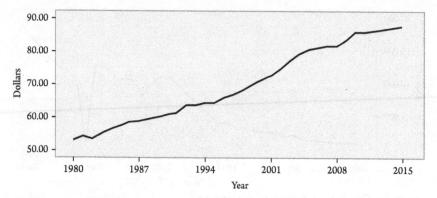

FIGURE 1.2. Net productivity per hour, 1980–2015
SOURCE: Bivens & Michel, 2015

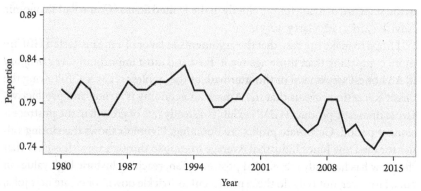

FIGURE 1.3. Labor share of corporate income, 1980–2015
SOURCE: Bivens & Michel, 2015

A more equitable distribution of spending power in the economy would foster both economic growth and economic stability.[2] The most affluent nation in the world *can* in fact ensure for all its citizens a minimum standard of living without incurring economic ruin—and indeed, our continued economic growth may *depend* on such a shift in our public policy.

Figures 1.2 and 1.3 show the trends in productivity and in shares of income going to labor since 1980. Figure 1.2 makes clear that there have been great advances in productivity in the recent past. This productivity, however, is *no longer dependent on human labor.* As a result, average wages have fallen or stagnated while corporate profits have ballooned—productivity increases result in the elimination of jobs and the creation of surplus labor. A buyer's market for labor naturally depresses wages. Figure 1.3 demonstrates the consequences of these transformations in the nature of productivity, in the falling labor share of corporate income since 1980.

Contemporary gains in productivity are almost entirely attributable to automation or "computerization" (Frey & Osborne, 2013). The process of automating
and consolidating tasks—thus eliminating jobs—is discussed in greater detail in
chapter 2. This process and the effects of technology on the economy more generally have been described as "creative destruction." This phrase is attributed to
economist Joseph Schumpeter, who derived the notion from Karl Marx's writings on capitalism. Schumpeter (1942, pp. 82–83) described creative destruction
as a "process of industrial mutation that incessantly revolutionizes the economic
structure from within, incessantly destroying the old one, incessantly creating a
new one." As it relates to technology, this process is often viewed as a force to be
resisted—as seen even in the titles of largely pro-technology works such as Erik
Brynjolfsson and Andrew McAfee's (2011) *Race against the Machine* and Martin
Ford's (2015) ominously titled *Rise of the Robots*. Perhaps we might better see technological change as a *liberator*. Could technology be the force that finally breaks
through what Robert Merton (1938, 1957) called the "pathological materialism"
of American society, opening other avenues through which members of society can
demonstrate and experience their worth? When we live in a time when human
beings have found a way to turn these tasks over to machines that do not tire, suffer repetitive stress injuries or psychological burnout, make errors in judgment,
or have any understanding of whether a task is "repetitive" or "demeaning" (Ford,
2015; Frey & Osborne, 2013), it becomes increasingly difficult to find the *intrinsic
value* of human beings performing unfulfilling, physically wearing, or dangerous
work—often for less than a living wage.

Additionally, outsourcing, or offshoring—that demon of populist politicians—
has ceased to be a relevant factor in U.S. labor market dynamics for quite some
time. Simply put, the jobs and tasks that *can* be offshored already have been. Certain types of work simply cannot be effectively outsourced, and these are the types
of jobs that have dominated the low-wage sector for decades. Chapter 2 explains
how outsourcing has shaped the contemporary labor market, as well as the reasons why its limits have largely been reached in terms of significantly impacting
the U.S. labor market, both currently and in future.

That the limits of offshoring have largely been reached leads to an unmistakable conclusion: the arguments that have been historically employed in favor of
minimal taxation of corporate profits are no longer defensible. The notion that
large corporations will simply pull up stakes and abandon their American opera-
tions for friendlier shores *simply does not hold water*.[3] A more appropriate level of
taxation of these surplus profits would also permit a more equitable distribution
of income shares, which would have two highly desirable effects: it would limit
the amount of "surplus profits" available to invest in high-risk speculative ventures,
which would reduce volatility in the economy; it would also allow for a more widespread distribution of purchasing power, which will drive sustainable economic
growth (Livingston, 2011).

Other changes that could facilitate the funding of a means-tested GBI include the aforementioned shifting of criminal justice priorities. A means-tested GBI administered at the federal level might also allow for the consolidation or elimination of fragmented half-measure assistance programs that have failed miserably at the goal of eliminating poverty and would likely perform better at the task of redistributing income shares and reducing inequality than our current antipoverty efforts.

Richard Wilkinson and Kate Pickett, in their 2009 book *The Spirit Level: Why Greater Equality Makes Societies Stronger*, present a multitude of analyses demonstrating better public health and other quality-of-life outcomes in societies characterized by lower levels of economic inequality. These outcomes include women's status, teen births, mental illness, obesity, and violence. The countries in the analyses that register the most favorable outcomes—the lowest levels of these social and public health problems—also tend to be those that subscribe to some notion of citizenship rights, as manifested in an adequate social welfare safety net that provides an income/standard-of-living floor.

The notion of citizenship rights has never fully taken hold in the United States, this being incompatible with the rhetoric that surrounds the "American dream" and its emphasis on "rugged individualism." Full participation in American society seems to morally require *labor*, even if that labor is dangerous, demeaning, or unfulfilling. Yet where has our stubborn adherence to this idea gotten us? And where is it likely to take us in future—when the economy clearly can no longer provide work for all?

Fiscal conservatives (and others) rightfully point out that we already spend a great deal, in dollar figures, on antipoverty programs—over ninety such programs exist at the federal level (House Budget Committee, 2014). These efforts, discussed at greater length in chapter 4, do not appear to be either an efficient or effective means to combat poverty. In 1965, 17.3 percent of all Americans lived with incomes below the poverty line. In 2012, this figure is barely unchanged, at 15 percent. Similarly, the 22.3 percent rate of child poverty recorded in 2012 is virtually unchanged from the 1959 figure of 26.8 percent (Council of Economic Advisers, 2014). It should also be noted that historic *patterns* in the distribution of poverty in America also remain consistent—female-headed households and African Americans today experience poverty at twice the average rate, much as they did prior to the War on Poverty and the Great Society.

In addition to the haphazard social welfare spending that remains after the Clinton administration and the 104th Congress "ended welfare as we know it" in the late 1990s, we should also consider the role of what Christopher Howard (1999, 2007) has called the "hidden welfare state" (see also Caputo, 2011). Howard uses this term to refer to *tax expenditures* with a social policy bent. Tax expenditures are foregone tax revenues. Tax expenditures serve to redistribute income shares for the purpose of incentivizing socially desirable behaviors. They do so by exempting particular kinds of income from taxation. Examples include the mortgage interest tax deduction, the tax exemption of employer contributions to pension funds, and capital gains on assets transferred at death. A recent report published by the Congressional Budget Office (2013) reveals that over 50 percent of the economic gains realized as a result of the tax expenditures that make up the hidden welfare state accrue to those households in the highest income quintile; 17 percent of tax expenditure benefits goes to the top 1 percent (Congressional Budget Office, 2013). This makes sense when considering the nature of the encouraged behaviors (e.g., homeownership, pension savings) and the resource position individuals and households must hold in order to be able to participate in these benefits. "Welfare" is alive and well in America—it is just that very little of it reaches actual poor people.

It also bears repeating that our massive system of incarceration is another way that we are *already paying* for the failure of the structural realities of the labor market to correspond with prevailing narratives. In fact, we pay quite handsomely for the luxury of this particular form of denial. As a nation, we spend a staggering $80 billion on costs associated with incarceration annually (Council of Economic Advisers, 2016a). We also pay, both literally and figuratively, in terms of the collateral costs, which encompass consequences for individuals, families, communities, and our social priorities. Bruce Western and Katherine Beckett (1999, p. 1052, emphasis added) have observed that "while European social policy is redistributive, the employment effects of U.S. incarceration exacerbate inequality. Comparative research shows that tax and transfer policies lifted about half the nonelderly poor out of poverty in European countries in the 1980s. . . . Incarceration has the reverse effect. Because incarceration rates are highest among young, unskilled, minority men, the negative employment effects . . . are focused on those with the least power in the labor market. The penal system thus *deepens existing market inequalities*." When viewed as a labor market intervention, it is clear that the criminal justice system—specifically mass incarceration—is an expensive and socially destructive means of managing our profoundly deep cognitive dissonance about the economy. Recent trends in criminal justice reform foretell a decreasing reliance on incarceration as a means of managing surplus population. This, combined with the increasing pace of automation, will result in even greater labor market competition at the same time that the number of jobs is dwindling. However, like an aerial image of two trains improperly routed at opposite ends of the country heading toward each other on the same track—the metaphor that inspires this book's title—we have the ability to see the coming collision. This "long view" is obtained through historical trend analyses and a grounded understanding of the contemporary structural realities and trajectories of the economy and the criminal justice system and affords us the opportunity to prevent the tragic consequences of their convergence.

## HYSTERICAL DENIAL AND ITS DISCONTENTS

David Garland (1996, 2002) has written extensively about state responses to crime in late modernity. He notes that state actors are faced with an unresolvable contradiction—the intractability of crime and the concurrent necessity of governments to appear to be "doing something about it" in order to maintain legitimacy. The overwhelming punitive shift in criminal justice policy that gave rise to mass incarceration represents what Garland characterizes as a disproportionate response of *hysterical denial*. Faced simultaneously with the understanding that high levels of crime are normalized and that crime cannot be effectively controlled, governments engage in a two-pronged strategy of abdication and repression. The abdication comes in the form of "responsibilization"—or diffusing the responsibility for crime control to nongovernmental actors. The repressive dimension comes from the necessity, from the standpoint of maintaining state legitimacy, to appear to be "doing something about the problem." This, in Garland's scheme, explains the massive growth in prison populations in the past four decades— growth that has brought us to today's state of affairs—what we now collectively refer to as mass incarceration.

Garland's analysis focuses on more direct and repressive forms of social control—the growth of surveillance and criminal justice—but his ideas can certainly be applied in other policy contexts and are particularly applicable here. Hysterical denial as it manifests in discourse around the economy has always been a part of labor market regulation and welfare policy in the United States. Relatively meaningless statistics (such as the unemployment rate) are bandied about and compared to the last quarter or last year but are never placed in larger context (such as the unmistakable downward trend in the employment-to-population ratio [EPR] in the last half century). Job creation is discussed in a similarly decontextualized fashion, with emphasis placed on raw numbers of new jobs created each quarter and trumpeted calls for the "return to full employment." In light of the "jobless recovery," these announcements resemble nothing so much as Winston Smith's work in George Orwell's dystopia *1984* when he is tasked with re-creating press releases joyously announcing increases in the chocolate ration in order to "correct" the historical record.

Even the jargon used by economists to describe the causes of labor supply-demand incongruity is indicative of this denial. When the mismatch is caused by a shortage of needed workers, economists refer to this as *structural* unemployment. Unemployment that results from a lack of labor *demand*—a surplus of workers for whom no slots are available—is called *cyclical* by economists. This implies, of course, that equilibrium will somehow return and unemployment will diminish, bringing us back to that nirvana-like state of "full employment" at the coming of the next "cycle." Yet even a cursory examination of long-term economic trends—one need only flip through the figures in chapter 2—negates this optimistic premise.

Another form of this hysterical denial can be seen in the ramping-up of work requirements for receipt of welfare benefits toward the end of the twentieth century. The Personal Responsibility and Work Opportunity Reconciliation Act of 1996 (PRWORA) was the crown jewel in the Clinton administration's plan to "end welfare as we know it." The PRWORA not only eliminated the Aid to Families with Dependent Children (AFDC) program—the primary form of cash assistance to the poor—and replaced it with block grants to states and the federally administered Temporary Assistance to Needy Families (TANF) program—but it tied receipt of TANF and state-administered benefits to work requirements, as well as penalties (including ineligibility for *other* means-tested benefits such as child-care and transportation subsidies) for noncompliance with work requirements.[4]

Work requirements for assistance deny the structural realities of the labor market's inadequacy—the reason individuals turn to the state for relief is that *there are not enough jobs*. Workfare requirements also function as a form of responsibilization and state control, in some ways mimicking the "punitive turn" observed in criminal justice during the same period. By linking receipt of benefits to work-searching behavior, the state is seen to be "doing something" to avoid lazy freeloaders from taking advantage, reflecting and reproducing hegemonic beliefs about work and welfare.[5]

While it is important, in terms of the maintenance of sovereignty and legitimacy, to *appear* to be doing something about the problem of labor market inadequacy, it is also the case that the state must actually manage the crisis. Economist David Autor documents one of the ways that this has happened—specifically, the sharp rise in the rolls of individuals receiving Supplemental Security Income Disability Insurance (SSDI). SSDI, a form of GBI, was created in 1956 by an act of Congress amending the Social Security Act. The Social Security Administration (2021) defines disability as "the inability to engage in any substantial gainful activity by reason of any medically determinable physical or mental impairment(s) which can be expected to result in death or which has lasted or can be expected to last for a continuous period of not less than 12 months." In other words, recipients of SSDI are not in the labor market and are not expected to return. Evidence indicates that SSDI recipients as a whole do not return to work in any meaningful way. Fewer than 20 percent of recipients return to the labor market, and the vast majority (97.1%) of those who do work earn less than $10,000 per year (Fremstad & Vallas, 2013).

Between 1989 and 2009, the percentage of American adults aged twenty-five to sixty-four receiving SSDI benefits doubled from 2.3 percent to 4.6 percent (Autor, 2011, p. 5). This increase came about as a result of revisions to the eligibility criteria and *not* as a result of increasing disability in the working-age population. In

1984, the program's eligibility criteria were "liberalized," specifically allowing less easily disproven disabling conditions such as musculoskeletal pain and mental disorders (including substance abuse disorders), as well as changes in the eligibility criteria that place relatively greater weight on subjective determinations such as pain, and on the individual's ability to work (Autor, 2011, p. 5). There is no evidence that the swelling of SSDI rolls is a consequence of increased levels of disability in the working-age population. Economists Mark Duggan and Scott Imberman (2008) report substantial overall *gains* in the average health of older U.S. adults aged fifty to sixty-four, who account for 62 percent of disability recipients, and only a small expected growth effect owing to the aging of the baby boom generation. During this same period, however, the prime working-age (25–54) EPR declined from 80.1 in the last quarter of 1989 to 74.8 in the last quarter of 2009 (Bureau of Labor Statistics, 2017). The conclusion is obvious—that SSDI stealthily accomplishes some of the same functions of mass incarceration with respect to the labor market. It serves to artificially depress the official unemployment rate—4.6 percent of the population receiving SSDI and effectively out of the labor market is approximately equivalent to recent officially recorded unemployment rates, yet these individuals are "hidden" and therefore excluded from these calculations. This serves as a "pressure release" that masks the inadequacy of the labor market and facilitates the continuation of unsustainable narratives about work, worthiness, and the functioning of the economy.

## ORGANIZATION AND GOALS OF THIS BOOK

I wrote this book to sound an alarm—to draw some focus to a problem that seems to be receiving dangerously little attention, given the wide-ranging potential consequences. It is time once and for all to acknowledge the fact that the U.S. economy can no longer utilize the labor of all citizens who are "expected" to work and that this is the result of forces far beyond any individual's control. Current trends in criminal justice policy portend greater numbers of would-be workers in a labor market already unable to accommodate all who seek employment. We must cease pretending otherwise. The following outlines the structure of the arguments and proposals presented in the remaining chapters.

Chapter 2 offers an in-depth examination of the state of the labor market and the U.S. economy, explains how we have arrived at the current situation, and what this trajectory implies for future labor market dynamics.

Chapter 3 focuses on the current state of criminal justice policy reform vis-à-vis the reduction of the prison population. I identify three reform movements in criminal justice that have great potential to drive decarceration: diversion, reentry, and drug policy reform. These three movements are highlighted because they are at the center of a great deal of research and policy activity and because reforms in these domains have as their goal reducing (or at least curtailing the growth of) the prison population. Chapter 3 also reviews the recent experience of some states that have achieved a more rapid pace of decarceration, which suggests that current trends may well intensify, bringing more and more people into the labor market.

Chapter 4 offers a sociohistorical accounting of the American experience with work and welfare. This is an important dimension of the problem I identify in this work. Deeply rooted American attitudes present significant obstacles to policy changes of the type I identify as necessary to avert the collision course of the labor market and the criminal justice system. This chapter examines the ideological and historical background of the hegemonic significance of work in our cultural imagination and the ways in which welfare policy has reflected and reinforced these ideas. This chapter will also show that the overarching assumptions that have undergirded centuries of relief policy in the United States are false, including the assumption that cash payments to the economically distressed reduce labor output—an assumption that is invalidated by a mountain of empirical evidence, as well as the generalized perception that welfare assistance to the poor constitutes the only form of government transfers to citizens.

Chapter 5 describes the consequences that trends in the economy and trends in criminal justice reform portend. Reforms that place more people into a labor market already unable to provide work to all who seek it—combined with the increasingly ludicrous expectation that everyone should work, reflected in the paucity of available economic assistance—are going to exacerbate existing trends with respect to the demand for labor. Increasing numbers of young Americans are failing to engage with the formal labor market in any meaningful way; many of these individuals meet their economic needs by participating in a wide range of illegal activities, from drug selling to predatory crime. Failure to address this structural reality through government intervention will further perpetuate the devastating consequences already evident in communities that experience high rates of joblessness and house many residents with a tenuous relationship to the labor market.

In chapter 6, I present a proposal to address the collision course of the economy and the criminal justice system—a means-tested GBI. I also articulate suggestions for how to fund such an initiative by increasing corporate tax revenues. While the analyses presented rest on foundational assumptions (such is the nature of all such speculative analyses), there is a good argument to be made that providing GBI over a lifetime is *less expensive than prison*. Additionally, due to the nature and sources of economic growth in the past century, superstitions about the infeasibility of leveraging higher taxes on excess corporate profits are rendered utterly toothless.

In the concluding chapter, I offer what I hope is a convincing argument for taking seriously the notion of *citizenship rights*. Americans tend to be a proud people—proud of what America "stands for." I am a native-born U.S. citizen, and I personally find it difficult to get behind persistent and widening inequality; nor can I take much pride in a system that foolishly pines for "full employment" while devaluing and denigrating those for whom we provide no opportunity. This chapter also examines the nature of low-wage work in contemporary America; this review should provide a new perspective on the "nobility" of work for all.

I would be delighted if a means-tested GBI were to be considered on the grounds of citizenship rights and an essential respect for human dignity. However, I focus this book on matters less philosophical and more concrete. Simply put, we can't afford *not* to consider GBI in the face of the collision course of accelerating automation and the declining use of incarceration. We can no longer afford to ignore the growing numbers of "extra people" in American society that denial of these structural realities produces. We do so at great peril.

# 2 · THE U.S. ECONOMY IN THE TWENTY-FIRST CENTURY

Discussion of the economy seems to be everywhere. We hear and read about it in news reports, political campaigns, and everyday conversation. Is unemployment higher or lower than it was at the last quarter? How many jobs have been added or lost since the last quarter's accounting? The idea of *labor* as an intrinsic part of our humanity is a basic tenet of social and behavioral science. A sampling of thinkers who have considered this in depth in the nineteenth and twentieth centuries include Karl Marx, Émile Durkheim, Robert Heilbroner, John Kenneth Galbraith, William Morris, and John Maynard Keynes. All of these men recognized the centrality of an economy as a system for allocating resources throughout societies, as well as the significance of labor as an element of the social contract. In advanced capitalist societies, this distribution of resources is accomplished through the processes of production and consumption.

Yet in the twenty-first century, an honest evaluation of labor market conditions and trends leads to the unmistakable conclusion that the U.S. economy no longer operates in ways that are consistent with the conventional economic wisdom of the nineteenth and twentieth centuries. The first reality that needs to be addressed is this: the economy simply can no longer provide work for everyone. The numbers are irrefutable. For the past forty years, the economy has been characterized by a slack labor market—one in which the supply of labor consistently exceeds the demand. Economists rhapsodize about the "return of full employment," yet we have not experienced full employment (or anything close to it) *since the early 1950s* (Baker & Bernstein, 2014). The economy has changed in important and permanent ways. Existing narratives about the functioning of the economy no longer provide plausible or valid explanations for the state of affairs that exists today. The remainder of this chapter is intended to provide historical and social context—something generally lacking in discussions about domestic economic policy—as well as to drill deeply into the facts and figures in order to forge an accurate picture that offers a realistic assessment of the future of work in the United States.

## LABOR SUPPLY: "EXTRA PEOPLE"

Prior to the coronavirus (COVID-19) pandemic, the officially recorded unemployment rate had been hovering between 4 percent and 6 percent, or somewhere around 8.5 million people. The unemployment rate is in many ways a flawed and unsatisfying way of gauging the health of the economic system. Social scientists of all stripes are familiar with the limitations of the federal government's approach to the measuring of unemployment. One such limitation is that the unemployment rate obscures large differences between different groups of would-be workers. For instance, an overall unemployment rate of 4.6 percent in November 2016 is disaggregated into rates of 4.2 percent for whites, 8.1 percent for African Americans, and 5.7 percent for Latinos. The variation in unemployment rates seen in age/race/ethnicity groupings is even more striking. Table 2.1 shows unemployment rates by race/ethnicity and sex for the first quarter of 2016. The unemployment rate for African American men aged twenty to twenty-four is roughly four times the aggregate rate. The rates for African Americans in all age groupings are between two and six times the aggregate rate. Young workers in all racial/ethnic categories experience disproportionately high rates of unemployment compared to older workers. In light of the trends discussed below, this suggests the possibility that some segments of the younger working-age population—as well as future cohorts—may *never* engage with the formal labor market (Crutchfield & Pitchford, 1997; Witte & Tauchen, 1994). Among formerly incarcerated individuals, the Prison Policy Initiative recently reported that the rate of unemployment is 27 percent, noting that this rate is higher than the peak unemployment rate recorded during the Great Depression (Couloute & Kopf, 2018).

Another limitation in the calculation of the official unemployment rate is that the numerator is based on a count of only those who have been *actively engaged in searching for work in the past four weeks*, a criterion that fails to capture many jobless individuals. However, the Bureau of Labor Statistics also counts, on a monthly basis, those who are *marginally attached* to the labor market—defined as having looked for a job in the past twelve months but not the last four weeks (for any reason), as well as a subset of the marginally attached, called *discouraged workers*—those available for work and who have searched in the past twelve months but are not currently looking—for the expressly stated reason that they do not believe they will find a job. These individuals are not included in the numerator used to calculate the unemployment rate. These two categories—the marginally attached and the discouraged—presently total approximately 1.9 million people. *Underemployment*, or "involuntary part-time work," was estimated to be the state of affairs for another 5.7 million people in November 2016. If we sum these figures together, we are talking about, at a minimum, *sixteen million people* for whom the economy cannot provide work, let alone a job that pays a living wage.

TABLE 2.1    Unemployment rates disaggregated by race/ethnicity and age, 2016

|  | Men | | | Women | | |
|---|---|---|---|---|---|---|
|  | African American | Latino | White | African American | Latina | White |
| **18–19** | 21.7 | 13.5 | 14.7 | 17.6 | 14.5 | 12.8 |
| **20–24** | 16.6 | 11.0 | 8.4 | 10.7 | 7.7 | 7.1 |
| **25–34** | 10.1 | 5.0 | 4.9 | 10.4 | 5.8 | 3.9 |
| **35–44** | 8.4 | 4.1 | 3.6 | 7.6 | 5.2 | 3.6 |

SOURCE: Bureau of Labor Statistics

And that's just today's problem. When we consider recent trends in job growth vis-à-vis the growth of the labor force, it is evident that the economy cannot fulfill the function of providing employment for all who desire it on an ongoing basis. Martin Ford (2015) asserts that one million new jobs per year would need to be created simply to keep up with the growth in labor supply resulting from population growth alone. Furthermore, economists Lawrence Katz and Alan Krueger (2016) demonstrate that 94 percent of all jobs that *were* created since 2005 were of the short-term, contingent, contractual "gig" variety, *not* the type of full-time jobs that provide income security for individuals and families.

According to these measures, in today's economy there are at least sixteen million people whose labor cannot be put to use in a productive way that furnishes a reasonable standard of living. As will be demonstrated below, there is absolutely no reason to expect the situation to abate or to return to some theoretical state of equilibrium. In addition, many of the jobs that do currently exist are likely to be eliminated via technology and automation before long.[1]

## MEASURING LABOR MARKET DYNAMICS: LABOR SUPPLY

As noted above, the officially recorded unemployment rate has numerous limitations. Critics argue that it suffers from a severe downward bias as a result of the exclusion of discouraged and marginally attached workers—as well as those who are involuntarily underemployed—and that this serves to grossly underestimate the true state of economic distress. Additionally, the unemployment rate fails to capture large differences in subpopulations. However, there are many different ways of capturing labor market dynamics. Some alternative economic measures help to shed light on the phenomenon of the "jobless recovery" following the Great Recession. A number of these measures and their historical trajectories are reviewed below.

## BUREAU OF LABOR STATISTICS MEASURES OF LABOR UNDERUTILIZATION (U-1 THROUGH U-6)

While the unemployment rate is the most widely used and reported, the Bureau of Labor Statistics calculates six different indicators of *labor underutilization*. These are computed using data collected monthly from approximately sixty thousand households by the U.S. Census Bureau (USCB) as the Current Population Survey (CPS) and data from the Federal Reserve Economic Database (FRED). The CPS collects data on employment and job-seeking activities. These count data are used to calculate six different indicators that are simply called U-1 through U-6.

Measures U-1 through U-3 share the same denominator, which is the total *civilian noninstitutional population*, also referred to as the *civilian labor force*. The civilian noninstitutional population consists of all individuals aged sixteen and older living in the United States, excluding those housed in institutions (prisons, old-age homes, mental hospitals) and those who are on active duty in the military. These data are obtained from FRED. The numerator of U-1 is the number of persons unemployed fifteen weeks or longer (and who have sought a job in the past four weeks). This provides an estimate of the rate of long-term unemployment in the population. The U-2 numerator counts those who are unemployed as the result of losing their jobs or as the result of a temporary or contract job coming to an end and who have looked for work in the preceding four weeks. The indicator labeled U-3 is the most widely reported and represents the official "unemployment rate"—the numerator is the number of people who are not currently employed (defined as having done no paid work at all during the survey week), available for work, and have sought employment in the past four weeks.

The numerator of the U-4 indicator adds the number of unemployed workers as defined in U-3 to the number of discouraged workers and divides this sum by the civilian labor force plus the total number of discouraged workers. The U-5 numerator sums the total number of unemployed persons, discouraged, and marginally attached workers and divides this by the civilian labor force plus all marginally attached workers. The U-6 offers the most comprehensive measure of labor underutilization and adds involuntary part-time workers to the numerator used in calculating U-5, and divides by the same denominator used for the U-5 measure—the civilian labor force plus all marginally attached workers (Brundage, 2014; Haugen, 2009).

The numerators for measures U-1 and U-2 use a less inclusive definition of unemployment than U-3, while the opposite is true of U-4, U-5, and U-6. The U-1 through U-3 numerators include only those who have sought employment in the past four weeks. Figure 2.1 demonstrates that U-3 and U-6 have historically shown very similar trends, with the U-6 estimates reflecting a larger segment of the population experiencing economic distress.

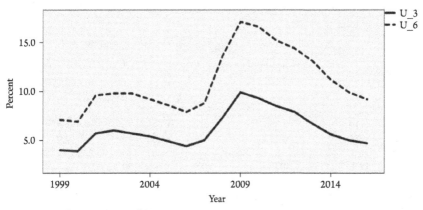

FIGURE 2.1. Measures U-3 and U-6, 1999–2016
DATA SOURCE: Bureau of Labor Statistics
NOTE: Yearly values reflect the estimate for December of that year.

## Employment-to-Population Ratio

The employment-to-population ratio (EPR) is another useful measure of labor utilization, particularly for assessing change and trends over time. The EPR is calculated in numerous ways. The simplest of these measures the proportion of the noninstitutional civilian population aged sixteen and older that did at least one hour of paid work (including self-employment) during the week of data collection.[2] This measure may better approximate the extent of joblessness in the population, as the denominator includes all noninstitutionalized civilian adults who are not working, regardless of the reason and without respect to employment-searching behavior.[3] For this reason, the EPR could be criticized as being overly inclusive, as the denominator does not differentiate those *not* seeking or desiring employment (e.g., full-time students, older workers who may be retired or disabled). On the other hand, one could make the case that the numerator is also biased upward; in using such a low threshold to define "employment," it treats one hour of paid work in the survey week as equivalent to a full-time, steady job. Nevertheless, the EPR is useful for understanding long-term trends in population and labor economics. Many find the EPR among those of prime working age (25–54) to be a more useful measure of labor market conditions. Trends in both of these measures tell a story that is inconsistent with the conventional economic wisdom and eternal faith that "enough" jobs will be created.

Figures 2.2 and 2.3 show trends in the EPR and the prime working-age EPR, respectively. The EPR measure for the entire civilian labor force shows marked decline associated with the Great Recession. While the overall EPR series has been trending upward in recent years, given trends in labor demand (discussed below), it seems unlikely that this will return to pre–Great Recession levels. In

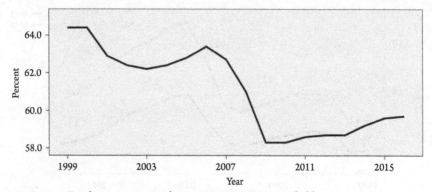

FIGURE 2.2. Employment-to-population ratio, ages sixteen and older, 1999–2016
DATA SOURCE: Bureau of Labor Statistics
NOTE: Yearly values reflect the estimate for December of that year.

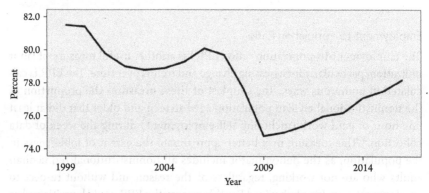

FIGURE 2.3. Employment-to-population ratio, ages twenty-five to fifty-four, 1999–2016
DATA SOURCE: Bureau of Labor Statistics
NOTE: Yearly values reflect the estimate for December of that year.

December 1999, the EPR was 64.4. By 2016, it had fallen nearly 5 percentage points, for a net decline of 7 percent. Figure 2.3 shows the trend in the prime working-age EPR. In December 1999, the prime working-age EPR was 81.5—meaning that nearly 82 percent of adults aged twenty-five to fifty-four were in the labor force. Figure 2.3 also illustrates the devastating effects of the Great Recession, as well as the "jobless recovery" that followed. The prime working-age EPR hit its lowest point, 74.8, in December 2009. Since then, it has feebly climbed back up to 78.2 in December 2016, reflecting a net decline of 4 percent over the past two decades.

Comparing the trends in the EPR and the prime working-age EPR, in light of the disaggregated unemployment estimates given in table 2.1, further underscores the effects on younger workers (and potentially on successive cohorts, given advances in automation technology, discussed below). The "rebound" seen after

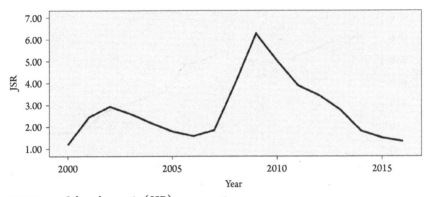

FIGURE 2.4. Job seekers ratio (JSR), 2000–2016
DATA SOURCE: Bureau of Labor Statistics
NOTE: Yearly values reflect the estimate for December of that year.

the recession is much more prominently reflected in those of prime working age—a great many of whom were *already* in the labor force prior to the recession, reflecting what might be called an *incumbency advantage*.

## Job Seekers Ratio

The job seekers ratio (JSR) reports the ratio of the number of unemployed workers seeking jobs and the number of available jobs. Figure 2.4 shows the trend in the JSR from 2000 to 2016. It is evident that there has been some "improvement" in this measure since the Great Recession, when the JSR hit a high of 6.7 in July 2009, but this figure still stands at 1.41 in 2016. Mishel and colleagues also provide an analysis comparing unemployed to job openings in different sectors of the economy to address the degree to which the mismatch may result from "cyclical" or "structural" causes. They find that job seekers outnumber job openings in all sectors of the economy. They conclude that the mismatch is not the result of a lack of qualified workers but simply a lack of available jobs (Mishel et al., 2012). It is important to note that this ratio only accounts for workers who are officially designated as "unemployed" by the Bureau of Labor Statistics. Discouraged and marginally attached workers are excluded, thereby exerting a significant downward bias on the JSR as a true measure of economic distress.

## Labor Force Participation Rate

The labor force participation rate (LFPR) is derived by adding the number of persons who are employed to those who are unemployed and actively looking for work and dividing by the civilian noninstitutional population. The LFPR is also calculated for the prime working-age civilian labor force (those aged 25–54). Trends in both measures demonstrate that overall labor force participation—attempted as well as actual—is in decline.

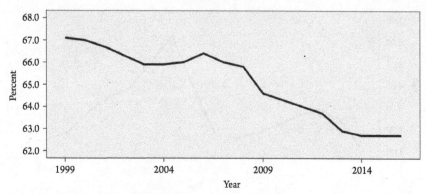

FIGURE 2.5. Labor force participation rate, ages sixteen and older, 1999–2016
DATA SOURCE: Bureau of Labor Statistics
NOTE: Yearly values reflect the estimate for December of that year.

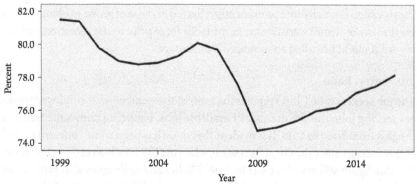

FIGURE 2.6. Labor force participation rate, ages twenty-five to fifty-four, 1999–2016
DATA SOURCE: Bureau of Labor Statistics
NOTE: Yearly values reflect the estimate for December of that year.

This measure excludes from the numerator those who have simply given up or who have never entered the labor market. However, these individuals *are* included in the denominator, and for that reason the LFPR provides a useful indicator of the size and trends of what might be called the "economically superfluous" population—the "extra people" at the bottom of the economic order.

Comparing trends in the overall and prime working-age LFPR series (figures 2.5 and 2.6, respectively) leads to the conclusion that the nature and structure of the *demand* side of the labor market portends vastly different outcomes for later cohorts in comparison to older ones. (This is also supported by the disaggregated unemployment statistics given in table 2.1.) Overall labor force participation peaked in 2000 and has been in steady decline ever since (Hipple, 2016); however, the postrecession recovery is much more pronounced in the prime-age series (figure 2.6) than in that for all ages. This suggests two things, which are both supported by evidence. The first is what might be called the advantage of *incumbency*, or of already being in the labor market in the first place. It also speaks to the lower labor force participation of younger cohorts (Autor & Wasserman, 2013; Hipple, 2016).

## DEMOGRAPHIC SHIFTS IN LABOR FORCE PARTICIPATION

There have been important demographic shifts in labor force participation that have significant implications for the meaning and salience of "work" in the United States. Of particular note are two related trends: increasing disengagement from the formal economy on the part of younger workers that is also evident in successive cohorts, and the declining labor force participation of men, in particular African American men.

### Age

Between 1994 and 2014, the median age of persons in the labor force increased 11 percent. This can be understood by examining the trajectories in the series of overall and prime-age LFPR over this period (figures 2.5 and 2.6, respectively). These figures demonstrate that older workers fared better than workers overall in the recovery following the Great Recession. Additionally, the labor force participation of those aged sixty-five and older has risen over the past two decades while labor force participation rates for workers aged twenty-four and younger have steadily declined for cohorts born in the 1960s and later (Council of Economic Advisers, 2016b; Hipple, 2016; Krueger, 2017).

The declining labor force participation for younger workers can be characterized as both a *period* and a *cohort* effect—much like the greatly increasing likelihood of incarceration for later cohorts as compared to older ones demonstrated by Becky Pettit and Bruce Western (2004, see also Western & Pettit, 2010), later cohorts demonstrate consistent declines in labor force participation in a monotonic fashion (Council of Economic Advisers, 2016b). The patterns we observe with respect to the trends in LFPR for younger workers reflect a consequence of being born at a particular time characterized by particular structural conditions—a slack labor market and ever-advancing robotic and machine technologies.

Mark Aguiar and colleagues (2017) examine trends in young men's (21–30) labor supply in a controversial analysis published by the National Bureau of Economic Research (NBER). Although some of their analyses and conclusions are debatable,[4] the authors document the sharply decreased labor force participation of young men in recent cohorts, identifying a "large and growing segment of this population that appears detached from the labor market: 15 percent of younger men [ages 21–30], excluding full-time students, worked zero weeks over the prior year as of 2016" (Aguiar et al., 2017, p. 1). They also find that among those in the labor force, hours worked by men aged twenty-one to thirty decreased by 12 percent between 2000 and 2015, compared to an 8 percent decline for men aged thirty-one to fifty-five. Aguiar et al. also note the increasing tendency of younger men—particularly those with low levels of education—to live in a household headed by parents or other close relatives, reporting an increase from 34 percent of men with less than a high school education residing in such circumstances in 2000 to 49 percent in 2015. Fully 67 percent of nonemployed men lived with a parent or other relatives in 2015, leading the researchers to conclude that "parents and close relatives are providing significant consumption insurance to younger men. . . . [Additionally], younger men experienced a rise, rather than decline, in measured happiness over the last 15 years" (Aguiar et al., 2017, p. 47). Leaving aside the more controversial claims of the analysis, the work of Aguiar and colleagues further adds to the evidence that a large-scale return to the labor force is an unlikely scenario for future cohorts of young men with low levels of education—the segment of the population most likely to engage in criminal activities and to be incarcerated.

## Sex

Over the past six decades, male labor force participation has declined, while female labor force participation has increased. These trends are shown in figures 2.7 and 2.8. One striking thing about the trend in both the male and female series is the consistency over time—the labor force participation rates of neither sex appear to have been greatly affected by economic downturns (Krueger, 2017). A report issued in June 2016 by the President's Council of Economic Advisers notes that with respect to males, "[labor force] participation at nearly every age has fallen for nearly every consecutive cohort of men, meaning that falling participation among prime-age men is largely a function of lower participation at all ages" (Council of Economic Advisers, 2016b, p. 2; see also Krueger, 2017).[5] These trends in labor force participation appear to be amplifying in successive cohorts.

The declining labor force participation of men, particularly those at prime working age is—and should be—a cause of some concern. Numerous authors have examined this "retreat from work" and the declining status of males in American and other advanced capitalist societies, or what has been termed the achievement gap between men and women (e.g., Council of Economic Advisers, 2016b; Eberstadt, 2015; Holzer, 2009; McDaniel et al., 2011; "Men Adrift," 2015a; Rosin, 2012; "The Weaker Sex," 2015b). Although women have made tremendous advances in terms of educational attainment and representation in high-paying fields of employment, gains in education for males largely stagnated in the latter half of the twentieth century, and with this stagnation came a contraction in their labor market prospects (Autor & Wasserman, 2013; McDaniel et al., 2011).

Economist Alan Krueger (2017) suggests an additional factor in prime-age men's labor supply trends—namely, the opioid crisis. Analyzing data from the American Time Use Survey, Well-Being module (ATUS-WB), he finds that "on any given

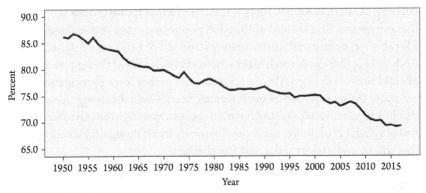

FIGURE 2.7. Male labor force participation rate, 1950–2017
DATA SOURCE: Bureau of Labor Statistics
NOTE: Yearly values reflect the estimate for December of that year.

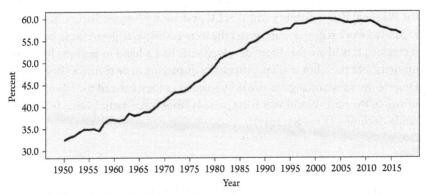

FIGURE 2.8. Female labor force participation rate, 1950–2017
DATA SOURCE: Bureau of Labor Statistics
NOTE: Yearly values reflect the estimate for December of that year

day, 30% of prime age, NLF [not in the labor force] men took pain medications, most likely an opioid-based medication. And these figures likely understate the actual proportion of men taking prescription pain medication, given the stigma and legal risk associated with reporting the taking of narcotics" (pp. 26–27). Analyzing linked data on opioid prescribing from the Centers for Disease Control and Prevention and the ATUS-WB in a regression analysis that controlled for other salient factors (such as rates of disability and manufacturing employment), Krueger finds that labor force participation rates have fallen more sharply in counties with higher levels of opioid prescriptions (p. 49).

The role of criminal justice system growth in the decline of male labor force participation has also been acknowledged by a number of analysts (Council of Economic Advisers, 2016a, 2016b; Autor & Wasserman, 2013; Western & Beckett, 1999; Western & Muller, 2013). It is estimated that approximately seventy million Americans, or one-third of the adult population, has a criminal record with a local, state, or criminal justice agency (Council of Economic Advisers 2016a; Rodriguez & Emsellem, 2011). Many scholars have also noted the suppressive effect of child support debt on African American male labor force participation (Holzer, 2009; Holzer et al., 2005; Link & Roman, 2017). Given the strong cultural forces that link work, masculinity, and financial success, as well as the existence of alternative (illicit) economies, these developments merit thoughtful scrutiny, a task that will be undertaken in the next few chapters.

Since 1950, the female LFPR has doubled. This development is the result of many factors, but among the low-wage segment of the workforce, the influence of welfare policy and practice likely plays a role (Boo, 2003; Eissa & Hoynes, 2011; Snarr, 2013). Chapter 4 describes the history of social welfare arrangements in the United States, highlighting the increasingly forceful work requirements on which receipt of benefits is contingent. Notably, both the Family Support Act (1988) and the Personal Responsibility and Work Opportunity Reconciliation Act (1996) expanded work requirements; given the near-exclusive targeted focus on female recipients, it is likely that these developments had a hand in pushing low-wage mothers into the labor market, potentially displacing male workers (Boo, 2003). Despite the substantial gains made by women as they entered the labor force in droves in the post–World War II era, female labor force participation is also currently declining (Krueger, 2017).

## Race

The trends in labor force participation by race are inexorably entwined with the trends observed by sex. When looking at trends in the LFPR among whites and African Americans of both sexes over the past several decades, *only* the labor force participation of African American women has grown. The steepest declines in the LFPR in the past few decades are observed among African American men. These trends have been evident for quite some time and reflect stagnation in educational attainment and progress for men in general (Autor & Wasserman, 2013; Council of Economic Advisers, 2016b; McDaniel et al., 2011).

African American males are the demographic group with the largest high school dropout rate and are the least likely to graduate from college (Holzer, 2009; McDaniel et al., 2011). For these reasons alone, they face an extremely difficult labor market. Anne McDaniel and colleagues (2011), in an analysis that disaggregates historical trends by race and sex, demonstrate differing patterns in educational attainment by race. For white males, college completion rates have barely increased since the 1960s, in contrast to the tremendous gains made by white women in the same time frame. White women's college completion rates increased by approximately 20 percentage points between 1960 and 2000, or an increase of more than 200 percent. College completion rates for African Americans also rose steadily in this period, although men's rates grew much more slowly than women's, and rates for both groups are far lower than the corresponding rates for white men and women.[6]

Over and above the decimation of labor demand for low-skill workers generally, there is much evidence that compared to other applicants, African Americans are particularly disadvantaged in the labor market. This has generally been explained by employer discrimination/preference to hire applicants of other racial/ethnic groups (Crutchfield, 2014; Holzer, 2003, 2006; Pager, 2003; Wilson, 1997). Ethnographic research reveals that a great many African American men react to these experiences in an arguably rational way, withdrawing from the formal labor market in the face of constant rejection and severely limited opportunities (Anderson, 1999; Crutchfield, 2014; Fader, 2013; Sullivan, 1989).

The decline in labor force participation among African American men is also connected to the phenomenon of mass incarceration. Pettit and Western (2004, p. 164) observe that "by 1999 imprisonment had become a common life event for black men that sharply distinguished their transition to adulthood from that of white men." Western and Muller (2013) note that in 2009, more than two-thirds of Black males under thirty-five had been imprisoned by that age, compared to 15 percent at the end of the 1970s (see also Pettit & Western, 2004; Western & Beckett, 1999). There can be little doubt that the decreasing likelihood of labor force participation observed in cohorts born after 1960, particularly among African American males, is related to the expanded reach of the criminal justice system.

## LABOR DEMAND: WHAT HAPPENED TO THE JOBS?

Economists have two ways of describing a mismatch between labor supply and labor demand. One kind of mismatch is what economists call *cyclical* unemployment—when there are simply more seekers of jobs than there are available positions to fill. This is the kind of mismatch that currently dominates in the contemporary U.S. labor market.

In addition to the sheer numerical inadequacy of labor demand, the *kinds* of jobs that are available have changed greatly in recent decades. Numerous analyses have demonstrated the *polarization* of the labor market, characterized by new job growth concentration in the highest- and lowest-skilled sectors of the market and a contraction of jobs in the middle sectors (Acemoglu, 2002; Autor & Dorn, 2013; Goos et al., 2014). Autor and Dorn (2013, p. 1556) report 30 percent growth in the employment share for "managers, professionals, technicians, finance, and public safety," over the period 1980–2005, as well as 30 percent growth in "service occupations." All other types of occupations exhibit declining shares, with the largest declines seen in the share of workers employed in "transportation, construction, mechanics, mining, and farm" and "production and craft" occupations (−54%

and –38%, respectively). Similar patterns have been documented in Europe and the United Kingdom (Goos & Manning, 2007; Goos et al., 2009). Workers at the low end of the skills spectrum are placed at an additional disadvantage in this highly competitive labor market as a result of more highly skilled workers "moving down the occupational ladder" into low-skill service jobs as jobs in the middle of the skills distribution are eliminated through automation (Beaudry et al., 2013).

Carl Frey and Michael Osborne (2013, p. 13) assert that "throughout history, technological progress has vastly shifted the composition of employment." However, the nature of this relationship has changed over time. In the nineteenth century, technological advancements in production capital had the effect of increasing aggregate labor demand. This is because in the early days of mass production, technological change generally worked to break down a complex task (e.g., building an automobile) into a series of simpler, routine tasks to produce on a larger scale, requiring a larger number of less-skilled workers to carry out these separate steps of the production process. However, mass production reduced labor demand for those with higher skill levels, such as artisans and craftsmen.

The relationship between technology and labor demand that was manifested in the early phases of automation is articulated in the *skill-biased model of technological change*. This model explains the premium placed on more-educated and more highly skilled workers, as technology tends to eliminate jobs at the lower end of the skills spectrum (Acemoglu & Autor, 2012; Goldin & Katz, 2008, 2009; Katz & Autor, 1999). However, the skill-biased model has been supplanted in recent decades; the behavior of the labor market vis-à-vis demand is now better explained by the *routine-biased model of technological change* (Goos et al., 2014). Advances in computing and machine learning have rendered many tasks previously thought to be dependent on human cognition automatable. Many processes comprising a nonroutine whole have been transformed into routine tasks. Frey and Osborne (2013) contend that the only real barriers to automating or "computerizing" any task currently requiring human labor are "engineering bottlenecks." A task can become automated if it is possible to detect patterns or to break it down into a series or group of component parts that *are* routine and predictable.

Many of these engineering bottlenecks are being conquered at a rapidly accelerating pace as "big data" comes to be harnessed and deployed in applications of machine learning. The availability of massive amounts of behavioral data has facilitated the transformation of nonroutine tasks into much more routine and predictable tasks as a result of being able to model for contingencies and refine algorithms such that they mimic or approximate the function as performed by human labor (Brynjolfsson & McAfee, 2011; Ford, 2015; Frey & Osborne, 2013). At the same time, the speed and analytic capabilities of machines have advanced at a staggering rate. Moore's law expresses the observation that computing power doubles about every two years; some technology pundits suggest eighteen months is a more appropriate window.

Industrial robots have already supplanted human labor in a wide variety of routine tasks. For example, it is increasingly likely that the package you recently received from Amazon.com was picked from the warehouse by a robot, packaged for shipment by a robot, and although a human postal or UPS carrier likely delivered it to your home (or to centralized locations such as Amazon lockers) it seems not far off to imagine the deliveries being entirely carried out by machines on a widespread basis in the not-too-distant future (Ford, 2015). Indeed, in March 2017, robots were delivering takeout food to customers in the Washington, DC area, and Amazon.com has filed a patent for delivery robots currently in development (Olson, 2018).

There are strong incentives, even beyond the acquisition of profit, to automate and replace human labor with machines. Of course, the profit motive is clear and intrinsic to the logic of capitalism; as the cost of computing power declines, even if wages are also falling, automation will be more attractive to business owners than human labor. Computers and robots have several advantages over human beings. They are not subject to fatigue over time, so their performance and outputs are more consistent; additionally, algorithms are free of discretionary human error and bias—apart from the inputs of the algorithm itself (Ford, 2015; Frey & Osborne, 2013).

It is also the case that many of the jobs vulnerable to automation are physically taxing and come with risk of injury and/or disability, such as checking electrical wires, monitoring nuclear reactors, and meat cutting and processing (e.g., Schlosser, 2001). Many do not pay a living wage (Bivens et al., 2014). Chapter 4 will address in more depth the ideological baggage that surrounds work, as well as some of the consequences resulting from policy decisions guided by that baggage. Specifically, the principle of less eligibility, a legacy of the British colonists, looms large in the history of American welfare policy. The principle of less eligibility posits that any economic and material relief provided by the state should be less appealing than the wages that could be had at the lowest-paying job. This reflects an overarching concern with what is known as the free-rider problem in economics. At one point in our economic history, this may have been a valid concern. After all, any society will fall into ruin if there are too many free riders—who will pull the cart? However, this kind of worry becomes irrelevant when we have robots to pull the cart for us.[7] Holding on to our concern about free riders requires a solid argument in support of the *intrinsic value* of work that is dangerous, uninteresting, and poorly compensated. Furthermore, we must also justify the belief that the performance of such work is the sole means by which an adult can be deemed fully worthy of participating in the rights and benefits afforded by virtue of being an American. In a world characterized by the economic and technological realities we currently face, this position is increasingly difficult to sustain (Desmond, 2018; Livingston, 2016).

Although the outsourcing or "offshoring" of jobs is a politically popular explanation for the economic difficulties faced by individuals that seems to offer a palatable solution, the impact of outsourcing on employment trends in the past several decades has been negligible. This is due to permanent changes in both the nature and the distribution of economic activity. Since 1970, outsourcing has all but ceased to be a numerically relevant factor in job losses and the shaping of labor demand. It is estimated that automation is responsible for 85 percent of job losses in the manufacturing sector in the past two decades (Ford, 2015; Solis, 2016). Indeed, manufacturing as a percentage of the U.S. labor force has been in decline since the 1950s, almost entirely as a result of advances in technology, specifically robotics (Ford, 2015; Frey & Osborne, 2013).

Similarly, the effects of globalization on contemporary economic activity in the United States are somewhat smaller than might be expected. Currently, services comprise slightly more than 80 percent of gross domestic product (GDP), and the vast majority of these services—also estimated to be over 80 percent—are purchased in the United States. To take a prominent example, goods and services made in China accounted for less than 3 percent of all consumer spending in an analysis of 2010 data. When consumer expenditures are disaggregated, the largest categories of goods made in China and purchased in the United States are in the areas of "apparel and shoes" with 35.6 percent of spending on goods made in China (24.9% of such expenditures are goods made in the United States) and "furniture/household equipment," which includes consumer electronics. Only 20 percent of such expenditures are for products made in China, and products made in the United States comprise 59.6 percent of expenditures in this category (Hale & Hobjin, 2011).

Globalization and outsourcing can only affect workers in "tradable markets"—which does *not* describe the vast majority of contemporary economic activity, nor the occupations and sectors that are growing at the fastest rates. Economic functions that require copresence, face-to-face interaction and that must be performed at a specific location cannot be "offshored" (Blinder, 2009). This applies to jobs such as food preparation and service and to personal services, such as haircuts, or caretaking of children or the elderly—the types of jobs in which we see the most growth in recent decades. Automation continues to threaten many jobs as advances in robotics and machine learning accelerate the pace of routine-biased technological change, but it seems the limits of outsourcing have largely been realized. This fact will prove important when we consider strategies to finance the policy solutions I propose to address and avoid the tragic consequences of the collision course of the economy and the criminal justice system.

## RACING THE MACHINES: THE EDUCATION PANACEA

In the parlance of economists, labor underutilization that results from a situation where labor *demand* exceeds supply is called *structural*. In this case, there are simply not enough qualified workers to fill vacant positions. This could speak to a "skills deficit" in the labor force. Attributing unemployment to an infelicitous match of skill demand and appropriately skilled labor supply fuels the idea that the solution—the thing that will bring us back to the elusive "full employment"—is more education. A college degree is presented as the solution to a lack of success navigating the modern economy. However, there is mounting evidence that the return on investment of a college education is in decline, and very little evidence to suggest that the skill pool in the civilian labor force is inadequate to fill the jobs that are available. As the foregoing will show, greater educational attainment for all does *not* appear to be the key to a stable economic future.

In light of the polarization of the labor market and the earnings differential observed for workers with college degrees, higher education is frequently presented as a panacea to reduce unemployment. However, the merits of these claims are the subject of some debate. It is absolutely true that college graduates fare better in the labor market than nondegree holders. However, evidence indicates that the bulk of this "premium" is attributable to the severe decline in wages and job openings for workers without a degree (Autor & Wasserman, 2013; Heller, 2012). When adjusted for inflation, real wages for college graduates have barely increased since 1979 (Bivens et al., 2014; Heller, 2012).

Another element of this debate concerns completion rates, which hover around 60 percent for those who enroll in institutions of higher education. Among those at the lower end of the income distribution, completion rates are even lower (Backes et al., 2015). The odds of degree completion must be included in any realistic assessment of the costs and benefits of higher education. Approximately 40 percent of students who enroll in four-year colleges fail to complete the degree in six years—this holds true even for students in the highest income quintiles (National Center for Education Statistics, 2017). Students at for-profit institutions have much lower completion rates than traditional colleges and universities, with fewer than 40 percent of students completing degree programs at these types of institutions (HELP, 2012). While there is some evidence for a small wage effect of having *some* postsecondary education, this falls far short of the wage premium that comes with a college degree (Backes et al., 2015).

Since the 1980s, the cost of college attendance has risen at a rate that is more than quadruple the rate of inflation. Students are assuming ever-larger debt burdens, regardless of degree completion status (Heller, 2012; HELP, 2012; Project on Student Debt, 2017). A majority of college students take out loans to finance their educational pursuits. Approximately 70 percent of graduates leave college with some debt; the average amount (approximately $30,000) represents a doubling of the student debt burden since 1992 (Project on Student Debt, 2017).[8] While students who graduate college do so with higher debt loads than those who do not complete the degree, there is some evidence that student loan debt results in harsher consequences for those who fail to complete degree programs.[9] Noncompleters are three times more likely to default on student loans, and 45 percent carry debt burdens that exceed their annual incomes. Unsurprisingly, unemployment rates are also very high among these individuals (National Center for Education Statistics, 2017).

Those displaced by falling demand for lower-skill labor are the target of the strategy that suggests that a college degree will secure a place in today's economy. The question we really should be asking is this: is college the solution for people struggling at the bottom of the wage and skills distribution? Ben Backes and colleagues (2015) offer an analysis that addresses this very question, analyzing educational and labor market outcomes in a longitudinal sample that integrates three large administrative data sets from the state of Florida. The study design permits comparisons between students originating from economically disadvantaged and nondisadvantaged households (as measured by eligibility for free or reduced-price lunch in high school), as well as other sociodemographic and educational performance variables. The authors report that disadvantaged students are about equally as likely as nondisadvantaged ones to enroll in two-year degree programs, but completion rates are about one-third lower for disadvantaged students. Similar patterns manifest for four-year degrees, but the gap in completion between disadvantaged students and others narrows to a differential of approximately 20 percent. Among the disadvantaged, women are more likely than men to enroll in and to complete degree programs, reflecting similar trends across the economic spectrum (Autor & Wasserman, 2013; McDaniel et al., 2011).

Backes and colleagues (2015, p. 21) do find "strong labor market outcomes for all post-secondary credentials," but they also report that some of the largest wage differentials are observed when comparing completers of vocational certificate programs and two-year degrees to high school graduates. Disadvantaged students who enroll in college degree programs with the intention of completing a four-year degree (regardless of enrollment institution type) also exhibit extremely low representation in the fields of study that yield the greatest returns in the labor market, a finding the authors attribute to lack of preparation at the secondary school level: "the low concentration in STEM fields by students in two-year institutions—who tend to come from disadvantaged backgrounds and/or with lower academic performance may reflect rational-decisionmaking" (p. 17). These findings suggest that a more measured and realistic assessment of the idea of college education as the path to a stable economic future, particularly for those at the lower end of the socioeconomic spectrum, may be in order.

A college degree fails to provide a universal guarantee of economic security in today's economy (Autor & Wasserman, 2013; Gabor, 2014). Similar to the patterns we observe with more recent cohorts in *all* segments of the labor market, newer cohorts of college graduates face a labor market that is increasingly less hospitable. Recent graduates register rates of unemployment that are at least twice the national average, though much lower than rates for young workers without a college degree (Gabor, 2014; Heller, 2012; Spreen, 2013). Wages for recent college graduates in entry-level positions have significantly declined since 2000, largely due to a brief period of strong wage growth in the second half of the 1990s (Bivens et al., 2014).

Additionally, over 40 percent of new graduates who are fortunate enough to secure employment can be considered *underemployed* in that they have jobs that do not require a college degree; approximately one-quarter are involuntarily under-employed in part-time work (Abel & Deitz, 2014; Gabor, 2014). It should be noted that although these outcomes are more pronounced for more recent cohorts of college graduates, the underemployment of college graduates in positions for which the degree is not required is by no means a recent phenomenon. Since 1990, one-third of all college graduates have been employed in positions not requiring a degree (Abel & Deitz, 2014). This slack in the market for college graduates is likely to intensify as advances in computing and machine learning threaten jobs previously thought to require human cognition (Ford, 2015; Frey & Osborne, 2013; Goos et al., 2014).

## INCREASING INEQUALITY

Heavily implicated in the story of our contemporary economy and how it functions for most Americans is deeply widening inequality—both between those at the very top and the very bottom and, increasingly, between those at the very top and everyone else. The Occupy protests of 2011 began on Wall Street but eventually spread to hundreds of locations in the United States and over seventy-five countries, bringing the issue of economic inequality to the forefront of national discussion.

Researchers at the Economic Policy Institute report that between 1973 and 2014, compensation for the median worker increased by a mere 8.7 percent, while for the *average* wage earner this increased 42.5 percent (Bivens & Mishel, 2015). What accounts for the skew? Well, it appears that the focus on the 1 percent by the Occupy movement was spot on. When we disaggregate the data by wage percentile, it seems that the late twentieth century's "the rich get richer and the poor get poorer" might be updated to "the ultra-rich get even richer, while the poor gain no ground"—or as Bivens and colleagues (2015, p. 11) state more precisely, "the higher the percentile in the wage distribution, the faster the wage growth." The cumulative increase in annual inflation-adjusted wages between 1979 and 2012 was 153.6 percent for the top 1 percent of wage earners; for those at the top 0.1 percent, annual wages increased at a staggering 337 percent over this period. The corresponding increase for the *bottom* 90 percent was 17.1 percent, reflecting a nearly tenfold disparity between the top 1 percent and the vast majority of American workers (Bivens et al., 2014, pp. 18–19; see also Piketty & Saez, 2003; Piketty et al., 2018).

Workers' wages no longer parallel productivity increases, as they did in the decades following World War II. Between 1979 and 2011, productivity grew by nearly 70 percent, while median compensation (wages and benefits) grew a mere 7 percent (Mishel et al., 2012, p. 381). Indeed, since the early 1970s, manufacturing productivity has grown at a rate four times greater than productivity gains in other sectors of the economy (Bivens & Michel, 2014).

Another aspect of increasing inequality concerns nonwage benefits (pension contributions, health insurance). Over the last three decades, the proportion of the labor force receiving such benefits has fallen, and the likelihood of having a job that provides such benefits is stratified by skill sector. Only 35.2 percent of workers with a high school diploma have jobs that provide pension coverage, while 55 percent of the college-educated workforce receive this employer benefit (Bivens et al., 2014). We can also observe deepening inequality in living standards by examining trends in income. For most Americans, the vast majority of income comes from wages (labor). Income gains over this period for typical workers resulted from increased work hours, not increases in wages. Nearly 30 percent of all workers earn poverty-level wages (Bivens et al., 2014),[10] often in increasingly insecure employment arrangements (Katz & Krueger, 2016; Weil, 2014).

It should also be noted that *all* of the wage growth for those below the median took place between 1995 and 2000. During these years, wages actually grew most quickly for those at the bottom of the wage distribution. This is attributed to the booming economy and consequently low rates of unemployment during this period, as well as to increases in the minimum wage (Bivens et al., 2014).

## INEQUALITY HINDERS ECONOMIC GROWTH

I stated above that the nineteenth- and twentieth-century narratives concerning the economy no longer provide plausible accounts of the actual functioning of the economy. As regard the evangelical belief in "full employment"—if we just return to full employment, everything will be rosy (this is perhaps the liturgy of the faith)—the foregoing review of trends in the labor market reveals this belief to be based *only* in faith. Another form of inaccurate orthodoxy about the U.S. economy concerns sources of economic growth. Central to the idea of a free-market capitalist economic system is the justification of unequal distribution of profit. Owners of capital assume significant risk, and a commensurate reward is needed to incentivize risky behavior, which is—in the near term—potentially injurious to one's self-interest. Surplus profits will be reinvested by successful owners of capital to create more capital, more capacity for labor utilization, and more jobs for all.

Unfortunately, this is not how things actually work in the real world. Indeed, as historian James Livingston (2011) points out, the reinvestment of corporate profit has *not* been a significant source of economic growth in the advanced capitalist economy of the United States for *nearly one hundred years*. Rather, since the early part of the twentieth century, periods of economic growth have been characterized by a shifting of income shares from profits to wages (Livingston, 2011, pp. 56–59).

It is macroeconomic orthodoxy that the engine of economic growth in a capitalist economy is the reinvestment of profits to expand the means of production—in this way, more jobs are created so that more people can labor and create more consumer goods. However, massive productivity gains negated the value of capital investment by the 1920s. Capital investment is driven by the age, quality, and adequacy of the capital stock, as well as technological innovation. Since the early twentieth century, massive technology-driven capital-saving innovations have taken place (Kuznets, 1961; La Tourette, 1965). Capital investment declined precipitously throughout the twentieth century, largely as a result of these technological "capital saving" improvements.

The profitability of increasing production is largely dependent on consumer demand, and particularly by the mid-twentieth century, capital reinvestment simply did not provide the best return. For this reason, since the second decade of the twentieth century, excess profits have been invested in risky, speculative ventures that offer potentially greater returns—*not* invested in ways that "create jobs" (Kuznets, 1961; La Tourette, 1965). In fact, this "surplus profit" is arguably unhealthy for the economy, given that it fuels speculative bubbles and crashes. This pattern holds when analyzing the Great Depression, the booming of consumer credit markets in the 1990s, and the housing crisis and global economic collapse of 2008 (Cassidy, 2009; Livingston, 2011).

The period preceding the Great Depression was characterized by great increases in productivity as well as a "fundamental shift of income shares away from wages and consumption to corporate profits, which produced a tidal wave of surplus capital that *could not be profitably invested in goods production*" (Livingston, 2011, p. 53, emphasis added). The shifting of income shares away from wages also meant that there was less purchasing power distributed throughout the population, diminishing consumer demand for goods. For this reason, rising profits were invested elsewhere—specifically, in the stock market, called by Livingston (2011, p. 55) "the single most important receptacle of the surplus capital generated by a decisive shift of income shares away from wages, toward profits" during this period. This fueled the runaway economic growth of the 1920s as well as the crash of 1929.

The period between the Great Depression and the early 1970s is generally considered a time of great prosperity in American history. And it was. However, this growth was in no way accomplished in the way that the fairy-tale narratives of mainstream economics suggest. The reinvestment of corporate profits played virtually no role in the growth and prosperity of this period. In the early part of this period, the New Deal's role in shifting some income away from profits and toward wages through the creation of work programs and the expansion of welfare programs, in addition to gains made by organized labor in the form of unionization and improved wages, redistributed some consumer purchasing power. Later on, growth was fueled by war-related production. Indeed, the growth of the "military-industrial complex" and federal spending played a significant role and even "stood in" for private investment well into the postwar era (Livingston, 2011, p. 53).

Another source of the shift from profits to wages resulted from the rise of the welfare state in the postwar period. In addition to the increase in transfer payments (which now comprise about 20% of national income), the development and expansion of relief programs in the 1960s was itself responsible for a great deal of job creation—comprising 20 percent of the labor force employed by some form of government by the 1960s (Livingston, 2011). The main point to be made here is that none of this growth was being fueled by private reinvestment of corporate profit. The driver of postwar prosperity was *consumption*, not investment. Consequently, inequality is a culprit in economic failure (Aguiar & Bils, 2015).

## CONCLUSION

An industrial economic system posited on scarcity has been unable to distribute the abundant goods produced. . . . Surplus capacity and unemployment have thus co-existed at excessive levels over the last six years. The underlying cause of excessive unemployment is the fact that the capability of machines is rising more rapidly than the capacity of many human beings to keep pace. *A permanent impoverished and jobless class is established in the midst of potential abundance."* (Ad Hoc Committee on the Triple Revolution, 1964, emphasis added)

These prescient words were penned nearly sixty years ago in a report produced by the Ad Hoc Committee on the Triple Revolution (1964), a group of activists, technology workers, and scholars working out of the Center for the Study of Democratic Institutions, a California think tank founded in 1959. The time period they reference is the late 1950s and early 1960s, and the "triple revolution" they warned about reflected concerns about fundamental changes in American society related to the domains of automation, the arms race, and human rights. Officially recorded unemployment rates during this time fluctuated between approximately 4 and 7 percent, very similar to those seen in our own recent history. Interestingly, these authors, writing in 1964, could easily be discussing the contemporary situation this book was written to address: "what is man's role when he is not dependent upon his own activities for the material basis for his life? What should be the basis for distributing individual access to national resources? Are there other proper claims on goods and services besides a job?" These questions are at the very heart of this book.

The economic trends reviewed in this chapter are of long standing and, importantly, predate the Great Recession of the late 2000s. We are, in a very real sense, rather late to the party in terms of addressing and reversing the likely consequences of the continuation of these trends. The next three chapters lay the groundwork for the policy proposals I offer in chapter 6. In chapter 4, I turn my attention to the cultural and ideological obstacles to these proposals by way of an examination of the origins, history, and outcomes of social welfare policy in the United States; chapter 5 highlights the likely consequences if we fail to conquer these ideological obstacles and choose to continue on our current course.

Prior to addressing these issues, the next chapter sets the stage with respect to the contemporary state of criminal justice in America. The ever-encroaching reach of the criminal justice system has impacted and distorted numerous societal institutions—for instance, readers will probably be familiar with terms such as the *school-to-prison pipeline*—but given the writing on the wall with respect to the relationship of human labor to the economy, recent trends in criminal justice reform portend even greater strain on the already inadequate economy as a means for distributing resources and utilizing the labor force. While these reforms are characterized by a bipartisan consensus (as were the reforms that built up the carceral state) and have been warmly embraced by criminologists, the potential societal consequences of decarceration vis-à-vis the distribution of the adult population merit a critical examination, given the economic realities described in this chapter. It is to these developments in criminal justice that we now turn.

# 3 · THE CRIMINAL JUSTICE SYSTEM IN THE TWENTY-FIRST CENTURY

The American criminal justice system is a complex machine with scope and reach of previously unimagined proportions. Currently, we find ourselves at the very beginning of the end of the era of mass incarceration. At present, approximately 1.4 million adults are housed in state and federal prisons. Another six million or so are under other forms of criminal justice supervision. This state of affairs has come about as a result of a series of deliberate policy choices over the past four decades. These include the shift from indeterminate to determinate sentencing in the 1970s, the net-widening consequences of the era of alternative sanctions in the 1980s, a growing interest in the incapacitation of dangerous offenders in the 1990s, reflected in a flurry of new habitual-offender sentencing provisions, and a state prison construction boom fueled by federal incentive grants (Auerhahn, 2003; Austin, 2016). Also underpinning much of this growth in incarceration was the devotion of unprecedented amounts of law enforcement, prosecutorial, and carceral resources to the "War on Drugs" ushered in during the 1980s during the Reagan and George H. W. Bush administrations.

It is by this point apparent even to the most casual observer of the American criminal justice system that the consequences of this unprecedented expansion of the state apparatus of surveillance and control have not been borne equally across all segments of American society. African Americans, particularly those at the bottom of the income and educational distributions, have been most deleteriously impacted by the decisions that brought about the current state of affairs. These consequences have been far reaching and pervasive, shaping not only the lives and life chances of those directly affected but also their families and communities, as well as the very character of the society in which we live.

Recently, there appears to be a groundswell of interest in reversing these trends. The phrase *mass incarceration* has now become part of the lexicon for much of the populace, and there is simply no positive spin on it. Mass incarceration has in

many ways become the discursive vanguard of the rapidly spreading disenchantment with the criminal justice system, serving as a generalized shorthand to represent the system in its entirety, disproportionately experienced by individuals and
communities of color.

This chapter examines these developments and offers an assessment of the contemporary state of American criminal justice. I begin with a brief historical accounting of the policies that shaped and grew the justice-involved population. I then
offer an inventory of the nature and consequences of the expansion of the carceral state. Following this, I examine three prominent reform domains in contemporary criminal justice. These are *diversion*, increased attention and resources
toward *reentry*, and *drug policy reform*. Each of these "movements" has the potential to contribute significantly to the reduction of prison populations. Finally,
I examine recent developments in decarceration. While the number of prisoners
housed in state and federal facilities has declined modestly since the 2009 peak,
several states have reduced their prison populations at a more accelerated pace.
California, for instance, has reduced its prison population by more than 25 percent
since 2006; New Jersey has seen a nearly 40 percent reduction over the same
period. These reductions have *not* been accompanied by attendant increases in
crime, and the policy changes that have made them possible have enjoyed
bipartisan support—as did the policies that created the prison boom. Given
the current degree of scrutiny and disapproval of American criminal justice—
not to mention a great deal of evidence that our current punishment practices
do little, if anything, to prevent or reduce crime—decarceration on a larger
scale appears as a likely possibility.[1] As chapter 2 demonstrated, the American
economy is no longer able to utilize the labor capacity of all who seek work;
justice-involved individuals returned to or retained in the community face an
increasingly inhospitable labor market. This is the issue at the crux of this book—
the collision course of criminal justice reform and the evolution of the twenty-
first-century economy.

## MASS INCARCERATION: HOW WE GOT HERE

How did the United States come to be the world leader in locking up its citizens?
The simple answer is this: we chose it. There is no room for argument on this point;
the prison population grew as a result of a series of deliberate policy choices. These
choices include the evolution of policing strategies that focus on target-rich environments, sentencing reforms that lengthen prison terms, as well as increased attention to the enforcement of drug offenses associated with the War on Drugs that
frequently carry stiff penalties. These choices have resulted in a prison population
that is disproportionately drawn from poor communities and from communities
of color; it has also resulted in unwaveringly high rates of recidivism and return
among released prisoners for decades.

At the beginning of the 1970s, the U.S. prison population had been stable for a period of approximately one hundred years. The rehabilitative consensus that was ushered in during the late nineteenth century held undisputed sway. In the face of rising crime rates, a generalized distrust of American governmental institutions, influenced by the Vietnam War, the Watergate scandal, and other forms of social conflict and division in the 1960s, the mid-1970s marked a point of departure. The rehabilitative consensus was roundly rejected, as indeterminate sentencing schemes and discretionary releasing authority in the form of parole boards were replaced by determinate sentencing (later supplemented with mandatory minimum sentences) and the abolition of discretionary parole in state after state. The increasingly politicized nature of issues of crime and justice, as well as an upsurge of urban violence attributed to a highly racialized "epidemic" of crack cocaine in American cities during the 1980s and 1990s also contributed to the selection of policy choices that resulted in an increase in sentence lengths as the rhetoric of "tough on crime" became a hegemonic narrative.

A great deal of the growth in prison populations that took place in the 1990s and 2000s has been directly attributed to drug law enforcement (Blumstein & Beck, 1999; Caulkins & Chandler, 2006; Mauer & King, 2007). Generally speaking, prison population growth is a function of two factors—admissions and length of stay. If either one rises, prison populations will grow. As the War on Drugs kicked into gear in the latter half of the 1980s—despite falling rates of illicit drug use that predated the crackdown by nearly a decade—mandatory minimum sentences were introduced into the federal system and reproduced in the states via the mechanism of incentive grants. The increase in law enforcement resources deployed for drug enforcement as part of our nation's War on Drugs was accompanied by upward trajectories in *both* prison admissions and length of stay.

These changes occurred in tandem with the lengthening of stay associated with the Violent Offender Incarceration/Truth in Sentencing Incentive Act (1994), which in exchange for federal monies for prison construction required that offenders convicted of certain offenses in the states serve at least 85 percent of their sentences prior to becoming eligible for release. Additionally, the 1990s saw a proliferation of "three strikes" habitual offender statutes across the nation. The consequences of these developments are demonstrated in figure 3.1, which documents this explosive growth.[2]

## THE CONSEQUENCES OF MASS INCARCERATION IN AMERICAN SOCIETY

Mass incarceration extracts a considerable toll on American society. Criminal justice expenditures total $80 billion per year—equivalent to the yearly funding allocation of the U.S. Department of Education (Stemen, 2017). However, this toll is not merely financial. Numerous scholars have considered the cultural and soci-

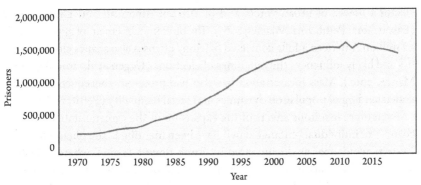

FIGURE 3.1. U.S. prison population, 1970–2019
SOURCE: U.S. Bureau of Justice Statistics

etal consequences of mass incarceration in America (e.g., Alexander, 2012; Gott-schalk, 2016; Loury, 2008; Travis et al., 2014; Wacquant, 2001). A great deal has also been learned in the past several decades about the collateral consequences of mass incarceration for the approximately twenty million Americans with felony records (Eberstadt, 2016; Travis et al., 2014) and the myriad ways in which these blight the lives of individuals, families, and communities. In addition to the obstacles faced by formerly incarcerated individuals seeking employment (these are considered in greater detail in chapter 5), these consequences include lasting detrimental impacts on the health status of incarcerated persons (Massoglia & Pridemore, 2015), enormously increased risk of death in the weeks immediately following release (Binswanger et al., 2007; Massoglia & Pridemore, 2015; Western et al., 2015), negative impacts of incarceration on the children of prisoners, the exacerbation of childhood poverty, inequality and life chances (Foster & Hagan, 2007; Sykes & Pettit, 2014; Wakefield & Wildeman, 2014; Wildeman, 2010), and increased crime resulting from damage to family and community social networks, which ultimately undermine collective efficacy in communities disproportionately affected by mass incarceration (Clear, 2007; Clear et al., 2003).

The scope of mass incarceration in the United States also distorts the democratic process and ideals upon which we pride ourselves as a nation. This comes about as the result of a number of deliberate practical and policy choices, including the U.S. Census practice of counting prisoners as residents of the counties in which they are incarcerated, rather than the place they voluntarily call home (American Civil Liberties Union (ACLU) et al., 2013; Kajstura et al., 2016; Travis et al., 2014). Urban residents contribute disproportionately to the prison population—in many states, the largest city contributes between 40 and 60 percent of the state prison population (Lynch & Sabol, 1997). Because prisons are frequently located in rural areas, this practice shifts political representation from more-diverse urban areas to less-populated and predominately white rural areas. This dilutes the electoral power of urban voters and of African American and Latino voters (Eason, 2017; Pettit, 2012; Wagner, 2005). The disenfranchisement of approximately six million American adults convicted of felony offenses also shapes electoral politics and likely influences the outcomes of elections (Uggen et al., 2016; Uggen & Manza, 2002). Mass incarceration has also had profound consequences for our understanding of population dynamics and racial inequality (Pettit, 2012).

Even more insidious effects of the expansion of the carceral state on the life chances of individuals entangled in it have been identified. The phenomenon of "system avoidance" as documented by Sarah Brayne (2014), whereby justice-involved individuals avoid contact with "surveilling institutions" such as banks, health-care providers, institutions of higher education, and of course, the formal labor market. Brayne's findings are remarkable for at least two reasons: one, she finds that these effects are present not just for formerly incarcerated individuals but for all levels of criminal justice contact (i.e., arrest, being stopped by police, conviction); additionally, she does *not* find similar avoidance behaviors for nonsurveilling (nonrecord-keeping) voluntary associations such as churches and other religious institutions and voluntary or community service organizations.

John Hagan and Holly Foster (2012a, 2012b) report on another significant form of "collateral damage" attributable to mass incarceration. In analyses of the nationally representative longitudinal National Survey of Adolescent Health (Add Health), they document wide-ranging impacts of parental absence in high schools characterized by high levels of incarceration, defined as 20 percent or more students with an incarcerated parent. Hagan and Foster find that high levels of incarceration in high schools have detrimental consequences not just for the children of prisoners but also for other students, *even those without an incarcerated parent*. Hagan and Foster find these effects to be persistent even when controlling for other factors that are known to influence educational outcomes, and for school-based variation. These "spillover effects" are observed in several measures of educational performance, including grade point average, college completion, and overall educational attainment, and appear to be invariant with respect to race. The researchers also observe that although

> African American fathers were much more likely than other fathers to be incarcerated, so the African American youth in the sample were more broadly impacted than other youth by paternal incarceration. . . . The broad-ranging intergenerational school effects of mass incarceration observed in this research indicate that the "long arm of the law" reaches far beyond the jails and prisons where inmates are held, with harmful collateral consequences for educational outcomes that extend more broadly across the geographic and temporal landscape of the national American sample we have examined. (Hagan & Foster, 2012, p. 279)

All of this serves to underscore that the impacts of mass incarceration are pervasive and entrenched within the fabric of American society while at the same time being concentrated among the most disadvantaged segments of the population.

## THE SOCIAL STRUCTURE OF MASS INCARCERATION IN AMERICA: CONCENTRATION

One of the most distinctive features of American criminal justice is its *concentration*. The negative consequences of the expansion of the carceral state are concentrated within individuals, within families, and within communities. David Garland has characterized the rise of mass incarceration as "an unprecedented event in the history of the USA and more generally, in the history of liberal democracy. . . . Imprisonment becomes mass imprisonment when it ceases to be the incarceration of individual offenders and becomes the systematic imprisonment of whole groups of the population" (Garland, 2001, p. 1; see also Feeley & Simon, 1992).

The impacts of the expansion of the carceral apparatus have been most keenly felt among African Americans, particularly among those who are most disadvantaged. The increased zeal for drug law enforcement that began in the 1980s and the net-widening that came about as a result of the priorities of the time greatly increased the risk of incarceration for all population groups. The risk of incarceration more than doubled for all Americans over the course of just twenty years. However, Becky Pettit and Bruce Western (2004) present an analysis that demonstrates the importance of base rates when analyzing changes over time. Pettit and Western compare the risk of imprisonment for two cohorts, born 1945–1949 and 1965–1969. They report that the cumulative risk of incarceration by the early thirties was 1.4 percent for white men in 1979 and increased to 2.9 percent by 1999; for African American men, the corresponding risks were 10.5 percent in 1979 and 20.5 percent in 1999.[3] Additionally, Pettit and Western's analysis highlights the concentration of incarceration among a particular subset of African American men:

> Imprisonment has become a common life event for recent birth cohorts of black non-college men. In 1999, about 30 percent of such men had gone to prison by their mid-thirties. Among black male high school dropouts, the risk of imprisonment had increased to 60 percent, establishing incarceration as a normal stopping point on the route to midlife. . . . Indeed, the lifetime risk of imprisonment roughly doubled from 1979 to 1999, but *nearly all of this increased risk was experienced by those with just a high school education.* (Pettit & Western, 2004, p. 164, emphasis added; see also Sykes & Pettit, 2014)

The distributional properties of criminal offending also exhibit patterns of concentration. Longitudinal cohort studies conducted in Philadelphia and Racine,

Wisconsin demonstrated that approximately 20 percent of those members who engaged in criminal activity were responsible for over 50 percent of the criminal behavior attributable to the entire cohort (Shannon, 1991; Wolfgang et al., 1972). These cohort studies documented delinquency, not adult crime, but similar distributional properties have been observed in samples of adult felony offenders (Chaiken & Chaiken, 1982; Kennedy, 1997; Wright & Rossi, 1986). As a consequence, criminal justice contacts are concentrated among those offenders whose greater level of activity disproportionately exposes them to such attention (Barnes, 2014; DeLisi, 2001a, 2010; Wright & Rossi, 1986). Recent research also offers some insight into the phenomenon of "heavy cross-system users"—a subpopulation of individuals with multiple deficits and challenges such as mental illness and substance abuse that bring them into frequent contact with the criminal justice system (Gladwell, 2006; Harding & Roman, 2017; Vaughn et al., 2011).

The impact of the criminal justice system is concentrated within families as well. The concentration of mass incarceration has profound implications for children and for childhood inequality (Gellar et al., 2011; Turney, 2018; Wakefield & Wildeman, 2014; Wildeman, 2010). It is estimated that more than five million American children have a currently or formerly incarcerated parent; nearly three million American children currently have an incarcerated parent (Glaze & Maruschak, 2008; Murphey & Cooper, 2015; Pew Charitable Trusts, 2010). Given the disproportionate racial impacts of mass incarceration, African American children are substantially more likely than white or Latino children to have an incarcerated parent. Nearly 25 percent of African American children born in 1990 experience the incarceration of their fathers by age fourteen—an 82 percent increase in the cumulative risk of paternal incarceration compared to African American children born in 1978 (Western & Wildeman, 2009, p. 237). For African American children with a father who did not complete high school, fully 49.4 percent experience parental incarceration. The corresponding figures for white children born in 1990 are 3.6 percent (incarceration of their fathers by age 14) and 7.1 percent (incarceration by age 14 of white fathers who did not complete high school). Using data from the Project on Human Development in Chicago Neighborhoods, a longitudinal data set that collected information on approximately six thousand children at three time points over the period 1994–2002, Christopher Wildeman and Sara Wakefield (2014) demonstrate that children with incarcerated parents are significantly more likely to experience the incarceration of other close family members, such as uncles and brothers, than other children.[4]

The concentration of criminal justice is also evident at the community level. This comes about as a natural consequence of policing practices that have evolved from a focus on "hot spots" (Sherman et al., 1989) to more sophisticated data-driven predictive policing techniques (Hardyns & Rummens, 2018; Kaufmann et al., 2019). Bernard Harcourt (2008) characterizes the manner in which contemporary policing strategies focus on the profiling of high-rate offenders—"the usual suspects"—as a *ratchet effect*, contributing to the concentration of criminal justice contact among individuals and specific neighborhoods:

> The logic of the ratchet in the policing context is simple: if the police dedicate more resources to investigating, searching, and arresting members of a higher-offending group, the resulting distribution of arrests . . . will disproportionately represent members of that higher-offending group. The basic intuition is that policing is like sampling: when the police profile frequent offenders, they are essentially sampling *more* among members of the higher-offending group. . . . This disproportion produces a distortive effect on our carceral populations and has a tendency to perpetuate itself. When the disproportion increases, it produces a ratchet effect with potentially devastating consequences for members of the higher-offending group. (pp. 147, 149)

The geographically concentrated nature of criminal justice intervention means that prisoners are disproportionately selected from a limited number of communities. Most incarceration episodes are less than five years in duration, leading to more than 25 percent of incarcerated individuals being released to these communities each year. This "churning" of population in impacted communities damages and disrupts already-fragile community networks and trust relationships, actually reducing the capacity of residents to deter and prevent crime (Clear, 2007; Clear et al., 2003; Gottfredson & Taylor, 1988; Lynch & Sabol, 2004; Piquero et al., 2006; Rose & Clear, 1998; Taylor & Auerhahn, 2015).

## MASS INCARCERATION AND CRIME

It is generally accepted among criminologists that the buildup of the carceral state has little relationship to crime rates, which declined or held steady during most of this period. Jeremy Travis and colleagues, in a 2014 report produced under the auspices of the National Academy of Sciences, observe that

> social science evidence has had strikingly little influence on deliberations about sentencing policy over the past quarter century. Many factors combined to increase sentence lengths in U.S. prisons. They include enactment of mandatory minimum sentence, truth-in-sentencing, three strikes, and life without possibility of parole laws; discretionary decisions by prosecutors to charge and bargain more aggressively and by judges to impose longer sentences; and decisions by parole boards to hold many prisoners longer, deny discretionary release altogether more often, and revoke parole more often. Some of these decisions were premised on beliefs or assumptions about deterrence, incapacitation, or both. From a crime control perspective, those beliefs and assumptions were largely mistaken. (p. 85; see also Nagin et al., 2009)

The relationship between incarceration and crime has been meticulously examined by scores of researchers over the past half century. The general consensus is that the net-widening that has resulted in the imprisonment of so many Americans has rendered marginal increases in incarceration insignificant in reducing crime (Auerhahn, 2003; Canela-Cacho et al., 1997; Liedka et al., 2006). An exhaustive review of studies examining the effects of criminal sanctions on offending behavior concluded that "even after years of research, we simply do not have knowledge with respect to key questions such as whether or not there is a connection between punishment policies intended to deter and perception of sanctions. We also have evidence of countless criminal justice policies . . . with no evidence that such laws effectively prevent crime" (Bushway & Paternoster, 2009, p. 144).

A great deal of attention has been focused on the historic "crime drop" that was observed in the latter half of the twentieth century. While the vast majority of this research examined developments in New York City in the 1990s, in particular changes in policing practices that focused on "broken windows" and quality of life or "nuisance crimes" (e.g., Blumstein & Wallman, 2006; Zimring, 2007), recent empirical analyses demonstrate that the crime drop was in fact global in nature and attributable to structural-demographic factors such as the aging of the population, decreased alcohol consumption, improved security and anti-theft technologies, and the economic prosperity of the 1990s (Baumer & Wolff, 2014; Farrell et al., 2011; Roeder et al., 2015; Stemen, 2017). This fact alone suggests that the unprecedented expansion of the use of incarceration in the United States likely had little to do with the crime drop. This crime drop coincided with the expansion of the use of incarceration in the United States, but estimates of the relationship between the two indicate a very weak relationship and one that essentially disappears when examining the relationship over time. Disaggregating the analyses by decade indicates that virtually the *entire* crime-reduction effect of increased incarceration took place in the period 1990–2000, with virtually no impacts in the first decade of the 2000s (Roeder et al., 2015). The most generous estimates of the impact of the buildup of the prison population suggest that at most 15 percent of the crime drop is attributable to increased incarceration; the majority of estimates range between 5 and 10 percent reductions in crime resulting from mass incarceration (Baumer & Wolff, 2014; Roeder et al., 2015; Stemen, 2017; Travis et al., 2014).

Perversely, there is disquieting evidence that criminal justice system interventions may serve to increase crime among the individuals and communities who experience them. Francis Cullen and colleagues (2011) undertook an exhaustive review of extant research concerning the effects of imprisonment on prisoners. After reviewing numerous systematic reviews and meta-analyses, they conclude that custodial punishments are no more effective than noncustodial ones at reducing recidivism (see also DaGrossa, 2018; Nagin et al., 2009). They also find evidence that prison actually increases recidivism, which is not surprising in light of the large and unwavering rates of recidivism we observe among released prisoners. They further report that "it is likely that low-risk offenders are most likely to experience increased recidivism due to incarceration" (Cullen et al., 2011, p. 60S). This last point is consequential in light of the massive net-widening that took place in the past forty years, exposing more and more low-risk offenders to the pains of imprisonment and the socially disintegrative effects thereof (Auerhahn, 2003; Brayne, 2014).

Similarly, research suggests that incarceration may have the perverse result of *increasing* crime in communities disproportionately impacted by mass incarceration (Clear, 2007; Stemen, 2017; Taylor & Auerhahn, 2015). Todd Clear and colleagues put forth the theory of coercive mobility (Clear, 2007; Rose & Clear, 1998). The geographic concentration of criminal justice interventions (including mass incarceration) results in the repeated removal and return of individuals to (highly disadvantaged) communities. This has the consequence of disrupting informal ·community networks and trust relationships, or collective efficacy, that function to deter and prevent crime (Clear, 2007; Gottfredson & Taylor, 1988; Lynch & Sabol, 2004; Piquero et al., 2006; Rose & Clear, 1998). Coercive mobility theory posits that thigh rates of incarceration will result in increased levels of crime in impacted communities: "In many disadvantaged inner-city communities, high rates of incarceration and reentry negatively affect the local economy, disturb family life, and most importantly disrupt social networks, all of which diminish the ability of residents to exert social control. Informal social control mechanisms are believed to be much more salient for crime control than the formal criminal justice system. . . . Therefore, increasing incarceration rates in already disadvantaged neighborhoods may actually increase crime rates in these neighborhoods by reducing the capacity for residents to regulate themselves" (Taylor & Auerhahn, 2015, p. 307).

## CONTEMPORARY CRIMINAL JUSTICE REFORM

In 2009, something historic happened: for the first time in more than forty years, the prison population stopped growing. It did not decline dramatically, but in light of the exponential growth in incarceration since the mid-1970s, this represents something significant. Figure 3.1 suggests that the task of undoing the prison population built with decades of layered sentencing reforms will not be a simple or easy undertaking. A recent analysis reported that if the current slow pace of decarceration remains, the prison population will decrease 50 percent by 2093—roughly three-quarters of a century from now (Ghandnoosh, 2018). However, there are several contemporary reform trends that may play a significant role in reducing prison populations in the future; additionally, quite a few states have achieved an accelerated pace of decarceration—some reducing prison populations by more than 20 percent in a very short time frame. Each of these developments will be discussed in turn.

Here, I focus on three significant developments in criminal justice reform. The first is criminal justice *diversion*, which includes programs designed to steer certain types of offenders away from incarceration, such as alternative disposition programs for first-time and nonviolent offenders, as well as the proliferation of "problem-solving courts" such as drug courts, mental health courts, and veterans' courts. The second is evidenced by an interest in *reentry*, embodied in research and policy initiatives designed to keep individuals from returning to prison in the face of a high and unchanging recidivism rate. Finally, there is evidence of growing interest in *drug policy reform*, reflected in the federal system in the Fair Sentencing Act of 2010, and at the state and local level in a multitude of initiatives and legislative reform in the area of cannabis decriminalization and legalization for medical and recreational use. In addition to these developments, a significant attitudinal shift toward illicit drug users is evident in the tone and tenor of the responses to the current "opioid crisis" in the United States. Recent legislative inquiries and proclamations regarding the import of this issue (as when President Trump declared the opioid crisis to be a "national public health emergency" in November 2017) portend potentially significant reform in American policy responses to illicit drug use.

## Criminal Justice Diversion

In the past twenty-five years, criminal justice diversion programs have proliferated throughout the United States. Rationales for pretrial diversion include reducing the strain on courts and prisons, as well as preventing recidivism among first-time or low-level offenders. This latter aim is achieved by the avoidance of formal justice system contact, processing, and sanctions, thereby avoiding the collateral consequences accompanying a felony conviction, as well as minimizing the disruptive effects of removing individuals from their families and communities.

The discussion that follows focuses primarily on reforms affecting the movement of individuals in and out of prison, with the potential to shift more justice-involved individuals from prisons to communities. This is done for two reasons. One is that "mass incarceration" has arguably become the touchstone for all the perceived failures of the criminal justice system. Another reason is a practical one. In chapter 6, I offer a policy proposal—a form of means-tested guaranteed basic income (GBI). The cost analyses that underpin this proposal are anchored by comparisons to the costs of incarceration. However, a great deal of reform in this area is evident at many points of contact with the criminal justice system. These include innovations in policing and crime prevention such as Crisis Intervention Teams (CITs) at the level of street-level law enforcement that represent another important form of criminal justice diversion (Center for Health and Justice, 2013).

The model of problem-solving courts (Berman et al., 2005; Huddleston & Marlowe, 2011; Wiener & Brank, 2013), also known as therapeutic jurisprudence in some circles (Bennett Cattaneo & Goodman, 2010), has proliferated in the past two decades, producing drug courts, mental health courts, veterans' courts, community courts, and domestic violence courts, among others. In addition to approximately three thousand drug courts, there are currently more than a thousand such problem-solving courts operating in the United States (Huddleston & Marlowe, 2011; National Institute of Justice, 2020). In each of these specialty courts, the objectives are twofold: to address the underlying causes of criminal behavior by providing a more comprehensive and appropriate range of responses to criminal behavior than that afforded by the traditional criminal justice system such as social services, counseling, job training, and health care; and to keep participants out of prison, with the aim of reducing exposure to the collateral consequences of conviction and incarceration. Both of these objectives are motivated by the ultimate goal of reducing recidivism.

Drug courts are the most prominent example of this trend. The first such court was established in Dade County in 1989; today, over three thousand such courts process over 136,000 individuals annually in the United States (National Association of Drug Court Professionals [NADCP], 2012; National Institute of Justice, 2020). Drug courts offer an alternative to traditional criminal justice processing for low-level, nonviolent drug offenders. The drug court model seeks to address the root cause of offenders' criminal activity (substance abuse) by providing treatment, counseling, and other services in addition to supervision and monitoring, usually in the presence of a deferred prosecution agreement.

In addition to specialty courts with a therapeutic bent, there has also been a great deal of growth in alternative disposition programs in the past three decades. Originally, these programs tended to target juveniles or youthful offenders. The desire to divert juveniles from the formal system of processing delinquents has roots in the findings of the Cambridge-Somerville study of delinquent youth that demonstrated iatrogenic effects of treatment—that is, the finding that many youths were harmed by criminal justice intervention (McCord, 2003). Since the 1990s, the number of alternative pre-adjudication programs has grown steadily. A census of such programs identified 298 programs and eighty statutory provisions in place in forty-five states and the federal system in 2010 (Center for Health and Justice, 2013).

Despite the difficulties involved in comparing different programs for evaluation purposes, the assessment of alternative disposition programs and problem-solving courts is largely positive. Many studies have shown the post-program trajectories of diversion program participants to be characterized by lower rates of recidivism than those of individuals who go through the traditional criminal justice process (Drake et al., 2009; Lange et al., 2011; National Institute of Justice, 2006; Shaffer, 2011; Wilson et al., 2006; Zarkin et al., 2012). Additionally, program costs have been shown to be much lower than traditional adjudication and dispositions (Aos et al., 2006; Center for Prison Reform, 2015; Drake et al., 2009; National Institute of Justice, 2006). Eric L. Sevigny and colleagues (2013) have presciently noted that the stringent eligibility criteria used in most drug courts limit their potential to reduce prison populations. However, given the increasing salience of evidence-based practices in criminal justice as well as the need to contain costs, combined with changing attitudes with respect to the nature of the "drug problem" and drug-involved individuals, it seems likely that these programs will continue to expand their reach, resulting in greater numbers of people avoiding prison and remaining in the community—and trying to gain a foothold in an increasingly hostile labor market.

Reentry

Nearly seven hundred thousand men and women—mostly men—are released from prison custody and returned to their communities each year (National Institute of Justice, 2013). For nearly four decades, empirical research has repeatedly demonstrated that clear majorities of released prisoners would be rearrested and/or returned to prison. An analysis of released prisoners in fifteen states (representing two-thirds of releases that year) found that 51.8 percent of those released in 1994 were returned to prison within three years of release (Langan & Levin, 2002). Nearly half of parolees released in 2000 failed to successfully complete their terms of community supervision were returned to prison or jail, a figure that had remained stable throughout the previous decade (Hughes et al., 2001). An analysis of state prisoners released in 2005 revealed that slightly more than two-thirds were arrested for a new crime within three years, and over 75 percent were rearrested within five years of release; these rates are even higher for younger releasees (Durose et al., 2014).

In recent years, there has been significant policy and research attention directed at altering these outcomes. In 2003, over $110 million in funding was provided by the National Institute of Justice to "develop, enhance, or expand programs to facilitate the reentry of adult and juvenile offenders" in the form of the Serious and Violent Offender Reentry Initiative (SVORI). The programs were intended to "improve criminal justice, employment, education, health (including substance use and mental health), and housing outcomes," targeting violent offenders and offenders aged thirty-five or younger (Lattimore & Visher, 2009). Over one hundred programs in sixty-nine agencies nationwide were included in the evaluation. Participants and controls were assessed at four points in time: thirty days prerelease, three, nine, and fifteen months postrelease. Although the results of the SVORI evaluation failed to show any difference in postrelease recidivism between program participants and nonparticipants, SVORI resulted in a uniquely rich longitudinal data set permitting exploration of numerous outcomes that has greatly expanded our understanding of reentry dynamics (e.g., Stansfield et al., 2017; Taylor, 2015a, 2015b, 2016).

President George W. Bush noted in the final moments of the 2004 State of the Union Address, "This year, some 600,000 inmates will be released from prison back into society. We know from long experience that if they can't find work, or a home, or help, they are much more likely to commit crime and return to prison." As Devah Pager (2007, p. 10) astutely observed, George W. Bush "became the first president ever to acknowledge the vast social problem associated with America's policies of mass incarceration. . . . While Bush's nod to the problem was modest and his proposed commitment of resources trivial, for a conservative Republican leader to propose new domestic spending programs to address this problem is a sure sign of its troubling significance." Pager's assessment was supported when the Second Chance Act (SCA) was signed into law by President Bush in 2008. The stated purpose of the SCA was "to reauthorize the grant program for reentry of offenders into the community in the Omnibus Crime Control and Safe Streets Act of 1968, to improve reentry planning and implementation, and for other purposes." Congress appropriated approximately $25 million (after a proposed allocation of $65 million) in 2009 to fund demonstration projects and innovative programs to facilitate the successful reentry of individuals released from prison; subsequent allocations of $170 million followed in 2010 and 2011. The SCA was reauthorized as part of 2018's First Step Act. Given the sustained interest in reentry—as well as President Trump's designation of April 2018 as Second Chance Month—it appears likely that reentry programs and research initiatives will continue to develop.

Although the programs included in the SVORI evaluation failed to demonstrate significant impacts on recidivism, other reentry initiatives (including reentry courts) show greater promise. With the tide having turned against mass incarceration, it is extremely likely that reentry will continue to command significant resources and attention, and as we learn more, we can expect greater improvement in outcomes. The end result? More people than before, trying to participate in the labor market, many of whom live under the Damoclean threat of having to demonstrate employment as a condition of their continued freedom. The potential consequences for these individuals (as well as for society at large), in the absence of legitimate opportunities to generate income, are examined in depth in chapter 5.

## Drug Policy Reform

In addition to the expansion of drug courts, a great deal of drug policy reform has occurred quite recently, much of it in the past decade alone. Significant policy and legislative changes have taken place at the federal, state, and local levels of government. At the federal level, tangible drug policy reform takes the form of the Fair Sentencing Act of 2010 (FSA). The FSA reduced the hundred-to-one disparity in the sentencing of crack cocaine and powder cocaine offenses established in the mandatory minimum penalties put in place as part of the Anti Drug Abuse Act of 1986. This disparity has been criticized for its profound racial implications (and lack of scientific basis) since its inception. Sentencing for crack and powder cocaine offenses was not equalized in the FSA, but merely reduced to a ratio of approximately eighteen-to-one.[5] To date, this has been the only lasting, meaningful legal action taken at the federal level vis-à-vis drug policy reform, although a great deal of *symbolic* activity has been in evidence.

In 1996, California voters supported Proposition 215, the nation's first medical marijuana law. Today, a majority of states have chosen to relax state statutes vis-à-vis the criminalization of cannabis for medical use.[6] This has arguably facilitated more open discourse regarding the question of cannabis policy. There has been a great deal of legislative activity at the state and local level. As of the time of this writing, seventeen states and the District of Columbia have passed laws legalizing cannabis for recreational use, joining the thirty-seven states already allowing the use of cannabis for a list of enumerated medical conditions. At the same time, decriminalization initiatives have been undertaken in many cities, including New York, Chicago, Los Angeles, Philadelphia, and Washington, DC. While cannabis possession accounts for a miniscule proportion of conviction offenses in state and federal prisons, these initiatives and policies may portend significant changes in the discourse and direction of U.S. drug policy.

Many factors are implicated in this generalized shift in drug policy. Certainly, the massive expansion of the prison population and the fiscal strain it continues to place on states is a significant element. Additionally, questions regarding the utility of the War on Drugs are now a prominent part of public discourse. Popular media representations such as David Simon's television series *The Wire* (2002–2008), Steven Soderbergh's Academy Award–winning film *Traffic* (2000), and Jenji Kohan's Netflix series *Orange Is the New Black* (2013–2019) have certainly had an effect on popular conceptions of the utility of the drug war and the criminal justice system in general.

More widespread awareness of the racial implications of drug law enforcement may also play a role in these developments. For example, in 2013, the American Civil Liberties Union published a report that received a great deal of exposure and attention on popular and social media. The report documented massive racial disparities in marijuana possession arrests state by state—the most common arresting offense nationwide. The analyses demonstrated that on average, African Americans were four times more likely than whites to be arrested for cannabis possession, despite similarities in rates of marijuana use.

The increase in opiate use in the twenty-first century—widely called the opioid crisis—also portends change in our current approach to illicit drug use. In late October 2017, President Trump declared opioid use in America a "public health emergency" (a proclamation that does little more than relax restrictions on how certain discretionary funds can be allocated within the federal budget). A great deal of attention is focused on this crisis as of this writing. It has been observed that the tone and tenor of discourse surrounding opioid use differs dramatically from earlier discursive frameworks; a recent photo essay contrasting images of the opioid crisis with that of the "crack epidemic" dramatically illustrates the portrayal of (white) opioid users as victims, as sick, as needing help, while the images of the crack epidemic overwhelmingly feature images of (Black) criminals being apprehended and brought to justice (Shaw, 2017). The demographics of those affected by the current increase in opioid use stand out as one explanation of these differences. Over 90 percent of heroin users initiating use in 2010 or later are white; these new users are also overwhelmingly suburban and equally split by sex (Cicero et al., 2014).

The newfound compassion toward illicit drug users (at least for opioid users) and changing attitudes and state laws regarding cannabis both strongly suggest that we may be entering an era of wider-reaching drug policy reform. Given that the buildup of the prison population can be laid almost entirely at the feet of the architects of the War on Drugs, the consequences of wider drug policy reform to prison populations may be quite significant.

Such changes in drug policy have the potential to reduce the numbers of men and women being caught in the carceral net in several ways. The first is simply by reducing the exposure of drug users to the criminal justice system, whether this comes about as the result of legislative reform, changes in local law enforcement policy, or even de facto decriminalization. Additionally, in a landscape where drug treatment is more widely available, other crimes, such as acquisitive crime that finances an individual's drug habit, might decline in frequency as well, indirectly reducing the flow of drug-involved individuals to prison. Finally, legalization may cause illicit markets to contract, reducing opportunities in the drug trade.[7]

Irrespective of *how* or *why* it happens, a shift away from the punitive social policy responses to illicit drug use employed during the last three decades has the potential to significantly increase the number of would-be workers in an economy that already lacks the capacity to employ all who are expected to work. As discussed in the section that follows, quite a few states have already implemented drug sentencing reform. These states have, unsurprisingly, experienced significant reduction in their prison populations. If these trends continue and advance even greater changes to drug policy, prison populations will surely decline at an accelerated rate, introducing more would-be entrants to the labor market.

Each of these developments in criminal justice reform have the potential to do the same thing—namely, to reduce the size of the prison population. This will result in more justice-involved individuals remaining in the community and the labor market. As the foregoing chapter demonstrates, the U.S. labor market is already deficient in terms of its ability to provide work for all adult Americans. A felony conviction automatically bars individuals from many occupational sectors, including health care and public sector employment (Pager, 2003). Additionally, some of the fastest-growing occupations in the contemporary labor market are service occupations that require a great deal of trust—for example, home health aides, private security, retail and restaurant businesses involving money handling—positions the justice-involved are not likely to be considered the best candidates to fill, particularly in a slack labor market where job seekers exceed job openings and employers can be choosy in filling open positions. Herein lies the "collision course" that is the subject of this book, where the failures of the economic system to provide work for all—a situation that will continue and likely intensify as advances in engineering and automation proceed—collide with criminal justice reforms designed to put more and more people into the labor market. An additional wrinkle is that frequently, working in the formal labor market is a condition of justice-involved individuals' continued freedom to live in the community (Apel & Sweeten, 2010; Zatz et al., 2016). The hegemonic salience of "work" for defining human worth (discussed in chapter 4) and the subsequent practical consequences of that—such as defining a successful reentry as one in which the justice-involved individual is employed full time—do not bode well for a future in which we are successful at reducing the numbers of Americans who are incarcerated.

## CONTEMPORARY IMPACTS OF CRIMINAL JUSTICE REFORM: DECARCERATION IN THE TWENTY-FIRST CENTURY

The U.S. prison population reached an all-time high in 2009, with more than 1.6 million adults contained in state and federal prisons. By 2016, the number of prisoners declined 6 percent (Ghandnoosh, 2018). While the overall pace of decarceration is slow, twenty-one states and the Federal Bureau of Prisons have registered double-digit reductions in their prison populations since 2009. Included in this group are states with historically high rates of incarceration. Mississippi, for example, achieved an 18 percent reduction in prison population between 2009 and 2016; Alabama, South Carolina, and Louisiana have registered similar declines over the same period (Ghandnoosh, 2018; Schrantz et al., 2018). It is also notable that included in the group of states that have experienced above-average reductions are those with large prison populations such as California and New York. Additionally, the legislative changes observed in virtually all the states decarcerating at an accelerated pace have been characterized by bipartisan political support (Austin, 2016; Mauer & Ghandnoosh, 2014).

The relatively accelerated scale of decarceration that has been seen in some states has been achieved through a variety of strategies. However, there are some commonalities among these states with respect to the mechanisms driving change. Just as the buildup of the prison population resulted from legislative and policy changes that increased both the flow of individuals to prison and the average length of stay, the recent downsizing of prison populations has been achieved primarily through legislative and procedural changes—in some cases, literally rescinding policies put in place two decades ago. The two approaches most commonly employed involve *increasing release rates* and *reducing rates of return* to prison for individuals supervised in the community (Schrantz et al., 2018). New Jersey exemplifies the latter trend, registering a 37 percent decline in the state's prison population between 2009 and 2016 by implementing a combination of diversion for defendants charged with drug offenses and increased rates of parole release (Ghandnoosh, 2018).

Several states that have achieved above-average reductions in prison populations have done so by rolling back the length-of-stay requirements adopted as part of the Truth in Sentencing provisions implemented in the latter half of the 1990s. These were part of the Omnibus Crime Bill of 1994 (the Violent Crime Control and Law Enforcement Act). The Violent Offender Incarceration/Truth in Sentencing Act (VOI/TIS) provisions of the 1994 act provided increased funding to states for the explicit purpose of prison capacity expansion, either through new construction or expansion of existing facilities, provided that states passed legislation requiring offenders convicted of violent offenses to serve 85 percent of their sentences prior to being considered for parole eligibility. For the most part, the provisions encompassed violent offenses, though drug offenses were also sometimes included (Ditton & Wilson, 1999). Thirty-five states responded to the incentive and enacted legislation that placed them in compliance. The implementation of Truth in Sentencing had predictable consequences in the form of increasing time served for violent offenders; these provisions effectively doubled the average time served for offenders convicted of violent offenses in state prisons (Ditton & Wilson, 1999).

Mandatory minimum sentences for drug offenses proliferated in the late 1980s and 1990s as well, further increasing average length of stay. In South Carolina, where the prison population has declined 14 percent, mandatory minimum sentences for drug possession were eliminated in 2010. In 2007, Rhode Island abolished mandatory sentences for *all* drug crimes; the state's prison population has declined 23 percent since 2009. Legislative reforms in New Jersey that resulted in the diversion of many defendants charged with drug offenses from incarceration contributed to a nearly 40 percent reduction in the state's prison population over the same period (Austin, 2016; Mauer & Ghandnoosh, 2014).

The increased attention given to reentry, and the reorientation of community corrections policy and practice is also influencing the pace of decarceration in some jurisdictions. Connecticut, California, South Carolina, Mississippi, and Rhode Island reduced return commitments to prison by at least 50 percent through a revamping of supervision procedures and better coordination of reentry resources and services. California successfully reduced the number of state prison inmates through a widespread revamping of procedures, incentives, and resource allocation formalized in State AB 109, also known as the Public Safety Realignment Initiative (PSRI) (Austin, 2016; Mauer & Ghandnoosh, 2014). These changes included deliberate efforts to reduce the rate at which parolees were returned to prison, particularly for technical violations. In 2009, parole violators comprised 40 percent of admissions to California prisons. A mere five years later, changes to parole revocation procedures implemented as part of the PSRI succeeded in slashing this rate by half. Parolees convicted of new criminal offenses comprised just 21 percent of prison admissions in 2013, while those returned for technical violations represented only 0.1 percent of admissions that same year (California Department of Corrections and Rehabilitation, 2013; Legislative Analyst's Office, 2009). Overall, California achieved a 26 percent reduction in the state prison population between 2006 and 2012 (Austin, 2016).

Also worthy of note is the profound influence that policy and procedural changes in a single municipality can have on the pace of decarceration at the state level. This is a function of the population dynamics of mass incarceration. The state of New York achieved a 26 percent reduction in the population of state prisoners between 1999 and 2012, as well as similar reductions in jail, probation, and supervised release populations. These reductions were entirely driven by changes in policing practices in New York City—reflecting the fact that more than 40 percent of the state's prisoners originate from New York City (Austin, 2016; Austin & Jacobson, 2013; Greene & Schiraldi, 2016; Mauer & Ghandnoosh, 2014; New York State Corrections and Community Supervision, 2016).

Marc Mauer and Nazgol Ghandnoosh (2014, p. 9) of the Sentencing Project observe that "the experience in New York, New Jersey, and California over more than a decade demonstrates that substantial reductions in prison populations can be achieved without adverse effects on public safety." These impacts were generally realized within just a few years after the implementation of legislative and policy changes and appear to be sustainable (Schrantz et al., 2018). Indeed, crime rates have fallen along with prison populations in nearly every state registering an above-average pace of decarceration (Ghandnoosh, 2018; Greene & Schiraldi, 2016; Schrantz et al., 2018).

The lion's share of research examining the effects of decarceration on crime have examined developments in California. These include California's 2014 Proposition 47, which required treating certain drug and property offenses formerly classified as felonies as misdemeanors, as well as requiring resentencing for prisoners serving felony sentences for the enumerated offenses. Bradley Bartos and Charis Kubrin (2018, p. 708) concluded, after a variety of methodologically sophisticated analyses, that "Prop 47 had no effect on homicide, rape, aggravated assault, robbery, and burglary. Overall . . . we find very little evidence to suggest that Prop 47 caused crime to increase in California."

Another body of research evaluates crime trends in the wake of the Public Safety Realignment Initiative of 2011. These studies generally find no increases in crime resulting from the reduced use of incarceration in California (Lofstrom & Raphael, 2013a, 2013b; Sundt et al., 2016). Evidence from New York City also supports the conclusion that large-scale decarceration was not accompanied by increased crime (Greene & Schiraldi, 2016). Also informative is the work of Douglas Weiss and Doris McKenzie (2010), who analyzed the spectacular reduction in incarceration rates in Finland over the period 1950–2000. At the beginning of the 1950s, Finland's incarceration rate was more than three times higher than other Scandinavian countries. Over a fifty-year period, Finland reduced its incarceration rate by more than half, bring their level of incarceration into line with neighboring countries, with no increase in crime attributable to the reduction in the prison population. This was done via similar reform strategies currently being employed in the United States (reducing the use of carceral penalties and mandatory sentences, especially for nonviolent offenses). These findings come as no surprise to criminologists and other analysts of the growth of the carceral state. The net-widening and resulting of changes to the composition of prison populations that occurred during the prison buildup resulted in significant "dilution" of the average level of risk in prison populations (Auerhahn, 2003; see also Auerhahn, 2014; Auerhahn & McGuire, 2010).

## CONCLUSION: THE DOWNSIDE OF DECARCERATION

In recent years, a general disenchantment with the criminal justice system has been evident. In addition to public outcry, this disenchantment has taken the form of critical research on the actions and outcomes of the criminal justice system, as well as tangible legislative, policy, and practice reforms. While criminal justice reform is diverse and encompasses a variety of philosophies and strategies, in this chapter I have focused on three particular reform domains: diversion, reentry, and drug policy reform. Each of these reform movements has the potential to reduce the size of prison populations in the near future.

The relatively rapid cutbacks in the use of incarceration observed in numerous states provide a variety of blueprints for strategies and approaches that have been effective at achieving considerable reductions in prison populations over relatively short periods of time. Recent evidence demonstrates that several kinds of reforms—increasing release rates and decreasing rates of return for community-supervised offenders—have consistently succeeded in reducing prison populations with no corresponding increase in crime (Ghandnoosh, 2018; Schrantz et al., 2018). All of this strongly suggests that decarceration on a significant scale is a distinct possibility in the not-too-distant future, as more and more states come to terms with the expense and futility of mass incarceration.

These trends bode well for reducing the reach of the carceral state, a goal widely endorsed by academic criminologists (American Society of Criminology National Policy Committee, 2001). Decarceration is indeed cause for celebration. However, an economist may view these trends in a different light. Sociologists Bruce Western and Kathryn Beckett (1999) have demonstrated that high rates of incarceration in the United States serve to artificially suppress official unemployment statistics by effectively removing large numbers of working-age individuals from the labor market via incarceration. The consequences of the collision course that is the subject of this book are what we can expect when this safety valve becomes less effective, particularly in light of the picture of labor market dynamics and the diminishing availability of work. Chapter 4 explores the significance and meaning of work in America and highlights some of the implications and obstacles for the nature of the policy approach I propose in chapter 6 to ameliorate the consequences of the convergence of trends in criminal justice and the economy. Chapter 5 examines the consequences that may be expected if no attempt is made to do so.

# 4 · WORK AND WELFARE IN AMERICAN CULTURE AND SOCIETY

Social welfare policy in America reflects deep-seated ideological influences that have shaped the lives of those who find themselves at the bottom of the economic order for centuries. Welfare has always carried a stigma and is neither generous nor widely available. The limited economic assistance that has been available for the most disadvantaged members of American society has always been contingent on assessments of worthiness, which are defined by the recipient's relationship to the labor market.

The criteria for determining "deservedness" have historically been tied to cultural expectations and beliefs about who is expected to work. At present, two facts about the U.S. economy stand out: first, the United States is prosperous enough to provide a reasonable, dignified standard of living to all. Second, the economy, as it currently operates, *cannot provide work* for all of the adult Americans we have historically expected to work. These facts, combined with the seemingly inexorable connection between work and worth in our national consciousness, create a formidable challenge for American society.

At the same time that the American economy has undergone this transformation, criminal justice policymakers have begun to recognize, in increasingly meaningful fashion, that mass incarceration is an unsustainable distortion in a civilized society. The criminal justice reform movements and new approaches to policy and practice discussed in the previous chapter will result in even greater numbers of would-be workers expected to engage with an economic system that has no place for them. The chapter that follows this one details some of the likely consequences if we fail to take steps to avert this crisis. Before turning to these consequences, this chapter reviews the landscape of welfare assistance in America. This is important because of the significant overlap between the poorest Americans and the growing criminal underclass. We have reached a time in our history when it is imperative that we take stock of premises that have proven time and again to be both empirically invalid and incredibly dysfunctional. What follows is an examination of the origins and history of welfare assistance in America that focuses particular attention on the ideological origins and policy choices that have led us to our contemporary circumstances.

## THE ORIGINS OF WELFARE

The origins of contemporary attitudes and forms of public relief emerge throughout Europe during the transition from feudalism to capitalism in the early sixteenth century. Declining death rates resulting from improved sanitation and changing theoretical orientations in medicine combined with changes in social and economic arrangements resulting from the transition from feudalism to capitalism to create excess population—that is, population in excess of what could be absorbed by the burgeoning capitalist economy. Increased mobility resulted in the accumulation of greater numbers of paupers and beggars in rapidly growing cities, and "the problem of the able-bodied poor" came to shape welfare policy and the structure of aid in ways that persist to this day (Katz, 1989).

In the Middle Ages, assistance to the poor had a very different character than it does in the modern period. This responsibility was largely assumed by the church (Katz, 1989; Piven & Cloward, 1971; Wagner, 2005). Almsgiving was seen as a "means of personal salvation, and one-third of parish church funds were set aside for this purpose" (Piven & Cloward, 1971, p. 15). Sociologist David Wagner (2005, p. 4) elaborates: "In medieval Europe, before the poor and other groups such as the 'mad' were stigmatized, *hospice* or a place of hospitality was a central part of European society in which a stranger—often poor, sometimes just a wanderer—was welcomed. While all sectors of society played a role in hospitality, the monasteries came to play a key role in care of the poor. . . . Alms as charity was similarly a social obligation in Europe. The term *almshouse* in its original usage conjured up a house in which poor people or wanderers or others could be aided."

By the early sixteenth century, the responsibility for aiding the poor shifted from the church to the state. Sociologists Frances Fox Piven and Richard Cloward (1971, p. 15) identify the explicit "takeover" of the responsibility of the poor by the state in an act of the British Parliament in 1531 which forbade individuals from aiding the poor outside of this state apparatus as well as prescribing severe punishment for those seeking aid outside of these sanctioned arrangements.

Piven and Cloward also highlight the role of state sovereignty and legitimacy in the state's appropriation of assistance to the poor. They note that in addition to whatever humanitarian and social welfare concerns motivated the state's appropriation of the responsibility for the poor, the *visibility* of such poverty, coupled with the threat of civil unrest, also spurred elites to action (Piven & Cloward, 1971; see also Garland, 1996, 2002). Piven and Cloward (1971, pp. 9–10) offer a description of these developments in sixteenth-century Lyons:

A French town that initiated such an arrangement early in the sixteenth century was Lyons, which was troubled both by a rapidly growing population and by the economic instability associated with the transition to capitalism. . . . All this was very well as long as the newcomers could be absorbed by industry. But not all were, with the result that the town came to be plagued by beggars and vagrants. . . . The economic distress resulting from population changes and agricultural and other natural disasters which had characterized life throughout the Middle Ages was exacerbated by the vagaries of an evolving market economy. Consequently, turbulence among the poor reached a new pitch. By 1529 food riots erupted, with thousands of Lyonnais looting granaries and the homes of the wealthy; in 1530, artisans and journeymen armed themselves and marched through the streets; in 1531, mobs of starving peasants literally overran the town.

Piven and Cloward (1971, p. 11) also note that "most of the features of modern welfare—from criteria to discriminate the worthy poor from the unworthy to strict procedures for surveillance of recipients and measures for their rehabilitation— were present in Lyons' new relief administration."

Differentiating (and ensuring that aid did not reach) the undeserving poor, whose circumstances were seen to be the result of their own choices and moral failings, from those who were seen as genuinely deserving of assistance has been a defining feature of welfare since its inception. Salient criteria were based on the ability to work. Children, mothers, widows, the elderly, and the afflicted and infirm were deserving recipients of relief.[1] Those who could work, or who were expected to work, were not (Katz, 1989; Piven & Cloward, 1971; Torry, 2013). David Wagner (2005, p. 4) locates the origins of the connection between industry and worthiness within the Protestant Reformation and its theology: "a more punitive tradition arose in sixteenth-century Europe. . . . Initially in the areas where Protestantism first triumphed such as Holland, Switzerland, Germany and England, a harsher treatment of the poor and those were deemed unproductive ('indolent' or 'vicious') developed," and "two totally different ideas—hospitality and punishment—oddly enough became confused, at least when European institutions crossed the Atlantic to America."

## THE ORIGINS OF WELFARE IN AMERICA

The origins of contemporary American attitudes about welfare are often traced to the Elizabethan Poor Law of 1601. Three ideas that define contemporary welfare policy were established in the 1601 Poor Law. These are a *preference for local arrangements, a preference for "indoor relief"* over cash assistance, and the *formal establishment of a link between deservingness and one's ability to work.* The 1601 Poor Law made provisions for the collection of funds to be used for aid by local churchwardens; these officials were designated as "overseers of the poor." It also specified different ways in which aid might be provided, depending on deservingness; one practice that was transported to the American colonies was the leasing of the able-bodied poor for farm and domestic labor: "Perhaps the most shocking to us today is the auctioning of the poor to the lowest bidder. The ever-frugal early New England Yankees clearly prized economy above all else, and built in few safeguards against abuse. . . . Some people clearly had sponsors, the same family taking the person year after year. But in an extreme case, the widow Sarah Dill was auctioned off for fourteen years and went to fourteen different households" (Wagner, 2005, p. 8).

The American colonists favored assistance arrangements that were local, reflecting the idea that the poor in a community were the responsibility of and best handled within the community (Katz, 1989; Piven & Cloward, 1971). The preference for local assistance arrangements continues to be reflected in American welfare policy, via the mechanism of federal block grants to the states to administer economic assistance to the poor.

Beginning the tradition of creating coercive institutions to contain those failing to conform to social norms (reformatories, insane asylums, prisons), there were different types of repositories for the unfortunate based on assessments of deservingness. The relatively benevolent poorhouse or almshouse coexisted with the workhouse—also sometimes named more explicitly a house of correction (Gilliom, 2001; Katz, 1989; Piven & Cloward, 1971; Torry, 2013; Wagner, 2005): "Out of a new consensus that suggested 'repressing' pauperism and beggary came another institutional invention, the workhouse. The workhouse was meant as a correctional institution in which actual discipline (cells, bread and water, instruments of punishment such as the ball and chain and later the treadmill) was to be imposed on the 'unworthy poor,' usually men of working age, who were vagrants, beggars, 'indolent,' petty criminals, or intemperate. They would be housed only on condition of hard work" (Wagner, 2005, pp. 4–5).

The explicit connection between poverty and criminality comes to be forged throughout the next two centuries. The modern prison is a direct descendant of the workhouse (Wagner, 2005). The figurative construction of the "sturdy and vicious beggar" emerges as an object of deterrence and criminal punishment. The preference for local arrangements and indoor relief meant that some communities were forced, due to resource limitations, to house the poor in a single institution; the contradictions this created with respect to making distinctions between the worthy and unworthy poor were resolved, in part, by conferring questionable moral status on *all* the poor (Gilliom, 2001; Katz, 1989; Wagner, 2005).

Another defining feature of American welfare policy, also adopted from Mother England, is the *principle of less eligibility*. In response to changing economic conditions in Britain, the Poor Laws were amended in 1795 to permit for the provision of cash assistance to the needy in order to supplement low wages (Piven & Cloward, 1971). This raised concerns regarding the potential effects on wages and labor supply and fanned fears that the able-bodied would shirk labor if relief was available (Piven & Cloward, 1971; Torry, 2013). The Poor Law Amendment Act of 1834 (also known as the New Poor Law) grew out of response to these concerns. The 1834 *Report of the Poor Law Commissioners to Parliament* and the act itself expounded on the hazards of outdoor relief and made provisions for the construction of workhouses, as well as delineating strict rules and procedures for their operation. In addition to essentially abolishing outdoor relief, the 1834 act explicitly codified the principle of less eligibility: "Into such a house no one will enter voluntarily; work, confinement, and discipline, will deter the indolent and vicious; and nothing but extreme necessity will induce any to accept the comfort which must be obtained by the surrender of their free agency, and the sacrifice of their accustomed habits and gratifications. . . . . The first and most essential of all conditions . . . that his situation on the whole shall not be made really or apparently so eligible [i.e., desirable] as the situation of the independent laborer of the lowest class" (*Report of the Poor Law Commissioners to Parliament* [1834], quoted in Piven & Cloward, 1971, pp. 33–35).

The 1834 law legislatively formalized—indeed, made compulsory—the institution of *deterrent relief practices* designed to discourage individuals from seeking aid and to keep assistance rolls at their minimum. The state was willing to assume the burden of aiding the severely destitute—but only on condition that they could ensure that "the funds of charity are not wasted by idleness and fraud" (quoted in Piven & Cloward, 1971, p. 34). This orientation was seen as necessary to deter the unworthy from falling into idleness and worse—dependency. "The indoor relief of the poorhouse requires the poor to live within the walls of a total institution, often in uniform, and under strict rules of behavior and mandates of forced labor" (Gilliom, 2001, p. 24). The 1834 act can be seen as severing the ties to medieval notions of the community's responsibility to care for the poor and strengthening the linkages between poverty, work, and punishment. Indeed, early in his political career, Benjamin Disraeli is said to have commented in 1837 that the New Poor Law "announces to the world that in England poverty is a crime" (Piven & Cloward, 1971, p. 35).

The American colonialists adopted and reproduced these orientations toward poverty, pauperism, and welfare in the practices they developed to aid the poor. In addition to the local administration of assistance, a preference for in-kind assistance, or "indoor relief" was established early on in the evolution of American welfare policy, as seen in the establishment of workhouses throughout the American colonies (Wagner, 2005). These preferences directly reflect ideologies about work, deservedness, and the causes of poverty.

It is important to keep in mind that these structural arrangements—in particular the preference for indoor relief and the principle of less eligibility—are inexorably bound up with the idea of *work* as the defining characteristic of worth. They are also based on a figurative construction of the poor as defective, untrustworthy, moral failures, or some combination of these undesirable traits. Underpinning the preference for indoor relief is the assumption that the recipient cannot be trusted to make good choices; because poverty was clearly the result of laziness, poor moral character, and poor decision making, the idea of providing cash assistance in the form of "outdoor relief" and granting the recipient discretion in how to use it was seen as extremely ill-advised. After all, the recipient of relief has obviously failed or is defective in some important way, or they would not be in the position to need assistance.

It is also instructive to reflect on the assumptions about human nature that underlie and motivate the principle of less eligibility. The poor are viewed as *wanting* to avoid work. If assistance without work provides an adequate standard of living, then people will choose indolence over industry. But are work norms really that weak? Or is it only the poor who suffer from this moral failing? These questions are beyond the scope of this analysis, but a wide array of empirical evidence contradicts this premise. Leonard Goodwin's detailed inquiry into the question, published by the Brookings Institution in 1972, investigated and compared the work orientations of over four thousand welfare recipients with middle-class, nonpoor individuals; Goodwin found no evidence of differences between poor and non-poor individuals with respect to their internalization of work norms. Additional evidence can be found in the existence of the "working poor"—or the nearly eight million adult Americans who do work but remain below the poverty line. Gould (2015) reports that 63 percent of the poor who are eligible to work, do, albeit frequently at below-poverty wages (see also Ehrenreich, 2009b; Guendelsberger, 2019; Newman, 2000; Shipler, 2005; Tirado, 2014).

## OTHER PERSPECTIVES ON POVERTY AND WELFARE

In 1972, Herbert Gans's provocative essay, "The Positive Functions of Poverty," appeared in the *American Journal of Sociology*. Gans delineated fifteen ways in which poverty "is useful to a number of groups in society" and concluded that "a functional analysis must conclude that poverty persists not only because it satisfies a number of functions but also because many of the functional alternatives to poverty would be quite dysfunctional for the more affluent members of society" (pp. 284, 287).

In their classic work *Regulating the Poor: The Functions of Public Welfare*, Piven and Cloward's (1971) convincingly argue that the entrenched beliefs that shape American welfare policy—the principle of less eligibility, distinctions between deserving and undeserving recipients, preference for local administration of relief efforts, and a preference for indoor relief—also serve to regulate the labor supply to suit the needs of the economic elite, as well as to manage civil unrest and threats to the political order. Piven and Cloward's rendering of the history of American welfare policy from the 1930s through the 1960s places particular focus on the relationship between political unrest and the expansion and contraction of the welfare rolls. These authors demonstrate that during this period, economic relief becomes more generous and inclusive during periods of political unrest. These expansions are temporary arrangements that serve to adapt to "hiccups" that occur in the evolution of a capitalist economy. Enforcement of work norms both during periods of generosity, which occur when labor demand is weak, and during periods of contraction, which occur when demand for labor is strong, demonstrates the primacy of the logic of capitalism. During periods of contraction, welfare administration is characterized by deterrent relief practices which include setting funding allowances far below subsistence levels as well as shaming and stigmatizing current and potential recipients (see also Gilliom, 2001; Gordon, 1994). This retains them in the labor pool and ensures owners of capital a comfortable labor surplus (Piven & Cloward, 1971; see also Caputo, 2011). The administration of relief at the local level provides functional adaptability to local labor market needs, which frequently differ across regional sectors of the economy (Piven & Cloward, 1971, pp. 130–145).

Michael Katz (1989, pp. 13–14) also notes the ways in which the ideological legacies retained and reproduced in the development of American welfare systems both supported the needs of the emerging capitalist economy and perpetuated the idea of "American dream" by linking moral concerns explicitly to ideas about work, worthiness, and the causes of poverty:

> The redefinition of poverty as a moral condition accompanied the transition to capitalism and democracy in nineteenth-century America. It served to justify the mean-spirited treatment of the poor, which in turn checked expenses for poor relief and provided a powerful incentive to work. In this way, the moral definition of poverty helped ensure the supply of cheap labor. . . . The moral redefinition of poverty followed also from the identification of market success with divine favor and personal worth. Especially in America, where opportunity awaited anyone with energy and talent, poverty signaled personal failure.

Insofar as the existence of the poor serves the interests of economic elites by suppressing wages and strengthening work norms, it becomes imperative to contain, control, and *know* the poor via practices and institutions of confinement, surveillance, and punishment (Gilliom, 2001). Arguably, these interests have been as influential as the hegemonic linkages among work, worthiness, and moral character in shaping modern American welfare policy.

What follows is a review of the historical evolution of welfare policy in modern America, the impact of these efforts on the reduction of poverty, as well as a discussion of wealth and income transfer in contemporary America that brings to light what has been called the *hidden welfare state* (Howard, 1997, 2007), challenging the widely held belief that "welfare" constitutes the only source of governmental income redistribution in America. This last point is an important one in refuting arguments that a means-tested guaranteed basic income (GBI)—the proposal I present in chapter 6—is inconsistent with American ideals, philosophy, and practice.

## THE BEGINNINGS OF MODERN WELFARE POLICY IN AMERICA: THE NEW DEAL

The Social Security Act of 1935 established three major economic assistance programs, all of which remain a part of our welfare apparatus, albeit in different, evolved forms. These are Old-Age, Survivors, and Disability Insurance (OASDI), commonly known as Social Security, Unemployment Insurance, and Aid to Dependent Children (ADC)—which became Aid to Families with Dependent Children (AFDC) in 1962 and Temporary Assistance to Needy Families (TANF) in 1996. This latter program differs from the other two in that Social Security and Unemployment Insurance[2] are entitlement or social insurance programs, with eligibility and benefit levels determined by well-documented formulas based on work participation and payroll taxes, while ADC/AFDC/TANF is—and has been since its inception—a pure "welfare" program for the (deserving) poor, administered locally via the mechanism of block grants to the states, which facilitated wildly varying benefit levels and administrative practices (Béland & Waddan, 2012).

The original provisions of the Social Security Act were intended to support elderly Americans, a group unequivocally considered deserving of economic assistance. Indeed, locally administered Old-Age Assistance Programs had been in existence in the United States since the 1920s, with twenty-eight states having such programs in place prior to the passage of the Social Security Act in 1935 (McGarry, 2013; O'Connor, 2004).[3] Benefits for widows and families were added to the program in 1939.

Concerns about free riders and malingerers were evidenced by what Robert Moffitt (2015, p. 731) described as "intense debate in Congress" about the inclusion of provisions for the support of disabled Americans in the Social Security Act of 1935. There were no federal support programs for the disabled until the Social Security Disability Insurance program was established in 1956, with stringent eligibility criteria limiting benefits to the most severely disabled.

Social Security remains the income transfer program with the greatest amount of popular support. The features and administration of Social Security reveal some of the reasons for this. Cognitive dissonance around aid to the less fortunate, or what economist David Ellwood calls "helping conundrums" that characterize the practice of providing assistance to the poor, reinforce and perpetuate distinctions of deservedness. Social Security challenges these "helping conundrums" the *least*. Receipt of Social Security benefits is directly tied to work effort—this is even reflected in benefit levels. The program is universal rather than targeted (assuming work). The logic and structure of benefits also emphasizes the traditional, idealized American family in linking deservedness to benefits for dependents of deceased (and universally male at the time of the program's inception) workers/ breadwinners. Perhaps most importantly, benefits accrue only to those who are unequivocally *not* expected to work—widows, orphans, and the elderly (Ellwood, 1988).

The administrative practices of Social Security differ from pure "welfare" programs as well. Deterrent relief practices meant to discourage the needy from seeking aid as well as surveillance and vetting of applicants characterize programs like AFDC, food assistance programs, and Medicaid, but not Social Security. Social Security *beneficiaries* are distinguished from welfare *recipients* by this lack of surveillance (implying trustworthiness): "entitlements redefined their beneficiaries as deserving, by the simple act of removing surveillance from recipients, while charity created more of the undeserving by intensifying the surveillance" (Gordon, 1994, p. 289; see also Gilliom, 2001). In contrast to the universal nature of Social Security, the ADC program initially had a very narrow target of intended recipients—widows with children and married mothers with disabled husbands (Moffitt et al., 2017). Until the expansion of the Earned Income Tax Credit (EITC) in the 1990s, AFDC (so renamed in 1962), an outdoor subsidy, was the flagship "welfare" program in America. Even though benefit levels were low and highly variable across states, program administration was characterized by intrusive surveillance (Connor, 1967; Funicello, 1993; Piven & Cloward, 1971). It is therefore unsurprising, in light of our strongly held beliefs concerning work, poverty, and worthiness, that TANF (the current incarnation of AFDC) has been decimated in the past three decades, while Social Security remains the untouchable "third rail" of American politics.

## THE GREAT SOCIETY AND THE WAR ON POVERTY

The next period of expansion of the welfare state took place in the 1960s as part of the Great Society reforms of the Johnson administration. The publication of Michael Harrington's *The Other America* in 1962 is widely credited with spurring public awareness of the problem of poverty in America. In his 1964 State of the Union Address, President Lyndon Johnson declared a "War on Poverty" and subsequently introduced legislation to establish numerous programs and offices to address the needs of the poor.

This expansion of generosity, however, continued to reflect ideas about the deserving and undeserving, with most new assistance programs targeting children and the elderly. These included the Food Stamp Program, created in 1964 (renamed the Supplemental Nutrition Assistance Program [SNAP] in 2008), and the establishment of Medicare, Medicaid, and Head Start in 1965 as amendments to the Social Security Act. John E. Schwarz (1988) observes that the welfare expansion of the Great Society was politically palatable because in the post-Eisenhower era of prosperity and low unemployment, it was easier to classify more of the poor as deserving of assistance. Schwarz reports that in 1960, half of all families in poverty had an employed head of household, and 25 percent of such families had a head of household who was employed full time (p. 22).

At the same time that these sweeping federal initiatives aimed to lift deserving Americans out of poverty, the available avenues for relief for those whose deservedness was ambiguous were still administered in ways that Katz (1989) characterized as "mean-spirited" as well as "pejorative and degrading" (pp. 14, 15). The pervasiveness of deterrent relief practices led one observer to comment, "The relief programs are notorious for the varieties of humiliation they inflict on their clients" (Fraser, 1989, p. 152). Piven and Cloward (1971) provide a detailed and illuminating account of the ways in which low-wage labor force participation was "enforced" via the methods of administering relief during the welfare expansion of the 1960s. These included excessively burdensome application requirements designed to keep applicants off the rolls, as well as intrusive surveillance practices including the now-infamous "midnight raids" at the homes of AFDC recipients, whose aim was to root out violations of man-in-the-house eligibility restrictions (see also Connor 1967; Gilliom, 2001; Gordon, 1994).

These practices serve multiple ends. By expanding the principle of less eligibility to encompass quality-of-life considerations, they reinforce dominant ideologies about deserving and undeserving recipients, about the deviousness of the moral failures requiring assistance, as well as ensuring a labor surplus:

> Market values and market incentives are weakest at the bottom of the social order. To buttress weak market controls and ensure the availability of marginal labor, an outcast class—the dependent poor—is created by the relief system. This class, whose members are of no productive use, is not treated with indifference, but with contempt. Its degradation at the hands of relief officials serves to celebrate the virtue of all work, and deters actual or potential workers from seeking aid. . . . The main target of these rituals is not the recipient . . . but the able-bodied-poor who remain in the labor market. It is for these people that the spectacle of the pauper is intended. (Piven & Cloward, 1971, pp. 165, 175; see also Garfinkel, 1956; Halpern-Meekin et al., 2015).

## THE NEGATIVE INCOME TAX EXPERIMENTS AND THE FAMILY ASSISTANCE PLAN

Beginning in the late 1960s and continuing through the end of the 1970s, the U.S. government quietly engaged in an ambitious program of experimentation with negative income tax (NIT), a form of means-tested guaranteed income.[4] These experiments grew out of the newly created Office of Economic Opportunity (OEO), established in 1964 with Sargent Shriver serving as its first director.[5] The OEO was responsible for administering the programs enacted as part of the Johnson administration's War on Poverty. Between 1968 and 1976, four NIT demonstration projects were conducted. The New Jersey Income Maintenance Experiment ran from 1968 to 1972, and its participants were two-parent families in Trenton, Paterson, Passaic, and Jersey City, New Jersey, and Scranton, Pennsylvania (N = 1,357). In Gary, Indiana, the Gary Income Maintenance Experiment (GIME, 1971–1974) enrolled approximately 1,800 single- and two-parent African American families (the other NIT experiments enrolled participants from diverse racial/ethnic groups). The Rural Income Maintenance Experiment (RIME, 1970–1972) enrolled 809 families in three counties in North Carolina and Iowa to gauge the impact of NIT on rural populations. The most ambitious of the NIT experiments—the Seattle and Denver Income Maintenance Experiments (SIME/DIME) ran between 1970 and 1976, enrolling nearly five thousand families over the duration of the experiment.[6] The Seattle-Denver experiment was the only one to include childless families (about 10% of the sample).

It is an understatement to say that the primary focus of these experiments concerned questions of the labor supply response to NIT. The entire enterprise was undertaken with the seemingly single-minded goal of determining whether this approach to reducing poverty would create a mass of layabouts. Overall, the findings of the NIT experiments revealed fairly minimal labor supply impacts, with workers reducing their work hours between 7 and 17 percent from a baseline of thirty-five hours per week on average, per household. This work reduction was more commonly seen in secondary and tertiary earners and in teens and young adults (Burtless, 1986; Levine et al., 2004).

Two other facts are important to note about the NIT experiments. The first remarkable feature of the NIT experiments was their scientific rigor. Participants were randomly selected for placement to experimental and control groups, and the behavior of each was comparatively analyzed. A variety of experimental conditions were assessed; these included variations in benefit levels, tax rates, and durations of assistance. This kind of classic experiment—also referred to as a randomized controlled trial—is considered the gold standard in applied policy research.

The second feature of the NIT experiments that stands out is that the structure of the programs themselves—the deliberately time-limited nature of the assistance—would have tended to *exaggerate* the labor supply response, which further strengthens the conclusion that NIT was *not* a disincentive to work. University of Wisconsin professor Harold Watts, one of the original NIT researchers, explains:

It was a short-term experiment. . . . Essentially leisure was on sale for a three-year period. When laundry soap is on sale, what do you do? You buy a lot of it. You might expect people in the experiment to act the same way. Not everyone will; someone who has a good job (it may not pay much, but it's stable) may not want to mess around with that by working less. . . . But by and large the poor families we were looking at didn't tend to have terribly steady jobs. . . . People did work less, but percentage-wise it tended to be in the single digits for men in particular. Some of the work response came from taking more time to look for work. Some of it came from cutting down hours, say from 65 to 60 hours a week, which doesn't seem like a tragedy. I don't remember finding anyone . . . who as soon as they got the grant, left the labor market and sat on the porch and whittled for three years. (Levine et al., 2004, p. 5)

Due to the finite time duration of the NIT experiments (the longest-running paid benefits for five years to some participant families), the minimal impacts on labor supply observed likely *overstated* the true impact on work effort. More recent evidence is available that further supports these already-robust findings. A small pilot study published in 2008 to evaluate the labor supply effects of a Belgian lottery that pays winners a lifetime annuity—thus simulating conditions similar to GBI—found similarly miniscule effects on labor market behavior. Fewer than 5 percent of winners reported any reduction in work hours whatsoever, and none actually left the labor market (Marx & Peeters, 2008).

While the principal research objective was to determine effects on labor supply, a great deal of data were collected on the participants of the NIT experiments. It was found that the income guarantees were associated with numerous positive outcomes. Among these findings were that many participants used the freedom from dire economic necessity to pursue education and training, particularly teens, young adults, and secondary and tertiary household earners (Hanushek, 1986; Levine et al., 2004). Primary wage earners in recipient households were also more likely to seek better-paying jobs when receiving the income guarantee (Johnson, 1980; Watts & Rees, 1977). Better health outcomes were reported for recipients (Gibson et al., 2020). Additionally, many benefits accrued to children in recipient households, including reductions in low birth weight (Kehrer & Wollin, 1979), better nutrition (O'Connor & Madden, 1979), lesser likelihood of living in poverty (Salkind & Haskins, 1982), and improved educational performance outcomes (Manheim & Minchilla, 1978; Maynard & Crawford, 1977; Maynard & Murnane, 1979; McDonald & Stephenson, 1979) relative to children in nonrecipient households.[7]

In August 1969, President Richard Nixon introduced a radical proposal to reform federal assistance to the poor during a television address to the nation. The Family Assistance Plan (FAP), which was largely designed by Daniel Patrick Moynihan, in his capacity of counselor to the president on urban affairs, proposed to provide a means-tested benefit equal to a full-time job at the federal minimum wage, administered as a NIT. However, the proposal was not couched in the language of citizenship rights or any sort of humanitarian concern for a basic income standard; rather, Nixon presented the FAP as a way of introducing "fairness" to welfare policy by invoking tropes about American self-reliance: "This new approach aims at helping the American people do more for themselves. It aims at getting everyone able to work off welfare rolls and onto payrolls. It aims at ending the unfairness in a system that has become unfair to the welfare recipient, unfair to the working poor, and unfair to the taxpayer" (cited in Steensland, 2008, p. 117). Despite the structuring of the program as a means-tested income guarantee (benefits for a family of four ranged from a minimum of $1,600 to $2,320 per year, depending on earned income[8]), Nixon took pains to distance the FAP from an income guarantee, openly rejecting the notion of citizenship rights and doubling down on the connection between work and deservedness: "A guaranteed income would undermine the incentive to work; the family assistance plan that I propose increases the incentive to work. A guaranteed income establishes a right without any responsibilities; family assistance recognizes a need and establishes a responsibility. . . . There is no reason why one person should be taxed so that another can choose to live idly" (cited in Steensland, 2008, p. 117).

Eligibility for benefits would be determined by two criteria: financial need, and that an adult in the household was "making a genuine work effort" by either working or by actively seeking work.

These work requirements, however, were not sufficient to sway the naysayers. Alex Waddan (1998, p. 205) notes that resistance came from both sides of the political spectrum; while conservatives focused on the issue of work disincentives, liberals objected that the benefit level was too low and "were unable to look past their animosity toward Nixon and overestimated their capacity to direct future reform of the welfare system." Although the FAP passed a vote in the House of Representatives, it failed to receive enough support in the Senate, and guaranteed minimum income vanished as quickly as it had come.

## THE RISE OF WORKFARE

The election of Ronald Reagan to the presidency in 1980 ushered in a new era of conservatism in American politics, which carried over into welfare reform. The welfare dependency narrative, bolstered by widely read critiques of the system such as Charles Murray's *Losing Ground* (1984), dovetailed nicely with calls to decimate "big government." Workfare—a concept introduced and promulgated in the formulation of the Nixon administration's FAP—was the answer. The Omnibus Budget Reconciliation Act of 1981 created the structural conditions necessary to defund welfare at the federal level by converting existing federal funding mechanisms to state-level block grants (Caputo, 2011). The flagship piece of welfare reform legislation during the Reagan-Bush era was the Family Support Act (FSA), which President Reagan signed into law on October 13, 1988. The FSA expressly connected receipt of benefits—even for those deemed deserving—to work effort.[9]

The decentralized nature of the legislation and the multiplicity of ideas for job training and placement programs resulted in the provisions of the FSA being under-actualized and underfunded. Unsurprisingly, female labor force participation in the low-wage sector began to rise following the passage of the FSA. "Welfare mothers" came to be "a potential source of cheap labor whose prospective wages would be insufficient to enable women to avoid abusive marriages or insecure jobs" (Caputo, 2011, p. 39; see also Boo, 2003; Gordon, 1994; Piven & Cloward, 1971).

## THE END OF WELFARE: THE CLINTON YEARS

During his campaign for the presidency in 1992, Bill Clinton promised to "end welfare as we know it." One of the lasting accomplishments of the Personal Responsibility and Work Opportunity Reconciliation Act of 1996 (PRWORA) was the conversion of AFDC to the TANF program, which boasted work requirements, a five-year lifetime limit on the receipt of benefits, and a requirement that paternity be formally established for all children receiving benefits. These reforms had predictable consequences; the TANF rolls fell dramatically. In 1994, approximately fourteen million women with children received ADFC benefits. In 2019, TANF benefits went to a mere two million recipients (Office of Family Assistance, 2020).[10] Mission accomplished!

It is debatable whether the reforms of the Clinton administration represented something new, or if they were merely a continuation of existing trends and tropes in the history of American welfare policy. Arguably, the PRWORA was *not* a radical departure from an already-mean-spirited, ungenerous, and distrustful system reflecting a strong belief in the intrinsic value of work as essential to human dignity. However, the lifetime caps on benefits, which accrued after five years of assistance as well as the ramped-up work requirements, even for recipients who were previously not expected to participate in the labor force (e.g., mothers of young children) suggest a new recalcitrance toward the provision of a minimum standard of living for all—an explicit rejection of the notion of universal rights of citizenship.[11]

Another enduring impact of the welfare reforms of the Clinton administration were reforms to the EITC, which comes to assume a prominent role in the nation's antipoverty efforts. This was partially accomplished through the elimination or contraction of alternative sources of support, as well as by linking the EITC to TANF and Supplemental Security Income (SSI) benefit administration procedures (Caputo, 2011).

## WELFARE WITH DIGNITY: THE EARNED INCOME TAX CREDIT

The federal EITC was first established in 1975, on the heels of the NIT experiments and concerns about rapidly swelling welfare rolls.[12] The EITC approach appealed to many stakeholders in the debates; it held the promise of encouraging work and the essential human dignity connoted by such (Congressional Research Service, 2021; Sykes et al., 2015). The EITC is a refundable tax credit, which means that eligible recipients may receive a transfer payment (in the form of a tax refund) if the value of the credit exceeds the taxes owed on income. Indeed, nearly 90 percent of the annual cost of the EITC takes the form of these outlays (Eissa & Hoynes, 2011).

At its inception, the EITC resembled other welfare programs in that it was fairly ungenerous. Although it was structured as a refundable tax credit, benefit levels were set such that all it did was offset the tax liability of eligible filers; this was intended to compensate for the increases in Social Security payroll taxes that had risen in tandem with Social Security benefit levels throughout the 1960s (Crandall-Hollick, 2018). Changes were made to the EITC via tax legislation in 1986, 1990, and 1993. Notably, it was greatly expanded in the 1990s as part of the program of tax and welfare reform undertaken by the Clinton administration with the intention of reducing the AFDC rolls.

Most earlier welfare income transfer programs (such as AFDC) had a fairly simple taxation structure whereby benefits would be reduced dollar for dollar after a certain income threshold. This arguably provides an effective disincentive to work, which is amplified if working also requires expenditures for childcare, transportation, and the like. However, unlike earlier programs of outdoor relief, the EITC has a system of thresholds and plateaus. During a plateau phase, as income increases, so does the benefit level. As income rises, the benefit is phased out, and at a certain income level, households are no longer eligible for the credit. Interestingly, the income eligibility caps—the point at which tax filers are no longer eligible for the credit—are approximately *twice the federal poverty thresholds*. The reason this is significant, and why I shall return to this point in chapter 6, is that the EITC clearly establishes an income floor, at least for deserving Americans.

Both the labor supply and antipoverty effects of the EITC have been widely researched (Eissa & Hoynes, 2011; Halpern-Meekin et al., 2015; Hotz & Scholz, 2006; Jones & Michelmore, 2018; Mendenhall et al., 2012; Schmieser, 2012). The 1993 changes to the EITC are credited with increasing the labor force participation of low-income single mothers (Boo, 1997; Edin & Shaefer, 2015; Eissa & Hoynes, 2011). Economist Andrew Leigh (2010) demonstrates that the EITC suppresses wages among the target population. As the nation's largest antipoverty program, it unquestionably helps many low-income families (Scholz & Levine, 2001). However, there are limits to the effect that the EITC can have on alleviating extreme poverty. It is estimated that only 80 percent of eligible tax filers claim the credit (Internal Revenue Service, 2020; Jones & Ziliak, 2019). Furthermore, EITC eligibility is based on earned taxable income, as defined by the Internal Revenue Service. Nearly 75 percent of EITC recipient households report annual incomes between $7,500 and $25,000 (Eissa & Hoynes, 2011). The largest proportion of beneficiaries are in the *second*, not the first, income decile, and nearly half of all beneficiaries are in the second and third income deciles (Eissa & Hoynes, 2011). Additionally, workers must be between the ages of twenty-five and sixty-five, excluding younger workers entirely.[13] This means that many of the very poorest Americans, those with a tenuous or nonexistent connection to the formal labor market, are ineligible for EITC relief.

The EITC also reproduces and reinforces hegemonic norms about family forms and deservedness, limiting assistance primarily to custodial parents. In 1993, the EITC eligibility provisions were expanded to provide some relief to childless individuals. However, benefit levels for childless filers are extremely low, with 2019 benefits maxing out at $529 per year, compared to maximum benefit levels of $3,526, $5,828, and $6,557 for households with one, two, or three or more qualifying children, respectively (Falk et al., 2019).[14] Accordingly, costs for childless recipients account for only 2 percent of total EITC expenditures (Eissa & Hoynes, 2011).

## THE IMPACT OF WELFARE POLICY ON ALLEVIATING POVERTY

More than ninety antipoverty or welfare programs exist at the federal level (House Budget Committee, 2014). Overall, these efforts do not appear to be either an efficient or effective means to combat poverty. In 1965, 17.3 percent of all Americans lived with incomes below the poverty line. In 2012, this figure is barely unchanged, at 15 percent. Similarly, the 22.3 percent rate of child poverty recorded in 2012 is virtually unchanged from the 1959 figure of 26.8 percent (Council of Economic Advisers, 2014). It should also be noted that historic *patterns* in the distribution of poverty in America also remain consistent—female-headed households and African Americans today experience poverty at twice the average rate, much as they did prior to the War on Poverty and the Great Society.

Nevertheless, there is also a strong case to be made that welfare—the transfer of spending power absent the exchange of labor—can be an effective means to improve the lives of Americans at the bottom of the economic order. John Schwarz (1988) marshals evidence that overall, by the late 1970s, the programs instituted and expanded during the welfare expansion of the Great Society succeeded in reducing poverty in America by 60 percent. However, these gains were not universally experienced among all the poor. The biggest winners, by far, were elderly Americans. Although no new federal income support programs were put in place by the Older Americans Act of 1965, this piece of legislation unequivocally and forcefully proclaimed that "adequate income in retirement" and "suitable housing" for the elderly were "national priorities" (McGarry, 2013). These priorities were reflected in increases to Social Security benefit levels by congressional action throughout the 1960s; annual cost-of-living increases in benefits became automatic in 1975.

When we evaluate the results of the 1960s War on Poverty at reducing poverty among the elderly in America, it is clear that welfare policy *can* be successful at improving the quality of life for large numbers of Americans. In 1959, 40 percent of Americans aged sixty-five and older were classified as living in poverty. In 2012, this rate was 9.1 percent, in contrast to the overall rate of 15 percent. Today, the elderly enjoy the lowest rate of poverty in America. Legislation and programs associated with the Great Society welfare expansion have been universally credited with bringing about this sea change in the standard of living for the elderly in the United States (Council of Economic Advisers, 2014; McGarry, 2013).

By contrast, historic trends in poverty for nonelderly Americans have shown little impact of antipoverty policy. Rates of poverty for nonelderly Americans are virtually unchanged since 1959 (Fontenot et al., 2018). These rates are 21.8 percent for children, 45.6 percent for African American children under the age of six, and 34 percent for single mothers (Council of Economic Advisers, 2014; Mishel et al., 2012). Furthermore, 44.3 percent of the poor live in "deep poverty," or at an income level that is 50 percent or less of the official poverty line (Mishel et al., 2012).

Schwarz's analysis of the nature of Great Society programs reveals the mechanics of the success of these programs. The welfare expansion of the 1960s took place during a period of abundant private sector growth, but this was *unrelated to the change in fortunes for the poor whose circumstances improved during this period.* The reasons for this are explained by both the types of assistance that were made available during this period, as well as the relationship of the beneficiaries to the labor market. With respect to program type, the forms of outdoor or quasi–outdoor relief programs—AFDC, SSI, and Social Security—target recipients who have either a tenuous or nonexistent relationship to the labor market. The same is true of the in-kind programs (food stamps, Medicare, Medicaid), whose primary beneficiaries are the elderly, children, and their mothers. In contrast, the third type of program that expanded in the 1960s—job training and placement programs—did not and *could not be expected to* have much impact on alleviating poverty. Children and the elderly are not expected to work. Therefore, poverty-reduction strategies that focus on work cannot be expected to be ameliorative in these populations; nor can they be expected to have much impact in sectors of the economy with slack demand for labor.

The findings from the extensive research on the NIT experiments demonstrate that fears of dependency and idleness resulting from the provision of a guaranteed income are utterly ungrounded. The reductions in work effort were miniscule and mostly realized among secondary and tertiary earners and primary childcare providers. Additionally, the provision of a stable income improved the circumstances of adults and children in recipient households in numerous ways. It should also be remembered that at present, the U.S. economy can no longer provide work for all Americans.

Government expenditures reflect hegemonic views about work and social worth. Expenditures for TANF are dwarfed by those for Social Security. In 2017, federal expenditures were $945 billion for Social Security and a mere $16.5 billion for the TANF program. This is consistent with Piven and Cloward's (1971, pp. 129–130) contention that "since 1935, Congress has always shown greater willingness to vote increases in the federal share of grants for the aged, blind, and disabled than for AFDC; and state-legislated limits on payments have generally reflected the same bias." An important, and largely invisible, exception is the swelling of the Social Security Disability rolls in the last two decades (Autor, 2011).

## TAX EXPENDITURES AND THE HIDDEN WELFARE STATE

Transfer payments, such as Social Security Disability or TANF subsidies, redistribute spending power in the economy without regard to labor exchange. It is a commonly held misconception that transfer payments constitute the *only* such redistribution on the part of the federal government. In fact, a substantial amount of spending power is redistributed via the mechanism of tax expenditures. Tax expenditures are foregone tax revenues, usually structured in such a way to exclude certain types or sources of income, or portions thereof, from taxation. From a functional economic standpoint, there is no difference between transfer payments and tax expenditures in that both redistribute spending power without regard to labor exchange. Because the costs of tax expenditures vary with economic activity (e.g., in a time of rising housing purchases, the amount of foregone taxes will also rise) and are available to all who meet eligibility requirements, there are no statutory limits on tax expenditure outlays (Howard, 1997).

The U.S. government subsidizes its citizenry via tax expenditures in order to encourage socially desirable behaviors (Congressional Budget Office, 2013; Faricy & Ellis, 2013; Howard, 1997, 2007). These include homeownership, saving for retirement, and the provision of health care through employers—this last articulating the status and value of work as a criterion of deservingness. If we interpret tax expenditures as fostering desired societal ends, one such goal is apparently the preservation of economic inequality. The majority of tax expenditure benefits accrue to the wealthiest segment of society. Over 50 percent of benefits find their way to those at the top 20 percent of the economic distribution; 17 percent of tax expenditures go to the top 1 percent; those at the bottom 20 percent of the income distribution reap a measly 8 percent of tax expenditure benefits (Congressional Budget Office, 2013). The largest single category in the tax expenditure budget is "housing and commerce," accounting for nearly 40 percent of foregone revenue. Given that many of these benefits *require* that recipients be of a certain income level in order to avail themselves of them (such as the ability to make a down payment to purchase a home), it is not surprising that this redistribution of spending power favors those at the top of the income distribution.

Even the EITC, one of the only tax expenditure programs that targets low-income recipients, favors those with higher incomes. Nearly 75 percent of EITC recipient households report annual incomes between $7,500 and $25,000; nearly half of EITC filers have some college education or more (Eissa & Hoynes, 2011; Kneebone & Murray, 2017). The largest proportion of beneficiaries are in the *second*, not the first, income decile, and nearly half of all beneficiaries are in the second and third income deciles (Eissa & Hoynes, 2011).

Tax expenditures are invisible to most Americans, and the beneficiaries are not stigmatized (Faricy & Ellis, 2013; Howard, 1997). Tax expenditures are rarely news making, as they are not subject to congressional appropriations approval. Some are written into the tax code as permanent provisions; others are subject to review only after the expiration of statutory time limits (Driessen, 2016). In the federal budget, tax expenditures are recorded as "revenue losses," *not* as spending, which further limits their visibility in the budgetary process. Interestingly, there is one exception to this accounting scheme: net refunds for the EITC, one of the few tax expenditures that specifically targets the poor, are treated as government spending in federal budget calculations.

The EITC showcases the stealthy side of tax expenditures. It is frequently touted as the premier antipoverty program in the United States, and as noted above, 90 percent of EITC expenditures take the form of transfer payments. These payments subsidize insufficient wages for low- to moderate-income households and establish a minimum income standard, much like a NIT. Yet the EITC bears none of the stigma of welfare; beneficiaries and other observers view the annual payouts as a tax refund, indistinguishable from those received by millions of other tax filers at all income levels—a view that is supported by its method of administration (Halpern-Meekin et al., 2015; Sykes et al., 2015).

The EITC and the Child Tax Credit (CTC) are the only major tax expenditures that specifically target the poor. The EITC is the single largest tax expenditure benefiting those at the lower end of the income distribution; expenditures for the CTC are slightly less (Congressional Budget Office, 2013). In 2013, expenditure levels for the EITC were roughly equivalent to those for the mortgage interest deduction and slightly less than those allocated to capital gains on death-transferred assets. Combined outlays for the EITC and the CTC are nearly equal to the tax expenditures resulting from foregone taxes on pension contributions.

## CONCLUSION

Piven and Cloward (1971, p. 22, emphasis added) effectively argue that "relief arrangements deal with disorder, not simply by giving aid to the displaced poor, but by granting it on condition that they behave in certain ways, and most important, *on condition that they work.*" The proposals and arguments I present in this book are consistent with the premise that providing economic subsistence to the poorest of our citizens reduces disorder, though I focus specifically on disorder of the predatory criminal variety. At present, the U.S. economy can no longer provide work for all its citizens, let alone work that provides a secure and sustainable family wage. The rapid progress of automation threatens even more jobs at the low end of the income and skills distribution. Recent trends in criminal justice reform portend the introduction or reintroduction of large numbers of would-be workers joining in on this fool's errand.

The contemporary implications of the early linkages between institutions and practices for "helping" the poor and those for the control of crime are obvious and, indeed, are core to this book. At the current moment in our history, the inability of the criminal justice system to continue to contain society's undesirables—explicitly defined as those who are expected to work but do not—is clear. As chapter 3 demonstrates, a national, bipartisan consensus has emerged that we must reduce prison populations; this movement is building steam such that it may rival the staying power of the rehabilitative ideal that held sway for a century. The prospects for the need for human labor in the American economy require that we rethink the connection between social worth and work. We are currently in a process of undoing the buildup of the carceral state, resulting in more and more justice-involved individuals struggling with, or disengaging entirely from, the labor market. Many of these individuals are at the absolute bottom of the distribution of income, skills, and hireability in highly contracted sectors of the economy. In chapter 6, I offer, in broad-stroke terms, an ameliorative policy solution that in some ways exploits the historic connections between prison and welfare—a means-tested GBI, available to all adults unable to earn sufficient income through work in the formal labor market, administered to individuals at the federal level.

Before we turn to possible solutions, the chapter that follows details some likely outcomes if our social policy choices continue to reflect ignorance about the current realities. Chapter 6 proposes a solution—a means-tested GBI for individuals who are unable to meet economic needs in the contemporary economy. However, deep and meaningful attitude change regarding both work and welfare are needed in order to most fully avoid the negative consequences we will surely face if economic support for the poor continues to be available only as it is under the current regime, and if recipients continue to be stigmatized and shamed for failing to provide for themselves and their families by engaging in paid work.

It is my hope that a frank exposition of these probable consequences will help to move the conversation in the direction of considering alternative ideas and solutions. In a world in which there is simply not enough work for all, our stubborn adherence to these hegemonic ideals prizing work as the sole indicator of social worth means abandoning a potentially ever-growing segment of our citizenry. But the drive for survival and the uncanny adaptability of the human spirit mean that some of these individuals will find ways to meet their basic needs—and if we do not decide, as a society, to share in the benefits of economic prosperity, the pursuit of those means of survival will diminish the quality of life for all. In the chapter that follows, I explore some of the likely consequences of failing to address the collision course of economic trends and decarceration in contemporary America.

# 5 · THE CONSEQUENCES OF DENIAL

We have thus far considered trends in two societal institutions that are on a collision course—the economy and the criminal justice system. We have also examined the origins and policy manifestations of the strong cultural presumptions that link worthiness, masculinity, and work. By now, it should be abundantly clear to the reader that the idea that every adult in America *must* work at a full-time job as a requirement for full participation in society's benefits and privileges is, at the very least, unsustainable. Beyond the practical unrealism of these antiquated moral narratives about work, masculinity, and "deservedness," our stubborn adherence to these notions causes harm to individuals, to families, to communities, and to society at large. Mass incarceration has been one denial-sustaining adaptation to these realities, but as chapter 3 demonstrated, this safety valve is not likely to be as accommodating or available in the foreseeable future. The exposition that follows details what I see as some of the obvious and foreseeable consequences of the denial of our contemporary circumstances.

## BARRIERS TO EMPLOYMENT AMONG THE JUSTICE-INVOLVED

Because the focus of this book is on the colliding trajectories of the economy and the criminal justice system, and all signs point to the introduction of greater and greater numbers of individuals bearing the stigmas and barriers of criminal justice system contact into the labor market, a brief review of the obstacles these individuals face is in order. This shall serve as backdrop for the exposition of the likely consequences of decarceration that follows.

That the justice-involved face enormous obstacles in the formal labor market is undisputed. A recent analysis reported an unemployment rate of over 30 percent among formerly incarcerated individuals, in comparison to rates of 4–6 percent in the general population (Couloute & Kopf, 2018). This statistic, however, fails to capture the true extent to which the justice-involved are disengaged from legitimate work—formerly incarcerated individuals are significantly more likely than similar individuals to be discouraged or completely out of the labor force (Apel & Sweeten, 2010; Council of Economic Advisers, 2016a; Looney & Turner, 2018). The proportion of men who are completely out of the labor force has more than doubled since 1970 (Kudlyak et al., 2011). Chapter 2 reviewed these trends with respect to African American men, the group most affected by the expansion of the criminal justice system.

Incarceration—and justice involvement more generally—suppresses employment, wages, and lifetime earnings (Gellar et al., 2011; Mueller-Smith, 2015; Pew Charitable Trusts, 2010). The low probability of success in the legitimate labor market leads many to withdraw entirely; Adam Looney and Nicholas Turner (2018) estimate that approximately one-third of men aged thirty years who are not in the labor force are either former prisoners or currently incarcerated. They further note that only about half of formerly incarcerated individuals report any legitimate earnings as long as four years postrelease: "Overall, the incarcerated fare poorly in the formal labor market after they are released. In the first full year after release about 49 percent of ex-prisoners earn less than $500 as reported on a W2 or tax return . . . 32 percent earn between $500 and $15,000, and only 20 percent earn more than $15,000" (p. 7).

Sociologist Devah Pager and colleagues have extensively documented the impacts of direct discrimination on the part of employers (Pager, 2003; Pager & Karafin, 2009; Pager, Western, & Bonikowski, 2009; Pager, Western, & Sugie, 2009; see also Holzer et al., 2006). In an effort to reduce racial discrimination in hiring, reformers in some cities have championed "ban the box" (BTB) policies in hiring.[1] These initiatives, in place in thirty-four states and the District of Columbia, encourage or require employers to remove the item on job applications that asks about former criminal convictions. This was reasoned to prevent discrimination at early stages of the hiring process. However, a growing body of research finds the opposite effect—racial effects in hiring were *more* pronounced in the absence of criminal history information, suggesting that statistical discrimination disfavoring nonwhite male applicants was significantly increased following the implementation of BTB. They report that BTB "has no significant effect on white male employment, but reduces the probability of employment. . . . For black men . . . we find net negative effects on employment for these groups: on average, young, low-skilled black men are . . . less likely to be employed after BTB than before. This effect is statistically significant ($p < 0.05$) and robust to a variety of alternative specifications and sample definitions. . . . The effects are larger for the least skilled in this group (those with no high school diploma or GED), for whom a recent incarceration is more likely" (Doleac & Hansen, 2016, p. 23; see also Agan & Starr, 2017, 2018). Jennifer L. Doleac and Benjamin Hansen also find evidence that the effects of statistical discrimination are persistent and, more disturbingly, *increase* over time. It is important to situate these results in terms of baseline rates of employment (see Pager, 2003). They report that the suppressive effect of BTB policies can reduce employment among young Black men by as much as 50 percent (p. 23). Additionally, the authors examined BTB in a variety of labor market contexts and found these effects to be even stronger in slack labor market conditions, as "employers are more able to exclude broad categories of job applicants in order to avoid ex-offenders when applicants far outnumber available positions" (p. 5).

The conclusions that can be drawn from the body of research on the difficulties faced by the justice-involved in the labor market are fairly obvious—justice-involved individuals fare worse than others in a labor market already populated with plenty of "extra people." We are currently on a course that will introduce even more and more of the justice-involved into labor markets that are already unable to use the labor of all job seekers. Some of the further consequences we might expect to follow are detailed in the exposition that follows. Steel yourself: it is not pretty.

## LOST GENERATION(S)

Despite quarterly proclamations regarding the unemployment rate, jobs created, and the like, a great deal of evidence strongly suggests that there is a growing segment of the population with an extremely tenuous connection to the labor market. This is not a recent development. In some parts of America, this was evident more than two decades ago, when William Julius Wilson (1997, pp. 52–53, emphasis added) wrote:

> Neighborhoods that offer few legitimate opportunities, inadequate job information networks, and poor schools lead to the disappearance of work. That is, where jobs are scarce, where people, rarely, if ever, have the opportunity to help their friends and neighbors find jobs, and where there is a disruptive or degraded school life purporting to prepare youngsters for eventual participation in the workforce, many people eventually lose their feeling of connectedness to work in the formal economy; they no longer expect work to be a regular, and regulating, force in their lives. In the case of young people, they may grow up in an environment that lacks the idea of work as a central experience of adult life—they have little or no labor force attachment. *These circumstances also increase the likelihood that the residents will rely on illegitimate sources of income, thereby further weakening their attachment to the legitimate labor market.*

Wilson (1987, 1997, 2009) documents the social isolation created by concentrated joblessness among the urban poor—in communities where the only successful role models are criminally involved, residents of concentrated poverty ghetto areas lack modeling that might attach them to the conventional labor market. He also details the obstacles that unemployed African American ghetto residents face in seeking legitimate employment, both as a result of employer bias and discrimination; these obstacles are sometimes exacerbated by "responses and adaptations to chronic subordination" (Wilson, 1997, p. 55; see also Wilson, 2009). Jamie Fader (2013, p. 103) recounts an example of one of these types of responses in *Falling Back: Incarceration and Transitions to Adulthood among Urban Youth*, her award-winning ethnographic study of justice-involved young men in Philadelphia:

> Searching for work involved intense ambivalence, which could explain why Sincere and his friends were getting high before venturing on their job search. We might well ask why they bothered to search at all when the risk of rejection was so high. . . . With failure likely, however, they needed a way to explain the lack of success. By showing up at the Center City Olive Garden as a group—and a visibly high one at that—they engaged in classic reaction formation behavior whereby people protect themselves against the likelihood of being denied something they seek by pretending they did not want it in the first place.

Fader (2013, pp. 111–112) further describes some of the impediments faced by the urban poor navigating the formal economy, from having to traverse what these men view as hostile "white spaces" in order to seek employment, to extensive online application procedures that "serve as an additional disadvantage to inner-city job seekers because they are less likely to have access to computers [and] less likely to be familiar with online environments." Repeated failed attempts also perpetuate the internalization of narratives that focus on individual responsibility (Wilson, 1997, p. 67), leading to further discouragement and detachment.

It is important to place Wilson's observations and analyses of Chicago's ghetto poor in the 1980s and 1990s in context vis-à-vis the evolution of the economy and the mismatch between labor supply and demand. At the time Wilson conducted this research, the mismatch was more distinctly *geographical*—that is, driven by the movement of jobs, particularly in manufacturing, out of central cities and into suburban and rural areas, as well as from the rust belt to the sun belt. This era was also marked by much growth in the service and information sectors of the economy. Unlike the contemporary labor market, jobs *were* more available than they are today—just not in the locations and sectors favorable to the urban poor. The difference today is evident in the trends in the last few decades in *all* measures of labor utilization and in the increase in discouraged and marginally attached workers discussed in chapter 2. Advances in automation technology, e-commerce, and the like have now *permanently reduced the capacity of the economy to accommodate all those who seek employment.*

Quantitative evidence also bears this out. Holly Foster and John Hagan (2007, p. 401) report that approximately 15 percent of American youth lack any substantial connection to either educational institutions or the labor market (see also Aguiar et al., 2017; Zelenev, 2011). Young would-be workers face enormous adversity in the labor market. Labor force participation rates for men, as well as those of younger cohorts, are in decline (Autor & Wasserman, 2013; Council of Economic Advisers, 2016b). Young men of color are particularly disadvantaged in the formal economy (Crutchfield, 2014; Fader, 2013; Pager, 2003; Wilson, 1997). African American males aged eighteen to twenty-four experience unemployment rates that are four times the national average. The likelihood that a nonemployed African American was in prison tripled between 1980 and 1999 (Council of Economic Advisers, 2016a). Our jails and prisons are filled to capacity (and frequently beyond) with young men of color—the same demographic group whose participation in the labor market has waned in the past decade. Economist Alan B. Krueger (2017, p. 2) also observes "a continued decline in the rate of transition for those who are out of the labor force back into the labor force." Age- and cohort-specific trends in unemployment rates as well as labor force participation further suggest that in some communities, larger and larger proportions of successive cohorts of young men and women may *never* engage with the formal labor market (see also Brayne, 2014; Crutchfield & Pitchford, 1997; Pettit & Western, 2004; Witte & Tauchen, 1994).

Criminal justice system involvement appears to magnify these disintegrative effects. Sarah Brayne examined the phenomenon of "system avoidance" among the justice-involved and found that any contact with the justice system increased the likelihood of an individual avoiding "surveilling institutions"—defined as organizations and institutions that keep formal records. These include banks, hospitals and other health-care providers, educational institutions, and the formal labor market. Brayne (2014, p. 385, emphasis added) observes:

> Given that involvement with the criminal justice system is highly stratified by race and class, the negative consequences of system avoidance will be similarly disproportionately distributed, thus exacerbating preexisting inequalities for an expanding group of already disadvantaged individuals. Furthermore, lack of attachment to important institutions such as hospitals, banks, schools, and the labor market leads to marginalization and impedes opportunities for financial security and upward mobility. As Haggerty and Ericson (2000:619) suggest, "efforts to evade the gaze of different systems involves an attendant trade-off." *That trade-off is full participation in society.*

The prospect of a "lost generation" is troublesome all on its own, but there is an unavoidable conclusion even more disturbing to contemplate. Our contemporary condition is not a fluke. Current trends in automation, as well as advances in engineering and artificial intelligence facilitated by the enormous amounts of behavioral data generated and gathered on a daily basis, will continue—about this there can be no doubt. This means that the labor market prospects for *future* generations will be every bit as bleak as those faced by today's young adults—a prospect abundantly supported by the data.

## MASCULINITY, WORK, AND CRIME

The gendered nature of the cultural expectations that surround work—the salience of the "provider" role to hegemonic ideals of masculinity—adds another dimension to the problematic convergence of decarceration-oriented reform trends in the criminal justice system and the economy-wide mismatch between labor supply and demand. The deep cultural associations among work, worth, and worthiness are inexorably bound up with idealized conceptions of men as "providers" and "breadwinners." As chapter 4 demonstrated, these ideas about work and masculinity could not be more clearly expressed in American welfare policy. With the exception of the recent expansion in availability of Social Security Disability Insurance benefits (Autor, 2011), there are no economic assistance programs available for poor men who are not custodial parents. Historically, welfare arrangements have been contingent on the *absence* of a man in the family unit (Moffitt, 2015; Piven & Cloward, 1971). These policies clearly reflect and reproduce hegemonic ideals of masculinity—defined by a man's success at working and providing for his family; the way to become a man is to succeed at these roles. Men who do not are considered failures and undeserving of assistance.

These expectations weigh heavily on young men in urban communities, who struggle to develop masculine identities (Anderson, 1999; Fader, 2013; Hagedorn, 1998; Wilson, 2009). Lacking legitimate or socially acceptable opportunities to express their masculinity—to "do gender," in the words of Candace West and Don Zimmerman (1987)—many young men find these needs are more easily met in the illicit economy. Crime is not exclusively, but predominantly, the province of young men—a demographic for whom the labor market as it is presently constituted is particularly inhospitable.

Urban ethnographers have documented thriving "off the books" economies in places lacking legitimate economic opportunities (Duneier, 2000; Fader, 2013; Hagedorn, 1998; Valentine, 1978; Venkatesh, 2006). For a significant number of Americans, "hustles," or income-producing activity that takes place outside of the formal economy, serve as one of a number of income sources used to make ends meet. Fader (2013, p. 104) observes that "work in the formal labor market is located at one end of a continuum of strategies to meet economic demands. . . . Most of the urban poor engage in a mix of strategies, including public assistance, paid employment, and forms of hustling" to make ends meet (see also Edin & Lein, 1997; Edin & Shaefer, 2015; Fagan & Freemen, 1999; Sullivan, 1989). In some cases, this secondary or underground economy serves as the primary economy for neighborhood residents (Duneier, 2000; Fader, 2013; Hagedorn, 1998; Venkatesh, 2006). Sociologist Sudhir Venkatesh (2006, p. 7) notes that "not all who participate are criminals, and not all activities are heinous." Some of these off-the-books income-generating activities are only "illicit" from a regulatory standpoint (e.g., selling homemade food without proper licensing or health inspections or cutting hair in one's home without a cosmetology license). However, a good deal of this underground economic activity is criminal, particularly the illicit drug trade, which provides constant opportunities for young men in urban communities to earn money.

In 1998, John Hagedorn published a revised edition of *People and Folks*, his seminal ethnographic study of gangs in Milwaukee during deindustrialization in the 1980s. In the chapter he added revisiting the subjects of the original research, Hagedorn provides evidence supporting his contention that "it is likely today that drug sales is the largest single employer of African American and Latino males in Milwaukee" (p. 199) and also observed that "economic restructuring has made neighborhood-based economic functions more important for lower-class peer groups. The drug economy is the most profitable kind of informal economic organization that rose to meet the needs of those victimized by deindustrialization. *One major impact of economic restructuring for poor communities has been a sharp reduction in the extent of the licit economy and the vast expansion of the illicit economy, especially the business of selling drugs*" (p. 198, emphasis original; see also Hutcherson, 2012).

Referencing Robert Merton's work on the "pathological materialism" of American society, as manifested in the trope of the "American dream," Hagedorn (1998, p. 197, emphasis added) characterizes the violence in the underground economy as resulting from "overconformity" to this ideal, stating that "high rates of male inner-city violence appear to be basically the product of the intersection of *poverty with masculinity*." When you overlay this dynamic with a paucity of legitimate job opportunities and the entanglement of widely held cultural beliefs about work and worthiness with hegemonic narratives of masculinity, young men's involvement in a violent shadow economy appears an inevitable consequence.

The multiplicity of opportunities coupled with low barriers to entry make the street-level drug trade an attractive option for income acquisition to young men of color, particularly in the face of perceived and real hostility and rejection in the formal labor market. Over and above the pressures created by economic need, opportunities in the underground economy also offer psychic benefits, as Fader (2013, pp. 102, 127) documents in her ethnographic study of community re-entry among juvenile justice-involved young men as they transition to adulthood: "Despite the dearth of working men in their communities, they experienced both internal and external pressures to get jobs. Although they knew that few men fulfilled the breadwinner ideal, they still believed it was the best way to achieve masculine adulthood and provide for their families. . . . Hustling offers them both income and a sense of masculine dignity. . . . The dual images of the 'own man' and the 'mama's boy' reinforce young men's desire to achieve financial independence in the only job that is always available" (see also Anderson, 1999; Crutchfield, 2014; Sullivan, 1989).

The ability to earn money and to at least partially fulfill some hegemonic masculine ideals makes work in the underground economy particularly attractive for young men in communities that offer few legitimate alternatives. These behavioral patterns are often reinforced when they father children, a not-uncommon occurrence among the subjects of Fader's research. It has been suggested that parenthood can serve as a "turning point" or a "hook for change" in the process of desistance from crime (Giordano et al., 2002; Laub & Sampson, 2003; Sampson & Laub, 1993), However, recent work illustrates the complexity of these relationships in contemporary urban cohorts. While fatherhood appears to offer young men a means of experiencing masculine roles denied them by limited economic opportunities, it comes with additional pressure to fulfill the role of "provider," an increasingly unattainable goal, at least in the legitimate economy. Fatherhood and family as a means of expressing and adhering to traditional conceptions of masculinity is undermined by their inability to sustain a reliable source of legitimate income. In addition to making demands for support, the mothers of the young men's children frequently have greater control over household resources, due to the mothers' eligibility for government assistance. Fader (2013, pp. 128, 106) observes that "ultimately the young men's marginal position in the labor market, coupled with their ambivalence about romantic commitments with their babies' mothers, undermined their ability to form stable families. Moreover, their precarious status in the family often led to further involvement in the underground economy, where respect was earned more easily and their masculinity was less likely to be challenged. . . . Unlike other milieus where these men feel they constantly come up short, such as fatherhood and legal employment, the streets offer them the illusion of control over their lives."

In the absence of legitimate work opportunities, coupled with barriers arising from their involvement with the criminal justice system, many young men respond to the additional economic pressures of fatherhood by resorting to criminal opportunities. Fader reports that all but two of the fifteen young men who are the subjects of her research return to the drug trade, despite their intentions to desist from crime. In a recent study examining the effects of visitation on recidivism postincarceration, Grant Duwe and Valerie Clark (2013) reported that while visitation generally had the effect of reducing or delaying recidivism, visits from estranged or former spouses were associated with increased criminal activity upon release (see also Bales & Mears, 2008). The intersection of economic need, a tenuous or nonexistent relationship to the formal labor market, and the pressures to adhere to hegemonic notions of idealized masculinity result in a variety of reinforcing dynamics that serve to keep young men in the illicit economy—further distancing themselves from the mainstream and from conventional societal institutions.

The current state and future trajectories of both the U.S. economy and the criminal justice system portend serious consequences if we continue to turn a blind eye to these converging trends. One of the consequences of denial of these structural realities vis-à-vis the capacity of the labor market, and the retention of greater numbers of would-be job seekers in communities instead of correctional institutions is not simply more crime but the growth and persistence of a *permanent criminal class*, unengaged with mainstream social institutions and denied the benefits of full membership in society such as participation in the democratic process (e.g., Uggen et al., 2016). As innovations in engineering and automation progress, the proportion of Americans who are economically superfluous will grow, and we can fully expect that these individuals will resort to any means necessary to survive in the absence of alternatives. Underground shadow economies will continue to provide opportunities to earn income. The next section considers the ways in which criminal justice reform may influence the nature and structure of these illicit opportunities and also considers ways in which the consequences described here can become far worse.

## CRIMINAL JUSTICE REFORM AND CRIMINAL OPPORTUNITY STRUCTURES

While expansion of the illicit economy and the consequent increase in criminal activity that seems an inevitable consequence of the collision course of these two American institutions should be sufficient to command our attention, we are faced with an even more disturbing possibility. Just as legitimate economic markets evolve in response to legal, technological, and societal changes, many signs point to changes in the distribution of criminal opportunities in the illicit market resulting in the wake of the convergence of criminal justice policy reform and the declining capacity of the economy to utilize the labor of all who are expected to work.

The effects of criminal opportunities on criminal behavior—in particular, the substitution of one form of criminal activity for another—have not been widely researched. Sociologists Richard Cloward and Lloyd Ohlin (1960) were among the first to identify the role of illicit opportunity structures in shaping the *type* of offending behavior engaged in by delinquent youth. Several recent illustrations from the contemporary research literature presage what might happen if criminal opportunity structures change substantially in response or adaptive fashion to criminal justice policy reform.

Consider this: if current movements in drug policy reform continue (specifically, the move toward legalization of currently illicit substances for recreational use at the state level), opportunities to earn money in the drug trade may decline. Market contraction may also come about as a result of the attention currently focused on the "opioid crisis." If some of the proposals currently being floated (President's Commission on Combating Drug Addiction and the Opioid Crisis, 2017) result in more widespread availability of drug treatment, this may reduce demand for illicit drugs, which could result in reduced opportunities to earn money in the illicit drug trade. If opportunities to generate income in the drug economy contract and conditions remain the same vis-à-vis the labor market and the absence of government assistance for men, these individuals will likely resort to other hustles to earn money. These hustles may take the form of more potentially more damaging and violent kinds of crime such as street or home invasion robberies.

The increase in urban homicide in the late 1980s and early 1990s during a period of general decline in both violent *and* nonviolent crime demonstrates the role of criminal opportunity structures and market structures in shaping crime patterns. This spike in homicide was almost entirely concentrated among young urban males and has been attributed to the rise of the crack trade (Baumer, 1994; Blumstein & Rosenfeld, 1998; Chauhan et al., 2011; Grogger & Willis, 2000; Messner et al., 2007; cf Bartley & Williams, 2015). Jeff Grogger and Mike Willis (1998) characterize crack cocaine as a "technological innovation" that influenced cocaine markets in two ways. The introduction of crack effectuated the tandem consequences of expanding cocaine markets to new populations of consumers as well as reducing barriers to entry for sellers. Increased competition among sellers generates conflict; in illegal markets, disputes are regulated largely through violence. This resulted in a sharp uptick in homicides among young urban males at the height of the crack epidemic—as well as a corresponding decline when demand for crack waned in the 1990s and markets contracted (Blumstein et al., 2000; Golub & Johnson, 1997).

Sarah Becker and Jill McCorkel (2011) analyzed data from the National Incident-Based Reporting System (NIBRS) from 2002 to 2008 to investigate the effects of gender and co-offending on offending behavior. They found that when female offenders worked with male co-offenders, not only did their criminal activity increase in extent and frequency, but it also changed the *types* of crimes in which female offenders engaged, a finding the authors characterize as "broadening" their criminal activities, and explain with reference to the existence of gendered criminal opportunity structures:

> "For the majority of crimes . . . the presence of male co-offenders increases a woman's likelihood of involvement in that offense category. . . . Specifically, women are several times more likely to be involved in gender atypical offenses like robbery, drug trafficking, burglary, homicide, gambling, kidnapping, and weapons offenses when they have at least one male co-offender compared to when they work alone or in a same-sex group. With the possible exception of homicide and rape, these crimes involve resources offenders working alone might find difficult to access—tools and raw materials, information, specialized skill sets, and distribution channels. (Becker & McCorkel, 2011, pp. 99–100)

James Wright and Peter Rossi (1986) conducted extensive survey research with a regionally varied sample of nearly two thousand incarcerated felons in eleven different institutions on their attitudes, motivation, and behavior with respect to gun use and gun carrying. The finding that most informs the current discussion was in the response to questions concerning these men's likely response to changes in handgun availability. The modal response from gun-carrying offenders was that they would substitute sawed-off shoulder weapons (shotguns) if cheap, low-caliber handguns were unavailable or prohibitively priced. From the standpoint of potential victims, this would be an undesirable consequence, as a hit at close range from a sawed-off shotgun can cause much graver injury than a wound from a .22 caliber pistol. Relatedly, Claire Sterk's 1999 ethnography of female crack users in Atlanta demonstrates the effect of market structures and supply dynamics on the behavior of illicit drug users. Several of the participants in Sterk's study reported a preference for other drugs, such as heroin and marijuana, but explain that they took up using crack when it came to dominate local drug markets and drug-using subcultures.

The work of ethnographer Randol Contreras speaks more directly to the issues considered in this book. In his 2013 ethnography *The Stickup Kids: Race, Drugs, Violence, and the American Dream*, Contreras documents the criminal activities of a group of young men in the South Bronx in the 1990s who shifted their income-generating activities from nonviolent drug sales to violent robberies in the wake of declining demand for crack, which resulted in market saturation:

> They had invested their prime years in the crack game, when most young people were preparing for the legitimate labor force. So they knew how to manage drug spots, negotiate drug deals, and act around drug dealers—everything that had little use in a service economy demanding more subservience, less masculinity, more education, less resistance, and more middle-class etiquette.... They put their hopes in drug robberies as their last chance at capitalist success. It was a long shot, but their American success clock was ticking, and they were running out of time.... It was too late to go back to school.... It was too late to undo a criminal record. (pp. 112, 114)

This is precisely the consequence that might be expected if current trends in the economy, decarceration, and drug policy reform continue. What's more, the localized nature of these effects means that communities that are *already* burdened with large-scale drug market activity will bear the (initial) brunt of a shift toward predatory crime. However, outward diffusion from areas of concentrated criminal activity is to be expected, as criminal opportunities dwindle as a result of areas becoming "fished out" (Davies, 2006; Rengert, 1996). This means that the apparent ability of the economically fortunate to shield themselves from these consequences is illusory; this is not a problem that can be contained or ignored.

The types of work available—often determined by the dominant regional or local industry—influence the kinds of jobs individuals have. For the growing corps of jobless individuals, frequently with little or no connection to the formal labor market, the availability of criminal opportunities—both in quantity and in kind—influences criminal behavior in similar fashion. Even in the absence of changing conditions with respect to street-level opportunities in the drug trade, the mismatch between legitimate labor market opportunities and the economic needs of the "extra people" at the bottom of the income distribution portends a dangerous future in America's cities and beyond if measures are not taken to address this crisis in a realistic fashion.

## JOBLESSNESS, ANOMIE, AND PERSISTENT PRECARITY

The specter of a permanent criminal class, increasingly disconnected from mainstream social institutions, should provide sufficient concrete impetus to consider new narratives and new policy approaches regarding the distribution of income and wealth in American society. Decarceration-oriented reforms in criminal justice are likely to intensify the deficiencies of the institutional capacity of the economy. Apart from the immediate and tangible social harms produced by the convergence of excess labor supply and hegemonic beliefs about work, worthiness, and masculinity, the overemphasis we place on work as the near-exclusive marker of a person's worth may result in profound and pervasive individual and societal consequences.

The discontents that arise as a result of purposelessness have been thoughtfully considered by many social scientists. Merton's classic description of anomie and pathological materialism certainly strikes a chord; but perhaps even more on point are the writings of Karl Marx and Friedrich Engels on alienation and anomie. The contemporary research literature teems with confirmation that the dislocation that accompanies joblessness, unemployment, placelessness in the economy is associated with a general decline in well-being, increasing the likelihood of a whole host of maladies including depression, substance abuse, marital difficulties, and health problems (Maynard & Feldman, 2011; Norris, 2016; Warr, 1987).

The consequences of the increasing instability of employment arrangements have led some to identify a growing segment of global societies as the "precariat." Guy Standing (2011, p. 27), one of the most prominent analysts of the precariat, estimates that "in many countries, at least a quarter of the adult population is in the precariat." The precariat is defined by the erosion of trust and security as relates to work and material survival, as well as the loss of "a secure work-based identity" (Standing, 2011, p. 9).

The insecurity that defines the precariat has profound behavioral implications, many of which are consistent with Standing's concerns about the political and moral consequences of precarity. Standing (2011, p. 21) expresses concern about the immediacy of day-to-day concerns in the lives of the precariat, foretelling "a mass incapacity to think long-term." Edin and Shaefer (2015, p. 57) characterize the lives of those in extreme poverty and insecurity as "lurching from crisis to crisis." These crises can engender a variety of seemingly poor choices that may represent the best of available alternatives (Tirado, 2014). These can lead to a variety of consequences, from chronic and persistent debt (Edin & Shaefer, 2015; Standing, 2011), or engaging in criminal activity in response to a financial crisis (Corman et al., 2006).

Members of the precariat also engage in a great deal of uncompensated labor. This may take the form of searching for a job with better wages and more consistent hours, time spent having one's person and belongings searched by one's employer—off the clock—as well as the general drain on mental "bandwidth" (Mullainathan & Shafir, 2013) that results from the uncertainty of scheduling shifts, requiring that workers be constantly available (Edin & Shaefer, 2015; Golden, 2015; Guendelsberger, 2019; Standing, 2011; Tirado, 2014).

Criminal justice system involvement intensifies the conditions of precarity. For example, criminal justice involvement can significantly add to debt among justice-involved individuals (Bannon et al., 2010; Link, 2019). Avoidance of mainstream social institutions (including the labor market) signals distrust in these institutions and also creates conditions conducive to criminal involvement (Brayne, 2014; Link & Roman, 2017).

Journalist Emily Guendelsberger explains, from a firsthand perspective, how this manifests among those living in precariat America. During a monthlong stint working as a picker in an Amazon warehouse during the holiday season, she describes the physical and mental exhaustion that follows a full-time schedule of eleven-and-a-half-hour shifts spent in constant motion, every movement tracked and timed by a handheld electronic device. She expresses surprise, however, at the effect this has on "more than just [her] body":

> As I inch out of the massive parking lot, I spot Darryl [a friendly co-worker] in the large huddle of people at the bus stop. It's freezing and miserable, and we're going the same way. I consider stopping to give him a ride. No. Fuck Darryl. I don't care. I don't want to make small talk. I don't want to delay my bedtime for however many minutes I'll have to go out of my way . . . so I pretend not to see him. . . . It's not a big deal, and I'm sure Darryl wouldn't hold it against me. But I like to think of myself as someone who'd offer a nice kid a ride home after a truly shitty day of work. Right now, though, exhaustion has shrunk my circle of empathy to the point that it's barely big enough for myself. (Guendelsberger, 2019, p. 56; see also Tirado, 2014)

Standing's analyses emphasize the potential political and moral consequences of the rise of the precariat, such as the appeal of neo-fascist politics and the erosion of empathy and trust. While these are undoubtedly important issues worthy of consideration, the focus of this work is different. My focus is on a relatively small segment of the precariat—those at the very bottom of the economic and social order, and the justice-involved in particular. In short, my lens is trained on what criminologist John Irwin (1985) called the *rabble*.

This book examines the consequences that result from the convergence of trends in the economy and the criminal justice system, with particular attention to the growing segment of Americans who live in the very deepest forms of poverty, in profound material insecurity, saddled with stigma and negative credentials courtesy of criminal justice system contact, minimal connections to mainstream social institutions (e.g., the formal labor market), and minimal or nonexistent forms of support from the government. These individuals are invisible in the hopeful discourse about job training and full employment (Edin & Shaefer, 2015; Ehrenreich, 2009b), but they are quite visible in the field of criminology and criminal justice (e.g., Chaiken & Chaiken, 1982; DeLisi, 2001a, 2001b; Irwin, 1985; Vaughn et al., 2011).

In light of current trends in labor force participation and the cultural pressures to work, however, these conditions will come to characterize more and more members of our society, unless Americans can summon the political will to avert this collision course. This will require receptiveness to new ideas and a willingness to abandon those that no longer provide a sustainable narrative.

## IS THERE A WAY OUT?

In the chapter that follows, I propose an approach that could prevent much of the inevitable tragedy of this "collision course." The proposal—a means-tested guaranteed basic income (GBI) for all adults who are unable to meet their basic economic needs via the labor market—may seem radical and unprecedented. However, as chapter 4 demonstrated, government establishment of an income "floor"—a level below which no American citizen should be expected to fall—is *not* a new idea. Since the 1960s at least, the idea has been advanced, interrogated, and investigated. Political and ideological barriers—or perhaps simply a lack of social and political will to include the poor in the spoils of the American dream— prevented it from being realized. In chapter 6, I hope to demonstrate both the value and the feasibility of this approach; it seems the *only* practical solution if we are to avoid the grave societal consequences that will surely result in the face of continued denial of our contemporary realities. Chapter 6 presents analyses that answer the questions that motivated this book such as, "When does it become a less expensive proposition to provide income than to repeatedly incarcerate?" I also offer, in broad-stroke terms, a mechanism for funding a means-tested GBI.

# 6 · A WAY FORWARD

We have now reached the point where we should consider solutions to the problems outlined in the previous five chapters. It is my firm conviction that so-called critical scholarship (a label I will not take exception to) in the current era must go beyond simply pointing out that there is a problem and suggest at least the contours of possible solutions or ameliorative measures. What follows is my attempt to take on this task.

My proposal is simple: the provision of a means-tested guaranteed basic income (GBI) stipend—an income floor—to any adult individual who is unable to earn enough to furnish a reasonable standard of living in the labor market. It is not my intention to present a fully and immediately executable proposal here. The primary goal of this work is to make the case—to sound an alarm—that something needs to be done to avert the potential consequences of the convergence of the trajectories of the U.S. economy and criminal justice system, a task I hope I have accomplished in the preceding chapters. What I endeavor to do here is to sketch out the parameters of a policy solution to avert the potentially devastating consequences of this collision course. What I propose, if implemented, would represent a profound change in American social policy and vision (although, as chapter 4 demonstrated, not as novel or alien as a contemporary observer ignorant of the negative income tax [NIT] era might think). The notion of *citizenship rights* is not one that has been particularly resonant in American culture and society, but there are innumerable reasons why changing that would be beneficial to us all. In addition to potentially averting some of the consequences vis-à-vis criminal activity in the absence of both work and of alternative sources of economic support, societies with lower levels of inequality are healthier and more sustainable in many ways (Wilkinson & Pickett, 2009).

Americans are fond of professing "love of country," yet it appears that some Americans' love is more justified than others. Those at the bottom of the economic order are there, and arguably remain there, in large part as the result of a wide variety of social policy choices impacting the poor. These policy choices are wide reaching and span the realms of criminal justice, the tax code, commerce, and even our national defense. If it is possible for the United States to ensure that none of its inhabitants fall below a minimum standard of living—and it does appear that this is so—policy choices that would enable such a state of affairs would seem more congruous with the adulation and nationalistic pride expressed by so many Americans.

I use the term *citizenship rights* in order to situate my work within an already-existing discourse about issues that are essential to this project. However, it is important to note that I use the term *citizen* in a colloquial, nonlegalistic fashion. Issues surrounding citizenship and immigration are extremely charged in the contemporary moment in the United States; incorporating even the broadest of implications from these debates lies far beyond the scope of this work. For the moment, my usage of "citizen" and "citizenship" should not be taken to subsume exclusionary legal criteria; rather, the term as it is employed here is closer to the meaning of "denizens" or "inhabitants."

Given the necessity of limiting the scope of this work, as well as a recognition of the power of the hegemonic narratives that surround work, worthiness, and masculinity, I present my proposals in broad-stroke terms. These ideals have been internalized by the economically less fortunate as well as those for whom the economic system is "working" (Goodwin, 1972; Halpern-Meekin et al., 2015; Newman, 2000); means-tested GBI absent labor exchange is going to be a tough sell for those who would be eligible for the benefits as well as those who will not. Because I believe that we are nowhere near the point of implementing such an initiative (although the severe economic downturn during the coronavirus [COVID-19] pandemic may have the effect of moving things closer to that point) and that our political and policy landscapes can and have undergone radical change in short periods of time, developing a hyperspecific proposal at this point in time does not seem a good use of time and energy. My intent is to contribute to the nascent discussion that is currently taking place about citizenship rights, GBI, economic inequality, the changing American economy, and the possibility of charting a new course.

My intent is to be as transparent as possible with respect to the estimates, which are admittedly crude. Although I offer some thoughts about how to read and interpret these estimates and what they might mean, it is ultimately left to the reader to determine what is possible. Detailed below are the sources of the input values. Additionally, a range of estimates are presented to account for variations in benefit levels, duration of support, and estimates of incarceration costs.

## INPUT PARAMETERS: ESTIMATES OF PRISON COSTS

Estimation of the costs of incarceration is one of the more straightforward and least controversial parts of this exercise. The standard method for determining the cost per prisoner is to divide the total expenditures on incarceration by the number incarcerated. Although the costs of incarceration do vary widely by state, these differences are aggregated for our purposes and an unweighted national average is used to estimate annual costs per prisoner. These input parameters are derived from an ongoing survey of state prison systems conducted by the Vera Institute of Justice in 2012 and 2016; the most recent figures, employed here, are available for 2015 (Mai & Subramanian, 2017). The estimate is based on a simple average, which is equal to $33,274 per prisoner annually. "Low," "medium," and "high" esti- mates are arrived at by using 100 percent, 150 percent, and 200 percent of this annual unweighted per-prisoner cost. Using the empirical average as the low estimate rec- ognizes that the methodology used to arrive at this figure does not incorporate costs associated with jails, policing, or courts; the medium and high estimates are likely a closer reflection of actual costs associated with incarcerating an individual.[1] Additionally, per-prisoner costs vary significantly by state, ranging from a high of $67,355 in New York to a low of $14,780 in Alabama. Seven states report spending more than $55,000 per prisoner each year. For this reason, a range of cost estimates are presented to provide multiple points for comparison.

It is by no means a simple task to define the "typical" individual's experience with incarceration. Nor, I will argue, is it a particularly fruitful one. In social sci- ence, the central tendency of distributions is often the focus of our attention— the average family size, the average number of miles traveled on holiday weekends— but sometimes what is "typical" is not the most relevant input. This is particularly so in skewed or asymmetric distributions, which characterize many social and behavioral phenomena. Skewed distributions are those that are populated with outliers—cases with atypically large (or small) values. These outliers, though few in number, can exert significant mathematical consequences on the distributions of quantifiable things. It is for this reason that the median family income is more commonly reported than the mean; as we all know, the American income distri- bution contains a small number of households whose income exceeds that of the vast majority, by multiple orders of magnitude. The simplicity of a mathematical average makes this value *less* representative than some other measures (e.g., the median) of what is "typical" when this is the case.

With respect to criminal behavior, the outliers at the right-hand tail of the distribution—the most active criminals—manifest severely disproportionate impacts and costs on the rest of society. For this reason, and also in light of the net widening that has taken place during the forty-year buildup of the prison popula- tion, understanding the potential ameliorative impact of a GBI is more complex than a comparison of the cost of an "average" prisoner (or "user of incarceration") to that of GBI. The existence of a subset of highly active offenders is undisputed and well documented (Chaiken & Chaiken, 1984; Kennedy, 1997; Moffitt, 1993; Shannon, 1991; Wolfgang et al., 1972; Wright & Rossi, 1986), as is the distinct but related phenomenon of "frequent cross-system users" (Gladwell, 2006; Harding & Roman, 2017; Vaughn et al., 2011). In addition to making disproportionate contributions to the amount of criminal behavior in society, individuals in both of these groups are incarcerated disproportionately—or rather, their utilization of incarceration resources *is* proportionate to their exposure to sanctions for criminal activities and behaviors (Barnes, 2014; DeLisi, 2001a, 2010; Wright & Rossi, 1986). Following the presentation of estimates, the implications of these patterns of use of incarceration vis-à-vis the proposals advanced here will be further discussed.

## ESTIMATES OF GBI PARAMETERS

### Support Level

The means-tested GBI scheme I propose would be available to adults (age 18 and older) who are unable to earn sufficient income to meet an established standard of living; this support would be available for the individual's entire adult life, if necessary. The analyses use the 2017 poverty threshold reported by the U.S. Bureau of the Census for a single individual, $12,488 per year, as the starting point. Given the numerous critiques and limitations of this measure—reflected in eligibility criteria for assistance programs that use a multiplier of the poverty line, such as the federal Children's Health Insurance Program (CHIP), as well as the phase-out limits for the Earned Income Tax Credit (EITC)—estimates are also reported for 150 percent and 200 percent of this level of support ($18,732 and $24,976, respectively) to provide a low, medium, and high estimate of support levels. As a point of comparison, at the time of this writing, the federal minimum wage stands at $7.25 per hour; this translates to an annual full-time gross income of just over $15,000—assuming a forty-hour workweek, which is also an unrealistic assumption for many jobs at the bottom of the income distribution (Golden, 2015; Guendelsberger, 2019).

### Duration of Benefits: Life Expectancy and Benefit Utilization

The true costs of a means-tested GBI are ultimately unknowable, in large part because of two related factors that are difficult to parameterize. These are life expectancy and benefit utilization. The long-term costs of a means-tested GBI, in the form I propose here, are influenced by life expectancy. Life expectancy varies as a result of many factors, including genetics, nutrition, and lifestyle. Many of these factors are inextricably intertwined with socioeconomic status, which is increasingly confounded with geography (Ansell, 2017; Chetty et al., 2016, Crimmins et al., 2011). In any case, the segment of the U.S. population that is most at risk for incarceration also shares a great deal of overlap with those at the bottom of the economic order and experiences shorter life expectancies, generally speaking. However, if we were to move in the direction I suggest (providing a means-tested GBI stipend to all who are unable to meet a minimum income standard through work), it is possible that some of the sources of disparity in life expectancy might attenuate, possibly resulting in increased costs over time as recipients enjoy longer, healthier lives as a result of freedom from dire economic necessity. This doesn't seem to be a reason to argue against it.

Another unknown is the length of time that individuals will utilize the benefit. The estimates presented here do not incorporate variations in benefit utilization, though the varying estimates of support duration allow the reader to make inferences about costs, interpreting the number of years of support to suit either purpose. Extant research on the duration of receipt of benefits suggests that most recipients may not require support for the duration of their adult lives (O'Neill et al., 1987). However, it is important to place earlier studies into context. As chapter 2 demonstrated, the economy of yesteryear is not comparable to today's economy. The polarization of labor demand, contraction in the low-wage sector, trends in the labor force participation rate, and other measures of connection to the formal economy—particularly when these are disaggregated by race and sex—suggest that *there may well be a segment of the U.S. population that remains permanently reliant on a means-tested GBI.* This may be something that we as a nation may have to accept. Although the cultural baggage surrounding work holds great power, is letting go of some of these incredibly dysfunctional ideas a more difficult pill to swallow than the reality of how this segment of the population has been managed up to this point—namely, mass incarceration?

Ultimately, there is no way to foresee in what ways the economy—and the currently economically superfluous population—may evolve in future and how this may influence benefit utilization. It may be the case (and I believe this is most likely) that the demand for human labor will continue to decline as more and more economic functions are supplanted by advances in automation technology; it may turn out that advances in technology will result in new ways of utilizing human labor in the economic system, causing the demand for low-skilled human labor to rebound. Another possibility is that a means-tested GBI may facilitate the development of human capital among some recipients as they pursue interests and training, which may influence their income-producing abilities, either through adaptation to the contemporary economic landscape or the development of skills that enhance their competitiveness (Riddell & Riddell, 2014; Teer, 2020).

This last point is an important one. Evidence from the NIT experiments of the 1960s and 1970s demonstrated that some recipients *did* use the freedom from economic necessity to pursue education and training. It should be remembered that these experiments were of limited duration and did not offer an expectation of stable support. We can only imagine what security and freedom from economic necessity could foster in some individuals. Perhaps a great artist, community volunteer, or a religious calling could be developed in the absence of constant pressure to survive.

The estimates I present below are intended to be transparent with respect to the underlying assumptions. Because of the lack of clear parameters that might allow for a straightforward cost-benefit calculation, estimates are presented from a range of points of view (annual, lifetime) and at a variety of levels of support. I leave it to the reader to evaluate the moral calculus of the policy choices that now confront us—that is, there are many considerations that might lead one to the conclusion that it might be best to implement a GBI scheme even if it costs *more* than incarceration.

*There are not enough jobs anyway.* Repeated failures in an unwinnable system push the justice-involved into illicit economies for survival, further distancing them from mainstream social institutions, resulting in the entrenchment of a permanent criminal class. That these systemic effects—patterned by the nature of mass incarceration—are so racially disparate also means that this permanent criminal class will be disproportionately African American, strengthening narratives that conflate blackness with criminality (Alexander, 2010; Wacquant, 2001) and contributing to racial polarization in American society.

## PROPOSED STRUCTURE OF BENEFITS

The consequences of the colliding institutional trajectories described in this book could be significantly ameliorated with the establishment of a program that provides for a minimum standard of living—an income floor—for all adults who are unable to obtain such income through labor exchange. A crucial difference between this and prior forms of welfare assistance is that it would be administered to individuals rather than households or "family units." The reasons for this should be clear by this point; the United States' pitiful social welfare safety net fails to provide any meaningful assistance to so-called able-bodied men. Chapter 5 illustrates some of the consequences of this gap—especially for men of color and the justice-involved population, for whom the contemporary labor market is particularly inhospitable.

Additionally, the beatification of "traditional" family structures is increasingly unrealistic, given trends in the living arrangements of children and adults in the United States. Figure 6.1 documents the steady decline in the two-parent family structure that has been assumed and exalted in American social policy over the past half century. It also demonstrates the consistently lesser likelihood that African American children will reside in two-parent households. Indeed, with fewer than 50 percent of African American children living in two-parent households, the modal circumstance for an African American child is *not* to be in such a family structure. The societal and behavioral consequences of a support system that fails to acknowledge these structural realities are already documented in crime statistics and in the nature of mass incarceration, which has also played a role in shaping these racial differences in family structure (Pettit & Western, 2004; Sykes & Pettit, 2014; Western & Wildeman, 2009). Meaningful change in the fortunes of the eco-

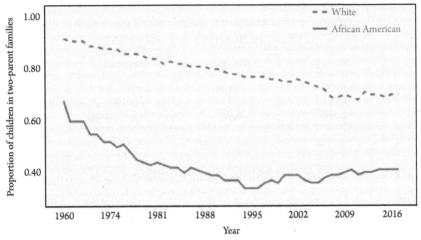

FIGURE 6.1. American children in two-parent families, 1960–2016
SOURCE: U.S. Bureau of the Census

nomically disadvantaged and their children, as well as the mitigation of severe economic inequality in the United States will be best served by letting go of romantic,
antiquated, and unrealistic notions—not just those linking work and social worth
but also those exalting idealized family structures that simply do not represent
the contemporary reality of a great many Americans.[2] Additionally, administering
assistance to individuals at the federal level via the already existing Social Security
Administration infrastructure may avoid some of the pitfalls we have seen in the
current practice of state-level benefit administration (as discussed in chapter 4).[3]

## ANNUAL COST COMPARISON OF PRISON AND GBI

Table 6.1 demonstrates that when the comparison is framed as a simple yearly per-
person expenditure, it is clear that the provision of a means-tested GBI—even
assuming the most generous support level modeled here—costs less than incarceration in a given year. Depending on which estimates are compared, the differential ranges between approximately $20,000 and $50,000 per person, per year.
However, things are far from this simple. Both GBI and mass incarceration represent policy choices over the long term. This necessitates an analysis that com-
pares these costs over time. The annual costs provide the input parameters for the
life-course estimates presented below. To determine the economic neutrality of
a policy of means-tested GBI in relation to mass incarceration, the relevant comparisons lie in the lives of those individuals who experience the sequelae of these
policy choices. The following section presents some comparisons of the use of
incarceration versus means-tested GBI over the life course.

TABLE 6.1    Individual-level annual cost of guaranteed
basic income (GBI) and incarceration

| GBI | Incarceration | Estimate |
|---|---|---|
| 12,488 | 33,274 | Low (100%) |
| 18,732 | 49,911 | Medium (150%) |
| 24,976 | 66,548 | High (200%) |

## LIFETIME COST COMPARISONS OF PRISON AND GBI

Tables 6.2 and 6.3 present estimates of the costs of incarceration and those of a means-tested GBI, considered at the level of the individual over time. Incarceration is measured as episodes of three years in duration. These tables reveal a zone in which the costs of GBI support over the life course of an individual can cost less than incarceration. Specifically, the "break-even" point for providing income support over the entire life course appears around five incarceration episodes, or fifteen years spent in prison.

The lifetime cost estimate for an individual subject to five three-year episodes of incarceration, using the middle-range estimate (150%) for prison costs, is $748,665. Any GBI scheme that costs less than this is defensible on grounds of economic efficiency. I fully acknowledge that this calculus is overly simplistic, as it implicitly assumes a complete substitution of GBI support for criminal justice costs. It is absolutely the case that some recipients of the means-tested benefit may engage in criminal behavior, perhaps for reasons unrelated to economic necessity (Katz, 1988); it may also be the case that some recipients may find the level of support insufficient and engage in criminal activities to supplement their income. It is likely that at least some of these individuals will become entangled with the criminal justice system.

It also does not consider the possibility that targeted individuals may *not* need to avail themselves of GBI support continuously throughout their entire lives. However, as I have repeatedly stated, these analyses are not presented as an implementable proposal but rather for illustrative purposes. The analyses are presented to show what is possible—if we are ready to move away from the destructive ideas and approaches that have gotten us to this point.

Tables 6.2 and 6.3 show the point at which—under the assumptions detailed above—means-tested GBI is economically neutral or advantageous relative to incarceration, when these are compared over the life course of an individual. Obviously, the lower the level of support, the longer that support can be provided at lesser expense. However, the analyses suggest that even the most generous scenario considered here (200% of the poverty line, or an annual income of $24,976 per year) can be provided for twenty-five years for less than the cost of fifteen years

TABLE 6.2    Individual life-course estimates of incarceration costs

| Years | Number of episodes | Cost per incarceration episode | | |
| --- | --- | --- | --- | --- |
| | | Low (100%) | Medium (150%) | High (200%) |
| 3 | 1 | 99,822 | 149,733 | 199,644 |
| 6 | 2 | 199,644 | 299,466 | 399,288 |
| 9 | 3 | 299,466 | 449,199 | 598,932 |
| 12 | 4 | 399,288 | 568,932 | 798,576 |
| 15 | 5 | **499,110** | **748,665** | **988,220** |
| 18 | 6 | 598,932 | 898,398 | 1,197,864 |
| 21 | 7 | 698,754 | 1,048,131 | 1,397,508 |
| 24 | 8 | 798,576 | 1,197,864 | 1,597,152 |

TABLE 6.3    Cumulative life-course estimates of GBI costs

| Support Level | | | Support years | Life expectancy |
| --- | --- | --- | --- | --- |
| 100% $12,488 | 150% $18,732 | 200% $24,976 | | |
| **749,280** | 1,123,920 | 1,498,560 | 60 | 78 |
| **724,304** | 1,086,456 | 1,448,608 | 58 | 76 |
| **674,352** | 1,011,528 | 1,348,704 | 54 | 72 |
| **649,376** | 874,064 | 1,298,752 | 52 | 70 |
| **624,400** | 936,600 | 1,248,800 | 50 | 68 |
| **561,960** | 842,940 | 1,123,920 | 45 | 63 |
| **499,520** | 749,280 | 999,040 | 40 | 58 |
| **437,080** | 655,620 | 874,160 | 35 | 53 |
| **374,640** | 561,960 | 749,280 | 30 | 48 |
| **312,200** | 468,300 | 624,400 | 25 | 43 |
| **249,760** | 374,640 | 499,520 | 20 | 38 |

of incarceration. Provision of a means-tested GBI over the *entire adult life*—modeled here as age seventy-eight—at the least generous benefit level estimated (100% of the poverty level, or $12,488 per year) is nearly equal to the cost of fifteen years of incarceration over that same life course.

A direct comparison of the lifetime costs of means-tested GBI to those of incarceration is not a task that can be accomplished with precision. In addition to the unknowability of the "typical" or average user of incarceration, the distribution of the duration of the income support benefit utilization among the recipient population is unknown. To reiterate, these analyses are presented as an illustrative jumping-off point to demonstrate, in addition to the arguments presented earlier in order to make the case for consideration of a means-tested GBI in light of economic and criminal justice trends, that the idea itself is, from an economic standpoint, neither ludicrous nor impossible.

## A NOTE ON POVERTY THRESHOLDS AND LIVING WAGE ESTIMATES

The Department of Health and Human Services provides estimates of the "poverty line" for different family configurations. These estimates have been the subject of intense criticism for decades. The formula used to create poverty thresholds is based on a method developed in the 1960s by Mollie Orshansky, an economist in the Social Security Administration—a method that has remained *unchanged for nearly sixty years.* The Orshansky method was quite simple. Famously mischaracterized on an episode of Aaron Sorkin's hit television program *The West Wing* in 2001 as based on food costs "in Poland during the Cold War," the actual origins of the dietary guidelines used to construct the poverty line thresholds are even more shocking. Rather, the basis of the formulas used to create poverty threshold estimates was the "emergency temporary low-budget diet," which purported to provide the minimal nutrients deemed at the time by the U.S. Department of Agriculture (USDA) as "adequate to sustain human life over short periods of time." It should be noted that this was *not* the same as the "minimum daily requirements" published by the USDA (these are now called dietary guidelines), which are "designed for professionals to help all individuals . . . and their families consume a healthy, nutritionally adequate diet" (USDA, 2021).[4]

Another serious limitation of the Orshansky method is the allocation of budget categories. The poverty threshold estimates established in 1963 relied on a 1955 study conducted by the USDA that indicated that one-third of the budget of families with children was spent on food. The cost of the market basket for the emergency temporary low-budget diet (a substandard nutritional regime by USDA's own standards) was simply multiplied by three to arrive at the "poverty line," with multipliers for various family sizes—treating adults and children as equal "mouths" to be fed.

The main problem with the federal poverty threshold estimates is that they are *still* calculated using the Orshansky methodology. Leaving aside the appropriateness of the assumptions vis-à-vis family food costs in 1963 (and the emergency temporary low-budget diet, apparently "good enough" for the poor), the failure of the Department of Health and Human Services to update the formulas used to calculate these thresholds is indefensible. Since the 1960s, the costs of housing, health care, transportation, and childcare have risen dramatically, while food costs have declined (Johnson et al., 2001).

The inadequacy of the poverty threshold estimates is reflected in U.S. antipoverty program eligibility requirements as well. The EITC, arguably the centerpiece

TABLE 6.4    Poverty and living wage estimates, 2020

| Family configuration | HHS poverty threshold | EITC phase-out | EPI budget estimate* |
|---|---|---|---|
| Single individual | $12,490 | $15,570 | $34,355 |
| 1 adult, 1 child | $16,910 | $41,094 | $56,889 |
| 2 adults, 1 child | $21,330 | $46,884 | $68,466 |
| 1 adult, 2 children | $21,330 | $46,703 | $76,778 |
| 2 adults, 2 children | $25,750 | $52,493 | $86,633 |
| 1 adult, 3 children | $25,750 | $52,493 | $96,763 |

*Based on residence in Omaha, Nebraska.

of American antipoverty policy since the Clinton administration, boasts income eligibility thresholds that are much greater than poverty line estimates. The income levels at which tax filers phase out of EITC eligibility reflect a more realistic vision than the poverty thresholds established by the Department of Health and Human Services, which are, for 2019, $12,490 for a single individual, and $16,910, $21,330, and $25,750 for families of two, three, and four, respectively. The income levels at which households are deemed as no longer needing the EITC to "lift them out of poverty" are set at $15,570 for a single individual, $41,094 for a single parent with one child, and $46,884 for a two-parent household with one child. For families with two qualifying children, the income threshold for eligibility is $46,703 for a single parent and $52,493 for married filers. Other programs, such as CHIP, administered by Department of Health and Human Services and the states to provide health insurance subsidies to low-income families, set income eligibility levels as high as 200 percent of the official poverty threshold estimates.

The Economic Policy Institute offers a tool on their website that calculates the annual income necessary for various family configurations to "attain a modest yet adequate standard of living" that utilizes more modern and appropriate budgetary allocations and cost estimates than the Orshansky method. Table 6.4 shows these values for the Omaha, Nebraska metro area (chosen for its modest cost of living and relative economic stability). Incorporating estimates for housing, food, childcare, transportation, taxes, and health-care costs, the calculator returns the following: approximately $77,000 for a family comprised of one adult and two children, $87,000 for two adults and two children, and nearly $97,000 for one adult and three children (Economic Policy Institute, 2020).

## THE IMPLICATIONS OF CONCENTRATION FOR A MEANS-TESTED GBI

Parameterizing a "typical" criminal career is difficult, if not impossible, to do with any degree of precision. However, we can draw some useful inferences with respect to the distribution and use of incarceration resources among the justice-involved population. It is clear that some criminal careers are characterized by multiple episodes of incarceration. It is not really possible to delineate the "typical" incarceration career for criminal offenders, and it would ultimately not be terribly useful. Like many behavioral distributions, criminal offending—as well as the utilization of incarceration resources—exhibits a long right-hand tail. Distributions characterized by a long right-hand tail contain small numbers of high-value outliers.

For our purposes, the individuals that populate the right-hand tail of the distribution of incarceration resources should be more salient than its central tendency. Whatever we call them—career criminals, life course–persistent offenders, or frequent cross-system users—these individuals use a disproportionate amount of criminal justice resources. It also seems reasonable to infer that a combination of deficits and criminal justice system involvement renders many of these individuals unlikely to have strong ties to the formal labor market and very likely to face adversity navigating it. As such, these individuals are *precisely the target of the means-tested GBI proposal I advance here,* insofar as ameliorating the consequences of the collision course described in this book.

In recent years, the impacts of frequent cross-system users have come to the attention of researchers and journalists. A population of individuals has been identified who manifest deficits in multiple domains, including poor physical and mental health, chronic homelessness and housing instability, and frequent interactions with the criminal justice system (Binswanger et al., 2007, 2012; Cuddeback et al., 2010; Greenberg & Rosenheck, 2008; Harding & Roman, 2017; James & Glaze, 2006; Mallik-Kane & Visher, 2008; Mumola & Karberg, 2006; Steadman et al., 2009; Vaughn et al., 2011). In a widely read 2006 *New Yorker* article, journalist Malcolm Gladwell introduced one of these individuals to a national audience. "Million-Dollar Murray" was, by all accounts, an affable man with severe substance abuse problems; his alcoholism brought him into contact with the criminal justice system on innumerable occasions. Gladwell interviewed Patrick O'Bryan and Steve Johns, two Reno police officers, who described the extent of system costs generated by these "frequent fliers." Johns stated, "I've been a police officer for fifteen years. . . . I picked up Murray my whole career. Literally. . . . It cost us one million dollars not to do something about Murray" (Gladwell, 2006, pp. 1–2).

While research and reporting about these frequent cross-system users has tended to focus on resource utilization systemwide, encompassing this group's costs in the arenas of emergency medicine, mental health, police, and jails, this group uses a disproportionate amount of prison incarceration resources as well. Research conducted by Courtney Harding and Caterina Roman as part of the Frequent Users System Engagement (FUSE) initiative, a reentry program administered through Chicago's Cook County jail that targets offenders with co-occurring disorders (in this case, a mental health diagnosis and a history of homelessness) reveals subpopulation groups that cycle in and out of the criminal justice system with alarming frequency. The *most* troubled group, accounting for 12 percent of the total sample, registered an average lifetime count of almost sixty arrests and nearly six incarceration episodes by the fourth decade of life (Harding & Roman, 2017, p. 519). While the proposals offered herein for a means-tested GBI will certainly not ameliorate *all* the adversity faced by those who are severely afflicted across multiple domains, it seems a likely proposition that the overall societal costs generated by these individuals can be lessened by addressing their deficits in a more appropriate manner than incarceration.

Michael Vaughn and colleagues (2011) analyzed data gathered from over 43,000 individuals in the National Epidemiologic Survey on Alcohol and Related Conditions (NESARC), which is a nationally representative sample of the noninstitutionalized U.S. population. Although the focus of the data source was not the criminal justice system, these authors identify what they term the "severe 5 percent"—so named because these individuals manifest high levels of "maladaptive externalizing behaviors" such as substance abuse, violence, and other forms of antisocial behavior that naturally lead to greater involvement with the criminal justice system.[5] These findings led the researchers to conclude that

> it is increasingly recognized that a relatively small pathological group exists, and this group will manifest problem behaviors early in life, engage in versatile and serious forms of maladaptive and criminal behaviors, and persist in antisocial behaviors long after more normative delinquents have desisted from crime. . . . The severe 5% class displayed high levels of virtually all types of externalizing behaviors . . . that are consistent with the career criminal, life-course-persistent offender prototype that exists in the criminological literature. (Vaughn et al., 2011, pp. 78–79)

With respect to prison use, Matthew DeLisi's work provides some more detailed insight on what he terms "extreme career criminals"—the heavy users of mass incarceration. DeLisi analyzed criminal activity and justice involvement in a sample of five hundred high-volume offenders in an urban jail population. These habitual offenders were identified as those with over thirty arrests; they comprised less than 2 percent of the jail population, but they were extremely active. The average career length of these five hundred offenders was twenty-one years; they averaged approximately sixty arrests over this period and amassed on average 3.48 lifetime episodes of incarceration, with the maximum reported at twenty-eight terms of incarceration (DeLisi, 2001a; DeLisi & Gatling, 2003). Disaggregating the criminal justice trajectories of high-volume offenders by offending patterns reveals even greater use of incarceration resources for high-volume *violent* offenders, who averaged between 4.31 and 5.29 lifetime incarceration episodes (DeLisi, 2001a).

The concentrated nature of the expansion of the criminal justice system—in particular, the concentration we observe in individuals' use of incarceration resources—has profound implications for the ameliorative proposals advanced here. It means that a means-tested GBI has the potential to maximize "bang for the buck" (see Kennedy, 1997). It also speaks to some containment of these costs; while the U.S. economy is unequivocally unable to utilize the labor power of all would-be entrants to the labor market, our economic health as a nation does depend on the continuing work effort of the vast majority of the working-age population. This fact, coupled with the power of hegemonic narratives that valorize labor as the only or most noble social purpose, means that the overwhelming majority of Americans will not be eligible for and will not avail themselves of this benefit.

As a result of the impossibility of formulating precise estimates and making precise comparisons, it is left to the reader to determine whether a means-tested GBI makes sense from a simple economic standpoint. Generally speaking, if one equivalent alternative costs less than another, this is an easy call—the lower-cost alternative would be clearly superior. Here, given the complexities, we are unable to make a determination based on a simple side-by-side comparison of costs.[6] However, it is apparent that there is a point at which a means-tested GBI benefit becomes the less expensive option relative to incarceration. It is also apparent that a means-tested GBI has the potential not only to avert some negative outcomes (e.g., predatory crime) but also to produce some positive ones. These include the investment in training, education, family, and community that can happen when individuals are freed from dire economic necessity. What benefit do we derive from another term of incarceration?

## HOW DO WE PAY FOR IT?

I stated earlier that contemporary critics of the current state of affairs have an obligation that goes beyond mere critique. It is not enough to simply point to and describe the problem; critical scholarship should at least suggest some plausible, concrete steps toward change. I have sketched out the basic parameters of a means-tested GBI for all American adults in need. My position on the role of the critical policy analyst necessitates that I offer some ideas or ameliorative solutions that may have some practical value. For the reasons detailed at the beginning of this chapter and above regarding the necessity of limiting the scope of the work, I leave it to other researchers to investigate the nuances of what I propose here as a starting point. However, I will attempt to convince the reader that the funding strategy I offer has value and should be developed.

The vast majority of taxes collected by the U.S. government are those on individual income. Corporate tax revenues account for only 7 percent of tax receipts. Corporate tax policy in America in the contemporary period reflects, at least in part, a concern about the outsourcing of American jobs (Clausing, 2013; Desai, 2002; Griffith & Miller, 2014; Serrato & Zidar, 2018). As demonstrated in chapter 2, outsourcing ceased to be a significant consideration in the disappearance of American jobs in the 1970s. Job depletion today is almost entirely attributable to advances in automation, and the vast majority of economic activity—as well as jobs at the low end of the income distribution—involves the provision of services and other transactions requiring copresence. Simply put, the jobs that could be "offshored" have already gone. The jobs that remain, particularly those at the low end of the skills distribution—cannot be outsourced. It's time to call this bluff.

Chapter 2 also demonstrated the negative consequences to the economy that come about in the presence of excess profits. The capitalist growth imperative dictates that profits be reinvested. When, as has been the case for approximately the last century, there is little need to upgrade capital stock and reinvestment in the original enterprise would be unprofitable, holders of excess profit invest in increasingly risky markets, leading to instability in the economy (Cassidy, 2010; Livingston, 2011).

Prior to the passage of the Tax Cuts and Jobs Act of 2017 (TCJA), the highest statutory rate assessed on corporate income in the United States was 38.9 percent, compared to an average rate of 25 percent in OECD (Organisation for Economic Co-operation and Development) countries. The TCJA introduced some sweeping changes to the U.S. tax code. With respect to corporate taxes, the TCJA lowered the maximum statutory tax rate on corporate income from 35 percent to 21 percent. In addition to lowering the maximum statutory tax rate on corporate income, the TCJA also made changes to the treatment of corporate income generated overseas.[7]

However, the statutory tax rate bears little relationship to actual taxes paid on corporate income. American corporations consistently pay less than the officially assessed tax rate. The Office of Tax Analysis, in the U.S. Department of the Treasury, report that the *effective tax rate* paid by U.S. corporate entities fell from an average of 26 percent in 2007 to 20 percent in 2011. Corporations in some industries pay even less, such as the effective tax rate of 18 percent paid across the "computer and electronics" industry and the 15 percent paid by entities engaged in leasing cars, equipment, and consumer goods (Office of Tax Analysis, 2016, p. 2).

While corporate profits have risen steadily over the past three decades, corporate tax revenues have fallen (Bureau of Economic Analysis, 2020; Desai, 2002). Economist Mihir Desai (2002) convincingly demonstrates that the disparity between "book income"—reported to shareholders as a measure of company fiscal robustness—and "tax income" for American corporations has intensified since the mid-1990s. He attributes this to increased tax avoidance[8] via sheltering activity, facilitated by the complexity of the tax code in which "firms are faced with enhanced opportunities for avoiding or evading corporate taxes" (p. 1). Desai concludes that "efforts by firms to circumvent tax payments are becoming more significant, cheaper to implement, and harder to detect" (p. 30).

The baroque structure of corporate taxation makes extensive use of tax incentives, whereby different categories of corporate income are taxed at different rates or not at all. This defines the corporate *tax base*. The tax base is more closely related to tax revenues than statutory rates (Griffith & Miller, 2014; Serrato & Zidar, 2018). The devil—depending on one's views on the appropriateness of corporate taxation—in this case, is truly in the details. Changes to the tax base are likely to have a greater impact on tax revenues than increasing the rate of taxation. Restructuring corporate taxation through tax incentives may be simpler and less politicized than changing statutory rates, given the "hidden" and esoteric nature of this process, and will likely be more effective at increasing revenues (Serrato & Zidar, 2018).

It is also worthwhile to consider the likely impacts on the taxed compared to those on the potential beneficiaries of a means-tested GBI. An increase in corporate tax receipts will likely have a very minor impact on the entities (the corporations themselves) and imperceptible impacts on any individuals indirectly affected by such changes to the tax code. Compare this to the likely impact on a recipient of a means-tested GBI stipend of the sort I propose here. This individual's day-to-day existence will be profoundly changed by the amelioration of economic insecurity (Mullainathan & Shafir, 2013). When we consider many of the issues affecting the urban poor and the justice-involved, such as the relationship of financial support to noncustodial fathers' access to children, spillover effects in schools, and impacts on the social health of communities, it becomes clear that a move in the direction I propose has the potential not merely to save money or to reduce crime but to strengthen families, and to lessen the burden on communities plagued by economic insecurity and crime.

## CONCLUSION

As I stated at the beginning of this chapter, a fully realized and executable proposal is beyond the scope of this work. My intention for this book has been to sound an alarm—to detail what I see as the collision course of trends in two American social institutions and the consequences that are likely to follow if we do nothing. Contemporary trends in the economy and the criminal justice system, when overlaid with existing social policy—specifically, economic assistance in the form of welfare—that reflects and reproduces dysfunctional and unsustainable narratives about the place and meaning of work in American society, masculinity, and antiquated idealized family structures will lead us into severe and profound consequences should we fail to do something to avert this crisis. I also stated at the outset that critical scholars have a responsibility to at least point the way to a solution; mere critique is no longer enough. This book began with the questions to which I have provided some answers in this chapter: what does a comparison of provision of an income floor to the most economically disadvantaged look like in comparison to the costs of incarcerating a significant portion of this segment of American society? From that initial seed grew the project that resulted in the book you are now reading. This question becomes timelier with each passing day, it seems, as states proceed with decarceration, placing more and more people into an increasingly inhospitable labor market. This trajectory now seems as immutable as the buildup of the prison population did in the late 1990s.

The final chapter of this book summarizes the evidence and conclusions amassed in this book. It also considers some features of low-wage work in the twenty-first century—apart from the difficulties related to earning a living wage, some insight into the conditions in which many of the most disadvantaged Americans labor under should provide a good push in the direction of abandoning outmoded ideals about the nobility of work. We have an opportunity to avert some of the tragedies that will surely result if we do nothing. Doing so will require that we abandon ideas that are both dysfunctional and false. It will require courage. It will also require decency.

# 7 · CONCLUSION
## Charting a New Course

> We cannot pretend that there are more important problems in our society, or that this circumstance is the necessary solution to other, more pressing problems—unless we are also prepared to say that we have turned our backs on the ideal of equality for all citizens and abandoned the principle of justice. We ought to ask ourselves two questions: Just what manner of people are we Americans? And in light of this, what are our obligations to our fellow citizens—even those who break our laws?
>
> —Glenn Loury, *Race, Incarceration, and American Values* (2008)

Over the last half century, the U.S. prison population grew dramatically, largely fueled by the enforcement of policies associated with the War on Drugs. Over the same period of time, the American economy underwent radical transformation. With respect to labor market dynamics, there now exists an entrenched mismatch between labor supply and labor demand. The former exceeds the latter across all sectors of the economy, but this mismatch is intensified at the low end of the income and skills distribution, and prospects are particularly bleak for more recent cohorts. The transformation of the labor market has been fueled primarily by advances in automation—advances that continue daily, indicating that these structural conditions are not likely to change; the demand for human labor will undoubtedly continue to decline.

Contemporary reform movements in criminal justice have been reducing prison populations since 2009. Three prominent reform domains that focus on decarceration are the proliferation of problem-solving courts and diversion programs, increased attention to reentry for justice-involved individuals, and drug policy reform. These reforms have as their goal keeping more individuals with justice system involvement in the community, out of prisons and jails, and subsequently in the labor force—introducing even greater numbers of economically superfluous people into a system that lacks the capacity to make productive use of their labor. Because the American economy is unlikely to evolve in ways that will absorb these individuals, alternative approaches to addressing the labor market discrepancy, and the consequences we can expect should we fail to do so, demand our attention.

I wrote this book because it seemed to me that no one was putting these two converging trends together. Possibly this results from the orthodoxies in different academic and policy realms. In economics, this manifests as the persistent belief in "full employment." In criminology, one such orthodoxy registers as "reducing prison populations is good." About this there is absolute consensus. The problem arises from the fact that social institutions exist in relation to one another, and the economy and the criminal justice system are—and always have been— intertwined in ways not immediately apparent to the casual observer or, frequently, to specialists and experts, given our field-specific blinders.

The primary contribution of this book, in addition to offering what is, I believe, a more realistic assessment of the current and likely future state of the economy than that which is frequently presented, is to highlight what I have called the dark side of decarceration—namely, that the shifting of justice-involved populations from custodial to community placement will further strain an economy that can no longer provide work for all Americans. If this reality is not addressed, predictable, wide-ranging, and extremely undesirable consequences will result.

The colliding trajectories of the economy and the criminal justice system necessitate re-examination of many of our deeply held beliefs about the nature of human beings in society, as well as our beliefs about the obligations of societies to the individuals who comprise them. In addition to the need to deeply examine and reconsider hegemonic narratives around work, worthiness, and masculinity, the time is right for some deep reflection on the *intrinsic value of work itself.* The default position—a holdover from America's colonial legacy—is that work is inherently *good.* Many of us (myself included) are fortunate to derive a great deal of gratification and enjoyment from our work. However, for many others, work is a necessary evil. It is merely a means of survival, and individuals' relationship to it may range from indifference to dread. Advances in automation are said to "threaten" many jobs that are dangerous, demeaning, and poorly compensated. I ask, how can the development of robots or automated systems that can take on some of these tasks, freeing up a human being to do something more interesting and fulfilling than, say, picking items for shipment in a warehouse for eleven hours a day for forty years, for wages that barely provide for basic necessities, be seen as a "threat"? How can we consider this anything but progress?

American welfare policy—in particular, the absence of economic relief for the "able-bodied" poor—reflects what David Ellwood (1988) identified as core American values: the intrinsic value of work, self-reliance, family, and community. As the review of relevant literature reveals, the underlying assumption that the poor do not want to work and will gleefully shirk labor if given any alternative (no matter how inadequate) is simply *not* supported. Rather, a substantial research literature warns that some of the strongest opposition to a means-tested guaranteed basic income (GBI) of the sort I am proposing may come from poor and low-income individuals. This research reveals that the poor—especially those who have received benefits in the past—internalize the same value structure that valorizes work and find the notion of "welfare" stigmatizing and unsavory. In their research on the Earned Income Tax Credit (EITC) reported in the 2015 book *It's Not Like I'm Poor: How Working Families Make Ends Meet in a Post-Welfare World*, Sarah Halpern-Meekin and colleagues describe how one of the subject families, Johanna and Mack, justify and explain the six-month period (some five years prior to the conversation) that Johanna received Temporary Assistance to Needy Families benefits, noting that

> like many others who have dealt with the cash welfare system . . . Johanna and Mack feel they must "explain away" Johanna's days on welfare. Their strong need to justify her reliance on government benefits reflects their palpable desire to distance themselves from the unpopular image of welfare recipients. As Johanna and Mack think back on this time in their lives, we hear familiar themes: it was only for a short time; it was only because Johanna was going to school to better herself and to increase her ability to be self-reliant through work; it was for the good of their child; and it was a terrible experience that she would do anything to avoid again. . . . Such justifications, and the implied condemnation of less virtuous others, are nearly ubiquitous among those who have had any experience with government aid. (Halpern-Meekin et al., 2015, p. 107)[1]

The stigma of welfare is without a doubt deeply entrenched. Indeed, this is an essential takeaway of Halpern-Meekin and colleagues' work—the EITC is not subject to the stigma of welfare. This is due to its linkage to "honest labor," consistent with our valorization of work as the most salient feature of worthiness and respectability, as well as the administrative features of the EITC. It is uniformly described and understood by recipients in the Halpern-Meekin and colleagues' research to be a *tax refund*, just the same as millions of hardworking Americans like themselves collect every spring.

As chapter 2 demonstrated, the nature of the American economy has changed in ways that render conventional narratives about its functioning unworkable. The driver of economic growth is no longer production; rather, it is *consumption*. Greater equality in the distribution of income will advance economic growth; inequality serves to stifle it. An additional consequence of economic inequality is the instability of the economy over the long term. Simply put, the capitalist imperative to increase returns on profits dictates investment of profits. However, when the limits of production have been reached, reinvestment in the enterprise that generated the profit does not provide a sufficient rate of return; in this situation, holders of this "excess profit" seek increasingly risky and speculative investment ventures in the service of maximizing returns. As a result, the economy becomes more volatile and susceptible to bubbles and subsequent crashes (Cassidy, 2010; Livingston, 2011). Therefore, a more equitable distribution of income would have the added benefit of stabilizing the economy by taking some of these profits out of the hands of risk-prone investors. We are all familiar with the expression "Money burns a hole in one's pocket." Here, concentrated wealth—in the form of excess corporate profits—threatens, on a cyclical basis, to burn down our entire economic system. Addressing the consequences detailed above with respect to crime would, as an added bonus, likely serve to stabilize the economy, minimizing the traumatic consequences of these new "business cycles" for many ordinary Americans.

## THE PRINCIPLE OF LESS ELIGIBILITY IN ACTION: LOW-WAGE WORK IN CONTEMPORARY AMERICA

We should also consider the realities of the kinds of jobs available to those at the bottom of the income and skills distribution. Emily Guendelsberger, a Philadelphia journalist, spent several months working at a series of low-wage jobs; she documented these experiences in her illuminating 2019 book *On the Clock: What Low-Wage Work Did to Me and How It Drives America Insane.* Over the course of a year, she worked at an Amazon Fulfillment Center, a call center, and a McDonald's restaurant. Guendelsberger's narrative makes clear that the pains of living at the bottom of the income distribution go beyond what could be solved by higher wages or greater representation in collective bargaining (the twin drums commonly beaten by "progressive" economists).

The nature of low-wage work has changed dramatically in the past few decades. Some of these changes are reflective of the changing nature of consumption patterns; for instance, the shift to e-commerce has resulted in warehouse work substituting for jobs that used to exist in the now-dwindling retail economy. These changes also include a remaking of the employment relationship itself, with third-party staffing firms acting as employer and as a contractor or vendor to the company where the employee actually works, rendering existing mechanisms for invoking labor-law protections utterly toothless (Guendelsberger, 2019; Weil, 2014). Other changes concern conditions of employment and working conditions.

Guendelsberger reports on a number of features common to all three workplaces. These include "lean" scheduling practices (guided by software) that determine minimum staffing levels at different days and times. These scheduling practices have two major ramifications: first, employees are informed of their schedules, at most, a week in advance and frequently with only a day before the week's schedule begins, making it nigh-impossible for workers to do things such as arrange childcare, schedule doctor appointments, or schedule family gatherings; apparently "work-life balance" is another thing that poor Americans are not deserving of. These practices are also designed to ensure that employees will work at their maximum intensity throughout their entire shift, never getting the chance to take a breath or have a moment of downtime. Guendelsberger (2019, pp. 245, 261) describes the ever-present line at the San Francisco McDonald's she worked at for two months: "There's *always* a line; we're *always* in the weeds. . . . Workers *and* customers . . . get slower service even as workers push themselves to work harder and faster than usual. Exhausted workers and impatient customers tend to create a feedback loop of frustration and negativity that makes for a really miserable day."

Other kinds of workplaces utilize the same "lean" staffing practices and heavy customer flows through quota systems. These take the form of an expected number of sales made or calls completed per shift, or an expected number of Amazon packing totes filled per hour. These quota systems are brandished like the sword of Damocles on a constant basis—reminding workers that they are subject to termination and dismissal at any time (Bruder, 2018; Guendelsberger, 2019; Soper, 2011).

In addition to employers' ability to define the conditions of the employment relationship, low-wage workers are also in no position to fight against practices that are commonplace but for many of us constitute great and offensive invasions of privacy. These include being barred from bringing personal items into the workplace, computerized systems that track and monitor employees' every second of time "on the clock"—including tracking how much time employees spend in the restroom (employees are cautioned if such time is deemed "excessive" by their supervisors—something, I need not point out, considered to be one of the most "private" things we do). At many workplaces, employees are subjected to searches at the end of their shifts (after clocking out, which frequently added thirty minutes to their time at work, unpaid).

These practices have profound impacts on the individuals subject to them. In their 2013 book *Scarcity: The New Science of Having Less and How It Defines Our Lives*, economist Sendhil Mullainathan and psychologist Eldar Shafir demonstrate the ways in which extreme material insecurity is detrimental to both cognitive capacity and executive function. These are both components of a larger concept they call "bandwidth," which encompasses decision making, cognitions, and even intelligence. While scarcity of all kinds negatively effects cognition and decision making, economic or material scarcity has qualitatively different consequences.

Amazon does not necessarily stand out as the "worst" employer, but it is one of the largest and as such has been the subject of a fair amount of investigative scrutiny. A series of articles published in 2011–2012 in the Allentown *Morning Call* revealed dangerous and demeaning conditions in Amazon's fulfillment center in the Lehigh Valley:

> Workers said they were forced to endure brutal heat inside the sprawling warehouse and were pushed to work at a pace many could not sustain. Employees were frequently reprimanded regarding their productivity and threatened with termination, workers said. The consequences of not meeting work expectations were regularly

on display, as employees lost their jobs and got escorted out of the warehouse. Such sights encouraged some workers to conceal pain and push through injury lest they get fired as well, workers said. During summer heat waves, Amazon arranged to have paramedics parked in ambulances outside, ready to treat any workers who dehydrated or suffered other forms of heat stress. Those who couldn't quickly cool off and return to work were sent home or taken out in stretchers and wheelchairs and transported to area hospitals. And new applicants were ready to begin work at any time. In a better economy, not as many people would line up for jobs that pay $11 or $12 an hour moving inventory through a hot warehouse. But with job openings scarce, Amazon and Integrity Staffing Solutions, the temporary employment firm that is hiring workers for Amazon, have found eager applicants in the swollen ranks of the unemployed. (Soper, 2011)

Communities lacking in legitimate economic opportunities frequently host thriving "off the books" economies that encompass both licit and illicit activities. These illicit economies provide opportunities for the generation of income as well as the expression of masculinity. For some, this serves as the primary arena of economic activity. Disengagement from the formal labor market also coincides with lack of engagement with other social institutions, particularly among the justice-involved.

Age- and cohort-specific trends in labor force participation, coupled with stark and increasing inequality in the distribution of income and wealth, portend the growth of an already-present *permanent criminal class*, increasingly divorced from mainstream social institutions—unless something is done to avert the collision course of the economy and the criminal justice system. We also face the possibility of more invasive and damaging forms of crime as the ranks of "extra people" swell and as criminal opportunity structures evolve and adapt to changing conditions, an inevitability in light of greater numbers of the justice-involved population remaining in their communities and competing for a pool of jobs that gets smaller every day.

Given the immutability of these trends in the economy and the criminal justice system, it is imperative that we as a society consider alternative redistributive and policy solutions—specifically, a means-tested GBI, to mitigate the consequences of this collision course of economic transformation and criminal justice reform. Concerns about free riders are both empirically unfounded and moot; the economic system is unable to make productive use of the labor of all who we have historically expected to work.

There may be concerns about the establishment of a two-tiered society in which the majority of Americans *do* work, but a minority may be dependent on GBI for a substantial part of their adult lives. I would respond that the distortions that mass incarceration has imposed throughout American society has *already* created such a tiered system of citizenship. Nearly six million Americans are disenfranchised as the result of a felony conviction; in four states, more than 20 percent of the African American voting-age population is barred from voting (Uggen et al., 2016). Additionally, Pettit and Western's (2004, p. 164) analyses of the increasing likelihood of incarceration in more recent cohorts unequivocally demonstrate that "by 1999 imprisonment had become a common life event for black men that sharply distinguished their transition to adulthood from that of white men.... Imprisonment has become a common life event for recent birth cohorts of black non-college men. In 1999, about 30 percent of such men had gone to prison by their mid-thirties. Among black male high school dropouts, the risk of imprisonment had increased to 60 percent, establishing incarceration as a normal stopping point on the route to midlife." *We already have a two-tiered society*. It is possible to attenuate severe economic inequality (which will also contribute to the overall health of a consumption-driven economy) by establishing a minimum standard of living. It is also possible that these inequalities need not be so very damaging and destructive to those who find themselves at the bottom of the economic order. However, the vision I offer in this book is absolutely dependent on a willingness to critically examine long-held but false ideas regarding welfare's effect on labor supply, the intrinsic value of work, work as the sole measure of worthiness, as well as obsolete models of how the contemporary American economy operates. It is a very tall order. The inevitability of continued technological advances, which will render more and more human labor unnecessary, will hopefully force these issues. Sooner is better than later; how many more generations are we willing to "lose" before we come to our senses?

I have offered some very rudimentary analyses and a range of estimates to serve as a basis for evaluating the relative costs of GBI and incarceration. While it is difficult to estimate the incarceration life course of a "typical" justice-involved individual, the analyses suggest that there is clearly a break-even point where it is economically neutral to provide GBI over the entire adult life, compared to incarcerating an individual several times over the course of that life.

I suggest that funding the means-tested GBI can be accomplished by increasing corporate tax revenues. This is best accomplished not through changes in statutory tax rates but rather through the redefinition of the corporate *tax base*—the amount of corporate income that is eligible for taxation at the statutory rate. Through perfectly legal means, the effective tax rate paid by American corporations is 40 percent less than what would be expected based on statutory rates. This results from the extensive use of tax incentives, which limit taxation on certain types of corporate income—these are "hidden" in the same way tax incentives are in the individual income tax system (Howard, 1999). The location of these kinds of decisions in the political process requires that only a few of our elected officials be committed to such changes to the tax code. Analysis of variation in the tax base at the state level suggests that widening the tax base is a more effective way of increasing tax receipts than is increasing statutory tax rates (Serrato & Zidar, 2018).

The unmistakable trends with respect to the labor market prospects of successive cohorts—successive generations—create a set of circumstances that absolutely require that some action be taken if we are to have any hope of survival. Forty percent of American children live in low-income households; as the prospects for low-income adults deteriorate, so do the life chances of their children. The deepening inequality we observe in the distribution of wealth and income in the United States threatens not only economic growth, but it also threatens the essential American vision and ideals—some of which are still quite viable and appealing. A change in the way we view the appropriate distribution of our nation's prosperity—breaking away from the idea that work is the only measure of worth, and of worthiness in participating in the full privileges and benefits of American society—is needed if we are to halt and reverse these potentially devastating trends.

The discourse of citizenship rights has never fully taken hold in the United States, this being incompatible with the rhetoric that surrounds the "American dream" and its emphasis on "rugged individualism." Full participation in American society seems to morally require *labor*, even if that labor is dangerous, demeaning, or unfulfilling. This could not be more clearly articulated in American welfare policy; what limited assistance exists is only available to a narrowly defined subset of "deserving" recipients. Decaying rural and urban areas characterized by high rates of joblessness, concentrated poverty, and high rates of crime show where our stubborn adherence to these ideas has gotten us.

Title I of the Older Americans Act of 1965 (reauthorized in 2016), a piece of legislation that established no federally administered programs but serves rather as a statement of values and ideals, nicely articulates the idea of citizenship rights:

> The Congress hereby finds and declares that, *in keeping with the traditional American concept of the inherent dignity of the individual in our democratic society*, the older people of our Nation are *entitled to, and it is the joint and several duty and responsibility of the governments of the United States* . . . to assist our older people to secure equal opportunity to the full and free enjoyment of the following objectives: (1) *An adequate income . . . in accordance with the American standard of living.* (2) The best possible physical and mental health which science can make available and without regard to economic status. (3) Obtaining and maintaining suitable housing, independently selected, designed and located with reference to special needs and available at costs which older citizens can afford. (4) Full restorative services for those who require institutional care, and a comprehensive array of community-based, long-term care services adequate to appropriately sustain older people in their communities and in their homes, including support to family members and other persons providing voluntary care to older individuals needing long-term care

services. . . . (7) *Participating in and contributing to meaningful activity within the widest range of civic, cultural, educational and training and recreational opportunities.* (Emphases added)

I can't think of a single defense of the notion that "American ideals" of dignity, a reasonable standard of living, and meaningful participation in their communities is something only the elderly are entitled to. Ethics aside, it's a dangerously foolish position to take at this historical juncture. If we remove all the references to age from the statement above, this provides an excellent summary of my vision with respect to citizenship rights.

As I stated at the beginning of this work, nothing would make me more proud to be an American than to see a proposal like the one I advance in this book established, motivated by ideals of citizenship rights and an essential respect for human dignity. However, even if we are unable to summon the collective will and generosity to do so, the trajectories of the economy and the criminal justice system that I have described in these pages should provide sufficient impetus to move in that direction. Simply put, we can't afford *not* to consider GBI in the face of accelerating automation and the declining use of incarceration. We can no longer afford to ignore the growing numbers of "extra people" in American society that denial of these structural realities produces; the consequences will be devastating. It is my hope that the alarm I intended to sound in this work will be heard and that necessary steps can be taken to avert this collision course and create a more inclusive society that values all of its members.

# ACKNOWLEDGMENTS

I am fortunate to have made the Department of Criminal Justice at Temple University my intellectual and professional home for the past two decades. I am tremendously grateful for the enduring support and enthusiasm of my wonderful colleagues; the graduate student colleagues who have passed through the department during this time have also been a constant source of inspiration and support. I have been talking about this project with anyone who would listen for quite some time, and over the years I received many valuable perspectives and ideas that informed the work in numerous ways. I thank you all for listening to me talk excitedly about robots and labor force participation for all this time, and I hope that you find the finished product deserving of your support.

I owe a special debt of gratitude to the students in my fall 2020 graduate seminar in criminal justice policy, titled "Mass Incarceration and Decarceration." Mea Agers, Jesse Brey, Steven Chen, Kate Kelly, Autumn Talley, and Lauren Perron—you were among the first to read the completed manuscript—fortuitously, just a few weeks before I submitted the final draft of the manuscript for publication. The opportunity to share my work with you and to receive your honest feedback was incredibly helpful and rewarding. More generally, our weekly meetings were a highlight during that truly challenging time in all of our lives. I feel confident in expecting great things from each of you in the future.

Special mention is due my friend and colleague Jamie Fader. In addition to her interest and support of my project, her contributions to this work are inestimable. Many conversations in which she shared with me her exhaustive knowledge of ethnographic research informed this work greatly. At the same time, her interest in the part of this work that deals with the state of the U.S. economy, as it relates to her current book—*Millennial Men on the Margins*—allowed me to feel that it was a more even trade than it probably was. Everyone should have a friend like Jamie.

Joe DaGrossa, former student and now colleague, also deserves special thanks. His support and enthusiasm for the work has been unwavering. Both his research and experience in the field—as well as his generosity in sharing both with me and my students over the years—has informed and contributed to the final product in ways that I hope he can see.

Peter Mickulas, my editor at Rutgers University Press, has shown unwavering support and enthusiasm for the project from the very beginning. I am also grateful to the production staff at Rutgers University Press, in particular those responsible for the cover design. Special thanks are also in order for the meticulous work of copyeditor Joyce Li and senior production editor Melody Negron.

Given the subject matter of this work, I would be remiss if I did not address the fact that as an academic, I am fortunate to have chosen a career and to have an employer that offers many rewards and benefits not available to the average worker in America. Periodic sabbaticals are one such benefit, and in my experience they are both wonderfully restorative and productive. In my opinion, this is a benefit that should be widely available to workers of all kinds. I owe thanks to Temple University for awarding me a sabbatical leave in 2016–2017.

Finally, I have a wonderful partner in Alex Muentz. He has endured a great deal in the service of my career, and his love and support have absolutely made this work stronger. This feeble attempt to thank him for all the ways he has enriched my life is absolutely inadequate, but I hope he knows how much I appreciate him. I am also thankful for my friends, who were always willing to talk with me about all aspects of this work, from robots to income subsidies. Their encouragement has strengthened my resolve that this book addresses an important crisis. As Jesse Brey, one of the students in my graduate seminar, put it as we discussed these issues: We don't have to live this way.

Kate Auerhahn
Philadelphia, Pennsylvania
December 2020

# NOTES

## CHAPTER 1 THE CONTOURS OF THE PROBLEM

1. Values are those at the close on January 31.

2. This disconnect between labor market opportunities and the hegemonic importance of work also creates other dislocations, both personal and social in nature. These include greater likelihood of depression, substance use, and other socially undesirable behaviors and outcomes (see Norris, 2016; Warr, 1987)

3. This is especially true since the passage of the Tax Cuts and Jobs Act (TCJA) of 2017, which established a territorial taxation model for corporate income generated outside of the United States.

4. Another example of the move "from welfare to work" can be seen in the distribution of income sources of the poor. Since 1996, the Earned Income Tax Credit (EITC) has provided more assistance to low-income families, in dollar terms, than traditional welfare assistance. The House Budget Committee (2014) reported that in 2012, expenditures on the EITC and similar tax credits aimed at the "working poor" amounted to four times the amount spent on the TANF program.

5. Macroeconomic "austerity" measures, such as reducing deficit spending, can also be seen as an example of the "responsibilization strategy" articulated by Garland (1996, 2002).

## CHAPTER 2 THE U.S. ECONOMY IN THE TWENTY-FIRST CENTURY

1. However, many of these jobs are unrewarding, dangerous, and do not provide a living wage. This begs the question, why are we so attached to this idea that "everyone works"? This will be addressed in chapter 4.

2. The definition also includes those working at least fifteen hours, unpaid, in family-owned businesses, as well as individuals who may not have worked in that particular week as a result of illness, vacation, childcare emergencies, and the like but who expect to return to stable employment.

3. These definitions and measures reflect the influence of hegemonic ideologies about deserving and undeserving recipients of relief—discussed at greater length in chapter 4.

4. The authors present a somewhat controversial analysis that examines the time use of young men using the American Time Use Survey (ATUS). They find that "the drop in market hours for young men was mirrored by a roughly equivalent increase in leisure hours" (Aguiar et al., 2017, p. 2) and assume a causal direction of this relationship that is debatable. To wit, the authors present that the availability of video gaming technology results in men choosing to withdraw from the labor force; however, given age- and cohort-specific trends in labor force participation and other measures of employment, it is entirely possible that the direction of this relationship is the reverse. It is just as likely a scenario that young men, thwarted and rejected by the formal labor market, spend more of their time playing video games as an alternative activity to work. Aguiar and colleagues *assume* an unwillingness on the part of young men to engage with the formal labor market.

5. Autor and Wasserman (2013) note that the decline in the prime-age male LFPR—particularly for African American males—is almost certainly *underestimated* due to the effects of mass

incarceration (see also Council of Economic Advisers, 2016a, 2016b; Pettit, 2012; Western & Beckett, 1999).

6. Black women's rates of college completion, though increasing, are still only half the rate at which white women attain bachelor's degrees (McDaniel et al., 2011).

7. I would also be remiss if I failed to point out that incarcerating large numbers of the populace is, as Francis Allen (1981, p. 12) put it, "an economic indulgence, and one beyond the means of most Western societies until near the end of the eighteenth century." Ironically, the decline of mass incarceration demonstrates that for labor markets at least, the sword cuts both ways.

8. The growth in student indebtedness is understandable in light of the restructuring of financial aid arrangements that took place during the Clinton administration. Reforms shifted the balance to favor loans over grants, which also had the consequence of expanding access to higher education opportunities.

9. Statistics regarding the fraction of students who take on student loan debt but fail to complete degree programs are difficult to come by. There is some evidence to support the inference that the proportion of student borrowers among those who leave college without a degree is similar, if not higher, than those who do complete degrees. The U.S. Senate Committee on Health, Education, Welfare, and Pensions (HELP) reported that fully 96 percent of students who enroll at for-profit colleges—which have much lower completion rates than traditional institutions—take on student loan debt; the corresponding figures for students at traditional four-year private and public colleges are 57 percent and 48 percent, respectively (HELP, 2012).

10. Bivens et al. (2014) note that the aging of the population and the attendant increases in the proportional contribution of government transfers (resulting from the successful commitment to government policy in raising living standards among elderly Americans in the 1960s) has served to mitigate the decline in incomes resulting from falling wages.

## CHAPTER 3 THE CRIMINAL JUSTICE SYSTEM IN THE TWENTY-FIRST CENTURY

1. The impacts of COVID-19 on prisoners in the United States are enormous; prisoners are an extremely vulnerable population with generally poor health status, reflected in substantially higher rates of both COVID-19 morbidity and mortality (Saloner et al., 2020). In response, some jurisdictions have been releasing those held in *jails*; prison releases have been relatively few at the time of this writing. However, it is entirely possible that the pandemic may accelerate the pace of prison decarceration.

2. During the eight years he served, President Bill Clinton oversaw the largest expansion of the prison population of any American president.

3. Pettit and Western find that while the risk of imprisonment by age thirty between 1979 and 1999 increased at the same rate for white and African American men, the base rates differ substantially, with African American men experiencing a cumulative risk of imprisonment that is six to eight times higher than white men. However, the massive expansion of incarceration increased the relative risk equally for both African American and white men. Racial disparity in incarceration exhibits "a pattern of stability" over the period of study, and while African American over-representation persists, it has declined in recent years (Pettit & Western, 2004, p. 164; see also Gramlich, 2019).

4. Additionally, the Cambridge Study in Delinquent Development, a multigenerational research effort that followed 411 men in South London and two previous generations, reveals strong evidence for the intergenerational transmission of criminal offending and conviction (Farrington et al., 2009; Farrington et al., 1975).

5. The precise ratio under the FSA is 17.86:1. This is an artifact of standardized measures. The original weights to compel a five-year mandatory minimum sentence (for first-time offenders) were five grams of crack cocaine and five hundred grams of powder cocaine. The FSA changed the amounts to trigger a five-year mandatory prison sentence to one ounce (28 grams) of crack cocaine and five hundred grams of powder cocaine. The FSA has a complicated legislative history (see Bjerk, 2017; Parks, 2012). The assessment of the accuracy of the definition of "fair" is left to the reader.

6. Interestingly but perhaps not surprisingly, the National Association of Drug Court Professionals (2012) has expressed opposition to cannabis policy reform: "NADCP unequivocally stands against the legalization of marijuana and the use of smoked marijuana as "medicine."

7. A contraction of illicit drug markets may qualitatively change urban crime patterns; this is considered in greater detail in chapter 5.

## CHAPTER 4 WORK AND WELFARE IN AMERICAN CULTURE AND SOCIETY

1. In the case of female, nonelderly recipients of assistance, sexual morality has also been highly salient in determinations of deservedness. This merits a fuller examination than the scope of this work permits. Excellent analyses of this aspect of welfare discourse are offered by Abramovitz (1996), Bell (1965), Day (1977), Gilliom (2001), Gordon (2001), and Katz (1989).

2. Because the main focus of this book is on the segment of the population with minimal attachment to the labor market, I do not address unemployment insurance here.

3. So-called mother's pensions also predated the Social Security Act in some locales. However, reflecting concerns about the sexual morality of female recipients (see note 1), support levels varied widely and were contingent on assessments of "suitability" of the home and the mother herself (Gilliom, 2001, p. 25).

4. NIT and GBI are different approaches to the redistribution of income at the operational level and have different operational burdens and consequences, but conceptually they share the same fundamental idea of an income floor.

5. The OEO was disbanded and its functions transferred to agencies operating in the states, as well as a reduced staff in the Office of Community Services in the Department of Health and Human Services under the Omnibus Reconciliation Act of 1981.

6. Mincome was a Canadian means-tested basic income program that ran in Manitoba between 1974 and 1979.

7. The impact of NIT on family dissolution has been the subject of some debate (Cain & Wissoker, 1990; Hannan & Tuma, 1990; Hannan et al., 1977, 1978). Effects, when found, were weak, and lacking context, the *meaning* of marital dissolution is not clear. It is possible that freedom from dire economic necessity enabled some low-income women the freedom to exit unhealthy or violent relationships.

8. These amounts are equivalent to $11,322 and $16,417 in 2020 dollars.

9. The Family Support Act also established a link between child support enforcement and receipt of benefits.

10. Additionally, the majority of funds earmarked for TANF are not disbursed as transfer payments. Only about 20 percent of TANF funds actually reach needy families in the form of cash assistance. The structuring of the block grants permits states to use TANF funds in a variety of ways, including job training programs. In some states, TANF funds have been used to supplant unrelated expenses in state budgets (Burnside & Schott, 2020).

11. Title I of the PRWORA also provided financial incentives to states demonstrating decreases in abortions and out-of-wedlock births, evincing a continued concern with sexual morality as a relevant component of deservedness for poverty relief.

**12.** Thirty states, the District of Columbia, Guam, and Puerto Rico have additional EITC programs; benefits and administrative structure vary widely (National Conference of State Legislatures, 2021). I focus discussion here on the federal benefit.

**13.** The lower age limit exists to avoid overlap and "double-dipping"; individuals are ineligible if they *can be* claimed as a dependent by another filer (regardless of whether they are so claimed). Reflecting the general tendency of welfare policy to beatify and enforce traditional definitions of "family," persons younger than twenty-five are only eligible for the credit if they are *married* with a qualifying child; single parents under age twenty-five are not eligible for the federal EITC.

**14.** The average benefit received falls far below these maximums, at $2,458 per filer (Internal Revenue Service, 2020)

## CHAPTER 5 THE CONSEQUENCES OF DENIAL

**1.** These policies vary widely in scope and enforceability. Some apply only to government jobs, while others affect all employers; they also vary in their powers of proscription and enforcement (Doleac & Hansen, 2016).

## CHAPTER 6 A WAY FORWARD

**1.** While the focus of this book and of the comparisons presented is prison incarceration, the processing, holding, and transport functions of jails and other auxiliary systems are also significant contributors to the costs of mass incarceration (Henrichson & Delaney, 2012).

**2.** My proposal targets *adults* as the beneficiaries of GBI. This approach brackets the problem of support of children and assumes that those adults who are parents will provide for children with the GBI stipend and other available assistance. At this point in time, despite the inadequacies of the extant programs to address child poverty, I am in no way suggesting that we dismantle these in favor of a single stream of support for those in extreme poverty; I am merely offering an idea in broad-stroke terms, with evidence to suggest that it is an idea worthy of consideration.

**3.** Administration of benefits through the Social Security Administration would also appease critics concerned with issues surrounding documentation and citizenship. Incidentally, it has been demonstrated that fear of legal consequences results in undocumented workers (with fraudulent Social Security numbers) contributing far more in taxes than they ever receive in benefits. Goss et al. (2013) report that undocumented workers contribute $12 billion annually to the Social Security Trust. Gee et al. (2016) estimate that collective state and local tax revenues received from undocumented immigrants total a similar amount annually.

**4.** Currently, the USDA publishes guidelines for four different "food plans." These are the Thrifty Food Plan, the Low-Cost Plan, the Moderate-Cost Plan, and the Liberal Food Plan. The Thrifty Food Plan is used to calculate the poverty threshold; the Liberal plan, which costs twice as much as the Thrifty plan, is used to calculate food allowances for military families (Lino, 2011).

**5.** Vaughn and colleagues also report that this segment of the population also manifests high levels of mental illness, which is consistent with other descriptions of frequent system users (Gladwell, 2006; Harding, 2020; Harding & Roman, 2017).

**6.** Another perspective for comparison is the estimation of the costs of crime to victims and to society at large. DeLisi and Gatling (2003) provide estimates of the societal costs inflicted by the extreme tail of the distribution of offending. These estimates average $274,610 per high-volume offender, per year but with great variation—the standard deviation is 372,942 and the maximum reported yearly cost estimate for an individual offender is over $4 million. Cohen (1998) estimates the victimization costs attributable to an individual high-volume offender to be $1.5–$1.8 million over the course of the criminal career. Welsh and colleagues (2008) estimate the costs incurred by a sample of five hundred active juvenile offenders between the ages of seven and seventeen to be between $89 million and $110 million over the ten-year period studied.

7. Prior to the TCJA's passage, corporate income earned in other countries was taxed under a *global* model, meaning that the U.S. rate was applied to all corporate income, regardless of where the economic activity that generated it took place. The TCJA introduced a *territorial* model for the taxation of corporate profits. In a territorial system of taxation, the prevailing tax rate in the country where the income is earned applies to the U.S. tax payment. Territorial tax systems are believed by some to discourage tax avoidance and sheltering activity.

8. Although tax avoidance and tax evasion both serve to suppress tax receipts, they are not reducible to each other. Tax avoidance describes minimizing tax liability by taking advantage of features and provisions of the tax code. As such, tax avoidance is a perfectly legal activity. This is distinguished from tax evasion, which describes unlawful manipulation or concealment of income in order to avoid taxation.

## CHAPTER 7 CONCLUSION

1. This phenomenon of distancing oneself from undesirable imagery or narratives and manifesting a presentation of self that is seen as "as good as" the normative ideal was called by Evelyn Brooks Higginbotham (1993) the politics of respectability; Michelle Alexander's (2010) discussion of same in the context of the divisive nature of mass incarceration among African Americans is a particularly helpful comparison here.

# REFERENCES

Abel, J. R., & Deitz, R. (2014). Do the Benefits of College Still Outweigh the Costs? *Current Issues in Economics and Finance, 20*(3), 1–11.

Abramovitz, M. (1996). *Regulating the Lives of Women: Social Welfare Policy from Colonial Times to the Present.* South End Press.

Acemoglu, D. (2002). Technical Change, Inequality and the Labor Market. *Journal of Economic Literature, 40*(1), 7–72.

Acemoglu, D., Autor, D., Dorn, D., Hanson, G. H., & Price, B. (2016). Import Competition and the Great US Employment Sag of the 2000s. *Journal of Labor Economics, 34*(S1), S145–S198.

Acemoglu, D., & Autor, D. (2012). What Does Human Capital Do? A Review of Goldin and Katz's *The Race between Education and Technology. Journal of Economic Literature, 50*(2), 426–463.

Ad Hoc Committee on the Triple Revolution. (1964). *The Triple Revolution.* Santa Barbara, CA.

Agan, A., & Starr, S. (2017). The Effect of Criminal Records on Access to Employment. *American Economic Review, 107*(5), 560–564.

Agan, A., & Starr, S. (2018). Ban the Box. Criminal Records, and Racial Discrimination: A Field Experiment. *Quarterly Journal of Economics, 133*(1), 191–235.

Aguiar, M., & Bils, M. (2015). Has Consumption Inequality Mirrored Income Inequality? *American Economic Review, 105*(9), 2725–2756.

Aguiar, M., Bils, M., Charles, K., & Hurst, E. (2017). *Leisure Luxuries and the Labor Supply of Young Men* [Working paper no. 23552]. National Bureau of Economic Research.

Alexander, M. (2010). *The New Jim Crow: Mass Incarceration in the Age of Colorblindness.* New Press.

Allen, F. A. (1981). *The Decline of the Rehabilitative Ideal: Penal Policy and Social Purpose.* Yale University Press.

American Civil Liberties Union (ACLU). (2013). *The War on Marijuana in Black and White.* https://www.aclu.org/files/assets/aclu-thewaronmarijuana-rel2.pdf

American Civil Liberties Union (ACLU), the ACLU of Florida, the Hip Hop Caucus, the Lawyers' Committee for Civil Rights Under Law, the Leadership Conference on Civil and Human Rights, the National Association for the Advancement of Colored People (NAACP), the NAACP Legal Defense and Educational Fund, Inc., and The Sentencing Project. (2013, September 30). *Democracy Imprisoned: The Prevalence and Impact of Felony Disenfranchisement Laws in the United States.* Submitted to the United Nations Human Rights Committee by a Coalition of 8 Organizations. The Sentencing Project. https://www.sentencingproject .org/publications/democracy-imprisoned-a-review-of-the-prevalence-and-impact-of -felony-disenfranchisement-laws-in-the-united-states/.

American Society of Criminology National Policy Committee. (2001). *The Use of Incarceration in the United States.*

Anderson, E. (1999). *Code of the Street: Decency, Violence, and the Moral Life of the Inner City.* W.W. Norton & Company.

Ansell, D. A. (2017). *The Death Gap: How Inequality Kills.* University of Chicago Press.

Aos, S., Miller, M., & Drake, E. (2006). *Evidence-Based Public Policy Options to Reduce Future Prison Construction, Criminal Justice Costs, and Crime Rates.* Washington State Institute for Public Policy.

Apel, R., & Sweeten, G. (2010). The Impact of Incarceration on Employment During the Transition to Adulthood. *Social Problems, 57*(3), 448–479.

Auerhahn, K. (2003). *Selective Incapacitation and Public Policy: Evaluating California's Imprisonment Crisis.* State University of New York Press.

Auerhahn, K. (2014). Sentencing Policy and the Shaping of Prison Demographics. In J. J. Kerbs & J. M. Jolley (Eds.), *Senior Citizens Behind Bars: Challenges for the Criminal Justice System* (pp. 21–42). Lynne Rienner.

Auerhahn, K., & McGuire, C. J. (2010). *Revisiting the Social Contract: Community Justice and Public Safety.* Nova Science.

Austin, J. (2016). Regulating California's Prison Population: The Use of Sticks and Carrots. *Annals of the American Academy of Political and Social Science, 664*, 84–107.

Austin, J., & Jacobson, M. P. (2013). *How New York City Reduced Mass Incarceration: A Model for Change?* Vera Institute of Justice, Brennan Center for Justice, and JFA Institute.

Autor, D. (2011). *The Unsustainable Rise of the Disability Rolls in the United States: Causes, Consequences, and Policy Options* [Working paper no. 17697]. National Bureau of Economic Research.

Autor, D. (2015). Why Are There Still So Many Jobs? The History and Future of Workplace Automation. *Journal of Economic Perspectives, 29*(2), 3–30.

Autor, D., & Dorn, D. (2013). The Growth of Low-Skill Service Jobs and the Polarization of the US Labor Market. *American Economic Review, 103*(5), 1553–1597.

Autor, D. H., Katz, L. F., & Kearney, M. S. (2008). Trends in U.S. Wage Inequality: Revising the Revisionists. *The Review of Economics and Statistics, 90*(2), 300–323.

Autor, D., & Wasserman, M. (2013). *Wayward Sons: The Emerging Gender Gap in Labor Markets and Education.* Third Way. http://www.thirdway.org/report/wayward-sons-the-emerging-gender-gap-in-labor-markets-and-education

Backes, B., Holzer, H. J., & Velez, E. D. (2015). Is It Worth It? Postsecondary Education and Labor Market Outcomes for the Disadvantaged. *IZA Journal of Labor Policy, 4*(1), 1–30.

Baillargeon, J., Binswanger, I. A., Penn, J. V., Williams, B. A., & Murray, O. J. (2009). Psychiatric Disorders and Repeat Incarcerations: The Revolving Prison Door. *American Journal of Psychiatry, 166*, 103–109.

Baker, D., & Bernstein, J. (2014). *Getting Back to Full Employment: CCF Brief #52.* Center for Children and Families, Brookings Institution.

Bales, W. D., & Mears, D. P. (2008). Inmate Social Ties and the Transition to Society: Does Visitation Reduce Recidivism? *Journal of Research in Crime and Delinquency, 45*(3), 287–321.

Bannon, A., Nagrecha, M., & Diller, R. (2010). *Criminal Justice Debt: A Barrier to Reentry.* Brennan Center for Justice.

Barnes, J. C. (2014). Catching the Really Bad Guys: An Assessment of the Efficacy of the U.S. Criminal Justice System. *Journal of Criminal Justice, 42*, 338–346.

Bartley, W. A., & Williams, G. F. (2015). *The Role of Gun Supply in 1980s and 1990s Urban Violence* [SSRN Scholarly Paper ID 2623253]. Social Science Research Network. https://papers.ssrn.com/abstract=2623253

Bartos, B. J., & Kubrin, C. E. (2018). Can We Downsize Our Prisons and Jails Without Compromising Public Safety? Findings from California's Prop 47. *Criminology & Public Policy, 17*(3), 693–715.

Baumer, E. (1994). Poverty, Crack, and Crime: A Cross-City Analysis. *Journal of Research in Crime and Delinquency, 31*(3), 311–327.

Baumer, E. P., & Wolff, K. T. (2014). Evaluating Contemporary Crime Drop(s) in America, New York City, and Many Other Places. *Justice Quarterly, 31*(1), 5–38.

Beaudry, P., Green, D. A., & Sand, B. M. (2013). *The Great Reversal in the Demand for Skill and Cognitive Tasks* [Working paper no. 18901]. National Bureau of Economic Research.

Beck, A. J., & Shipley, B. E. (1989). *Recidivism of Prisoners Released in 1983.* Bureau of Justice Statistics, U.S. Department of Justice.

Becker, S., & McCorkel, J. (2011). The Gender of Criminal Opportunity: The Impact of Male Co-Offenders on Women's Crime. *Feminist Criminology, 6*(2), 79–110.

Béland, D., & Waddan, A. (2012). *The Politics of Policy Change: Welfare, Medicare, and Social Security Reform in the United States.* Georgetown University Press.

Bell, W. (1965). *Aid to Dependent Children.* Columbia University Press.

Bennett Cattaneo, L., & Goodman, L. A. (2010). Through the Lens of Therapeutic Jurisprudence: The Relationship between Empowerment in the Court System and Well-Being for Intimate Partner Violence Victims. *Journal of Interpersonal Violence, 25*(3), 481–502.

Berman, G., Feinblatt, J., & Glaser, S. (2005). *Good Courts: The Case for Problem-Solving Justice.* New Press.

Bernstein, J. (2013, September 9). Why Labor's Share of Income Is Falling. *New York Times.*

Binswanger, I. A., Redmond, N., Steiner, J. F., & Hicks, L. S. (2012). Health Disparities and the Criminal Justice System: An Agenda for Future Research and Action. *Journal of Urban Health, 89*(1), 98–107.

Binswanger, I. A., Stern, M. F., Deyo, R. A., & Heagerty, P. J. (2007). Release from Prison: A High Risk of Death for Former Inmates. *New England Journal of Medicine, 356*, 157–165.

Bivens, J., Gould, E., Michel, L., & Shierholz, H. (2014). *Raising America's Pay: Why It's Our Central Economic Policy Challenge* [Briefing paper #378]. Economic Policy Institute.

Bivens, J., & Michel, L. (2015). *Understanding the Historic Divergence between Productivity and a Typical Worker's Pay: Why It Matters and Why It's Real* [Briefing paper #406]. Economic Policy Institute.

Bjerk, D. (2017). Mandatory Minimum Policy Reform and the Sentencing of Crack Cocaine Defendants: An Analysis of the Fair Sentencing Act. *Journal of Empirical Legal Studies, 14*(2), 370–396.

Blinder, A. (2009). How Many US Jobs Might Be Offshorable? *World Economics, 10*(2), 41–78.

Blumstein, A., & Beck, A. J. (1999). Population Growth in U.S. Prisons, 1980–1996. *Crime and Justice: A Review of Research, 26*, 17–61.

Blumstein, A., Rivara, F. P., & Rosenfeld, R. (2000). The Rise and Decline of Homicide—and Why. *Annual Review of Public Health, 21*, 505–541.

Blumstein, A., & Rosenfeld, R. (1998). Explaining Recent Trends in US Homicide Rates. *Journal of Criminal Law & Criminology, 88*(4), 1175–1216.

Blumstein, A., & Wallman, J. (2006). The Crime Drop and Beyond. *Annual Review of Law & Social Science, 12*(1), 125–146.

Boo, K. (1997, February 23). Reaching Up for the Bottom Rung. *Washington Post.*

Boo, K. (2003, February). The Black Gender Gap. *The Atlantic, 291*(1), 107–109.

Bourgois, P. (1996). *In Search of Respect: Selling Crack in El Barrio.* Cambridge University Press.

Brayne, S. (2014). Surveillance and System Avoidance: Criminal Justice Contact and Institutional Attachment. *American Sociological Review, 79*(3), 367–391.

Bruder, J. (2018). *Nomadland: Surviving America in the 21st Century.* Norton.

Brundage, V. (2014). Trends in Unemployment and Other Labor Market Difficulties. *Beyond the Numbers: Bureau of Labor Statistics, 3*(25).

Brynjolfsson, E., & McAfee, A. (2011). *Race against the Machine: How the Digital Revolution Is Accelerating Innovation, Driving Productivity, and Irreversibly Transforming Employment and the Economy.* Digital Frontier Press.

Bureau of Economic Analysis. (2020). *Corporate Profits*. https://www.bea.gov/data/income-saving/corporate-profits

Bureau of Labor Statistics. (2017). *US Bureau of Labor Statistics: Databases, Tables & Calculators by Subject*. https://www.bls.gov/data/#employment

Burnside, A., & Schott, L. (2020). *Policy Brief: States Should Invest More of Their TANF Dollars in Basic Assistance for Families*. Center on Budget and Policy Priorities. https://www.cbpp.org/sites/default/files/atoms/files/1-10-17tanf.pdf

Burtless, G. (1986). The Work Response to a Guaranteed Income: A Survey of Experimental Evidence. In A. H. Munnell (Ed.), *Lessons from the Income Maintenance Experiments (Conference Proceedings)* (pp. 22–52). Brookings Institution and Federal Reserve Bank of Boston.

Bushway, S. D., & Paternoster, R. (2009). The Impact of Prisons on Crime. In S. Raphael & M. Stoll (Eds.), *Do Prisons Make Us Safer?* (pp. 119–150). Russell Sage Foundation.

Cain, G. G., & Wissoker, D. A. (1990). A Reanalysis of Marital Stability in the Seattle-Denver Income-Maintenance Experiment. *American Journal of Sociology, 95*(5), 1235–1269.

California Department of Corrections and Rehabilitation. (2013). *Characteristics of Felon New Admissions and Parole Violators Returned with a New Term*. https://www.cdcr.ca.gov/research/wp-content/uploads/sites/174/2021/05/ACHAR_d2013.pdf

Canela-Cacho, J., Blumstein, A., & Cohen, J. (1997). Relationship Between the Offending Frequency (λ) of Imprisoned and Free Offenders. *Criminology, 35*(1), 133–176.

Caputo, R. K. (2011). *U.S. Social Welfare Reform: Policy Transitions from 1981 to the Present*. Springer.

Cassidy, J. (2010). *How Markets Fail: The Logic of Economic Calamities*. Farrar, Straus, & Giroux.

Caulkins, J. P., & Chandler, S. (2006). Long-Run Trends in the Incarceration of Drug Offenders in the United States. *Crime and Delinquency, 52*(4), 619–641.

Center for Health and Justice. (2013). *A National Survey of Criminal Justice Diversion Programs and Initiatives*.

Center for Prison Reform. (2015). *Diversion Programs in America's Criminal Justice System*.

Chaiken, J. M., & Chaiken, M. R. (1982). *Varieties of Criminal Behavior*. RAND.

Chauhan, P., Cerdá, M., Messner, S. F., Tracy, M., Tardiff, K., & Galea, S. (2011). Race/Ethnic-Specific Homicide Rates in New York City: Evaluating the Impact of Broken Windows Policing and Crack Cocaine Markets. *Homicide Studies, 15*(3), 268–290.

Chetty, R., Stepner, M., Abraham, S., Lin, S., Scuderi, B., Turner, N., Bergeron, A., & Cutler, D. (2016). The Association Between Income and Life Expectancy in the United States, 2001–2014. *Journal of the American Medical Association, 315*(16), 1750–1766.

Cicero, T. J., Surratt, H. J., & Kurtz, S. P. (2014). The Changing Face of Heroin Use in the United States: A Retrospective Analysis of the Past 50 Years. *JAMA Psychiatry, 71*, 821–826.

Clausing, K. A. (2013). Who Pays the Corporate Tax in a Global Economy. *National Tax Journal, 66*(1), 151–184.

Clear, T. R. (2007). *Imprisoning Communities: How Mass Incarceration Makes Disadvantaged Neighborhoods Worse*. Oxford University Press.

Clear, T. R., Rose, D. R., Waring, E., & Scully, K. (2003). Coercive Mobility and Crime: A Preliminary Examination of Concentrated Incarceration and Social Disorganization. *Justice Quarterly, 20*, 33–64.

Cobbina, J. (2019). *Hands Up Don't Shoot: Why the Protests in Ferguson and Baltimore Matter, and How They Changed America*. New York University Press.

Cloward, R. A., & Ohlin, L. E. (1960). *Delinquency and Opportunity: A Theory of Delinquent Gangs*. Routledge.

Cohen, M. A. (1998). The Monetary Value of Saving a High-Risk Youth. *Journal of Quantitative Criminology, 14*(1), 5–33.

Comfort, M. (2016). "A Twenty-Hour-a-Day-Job": The Impact of Frequent Low-Level Criminal Justice Involvement on Family Life. *Annals of the American Academy of Political and Social Science, 665*, 63–79.

Congressional Budget Office. (2013). *The Distribution of Major Tax Expenditures in the Individual Income Tax System.* https://www.cbo.gov/publication/43768

Congressional Research Service. (2021). *The Earned Income Tax Credit (EITC): How It Works and Who Receives It* (No. R43805). https://crsreports.congress.gov/

Connor, S. S. (1967). Social Welfare Regulation—The "Man-in-the-House" Rule—Moral and Economic Rationales—Denials of Equal Protection—Contrary to Primary Purpose of the Welfare System. *Harvard Civil Rights–Civil Liberties Law Review, 2*(2), 299–316.

Contreras, R. (2013). *The Stickup Kids: Race, Drugs, Violence, and the American Dream.* University of California Press.

Corman, H., Noonan, K., Reichman, N. E., & Schwartz-Soicher, O. (2006). *Crime and Circumstance: The Effects of Infant Health Shocks on Fathers' Criminal Activity* [Working paper no. 12754]. National Bureau of Economic Research.

Couloute, L., & Kopf, D. (2018). *Out of Prison and Out of Work: Unemployment among Formerly Incarcerated People.* Prison Policy Initiative. https://www.prisonpolicy.org/reports/outofwork.html

Council of Economic Advisers. (2014). *The War on Poverty 50 Years Later: A Progress Report.* Executive Office of the President of the United States, Council of Economic Advisers.

Council of Economic Advisers. (2016a). *Economic Perspectives on Incarceration and the Criminal Justice System.* Executive Office of the President of the United States.

Council of Economic Advisers. (2016b). *The Long-Term Decline in Prime-Age Male Labor Force Participation.* Executive Office of the President of the United States.

Crandall-Hollick, M. L. (2018). *The Earned Income Tax Credit (EITC): A Brief Legislative History* (no. R44825). Congressional Research Service.

Crimmins, E., Preston, S. H., & Cohen, B. (Eds.). (2011). *Explaining Divergent Levels of Longevity in High-Income Countries.* National Academies Press.

Crutchfield, R. D. (2014). *Get a Job: Labor Markets, Economic Opportunity, and Crime.* New York University Press.

Crutchfield, R., & Pitchford, S. R. (1997). Work and Crime: The Effects of Labor Stratification. *Social Forces, 76*(1), 93–118.

Cuddeback, G. S., Scheyette, A., Pettus-Davis, C., & Morrissey, J. P. (2010). General Medical Problems of Incarcerated Persons with Severe and Persistent Mental Illness: A Population-Based Study. *Psychiatric Services, 61*(1), 45–49.

Cullen, F. T., Jonson, C. L., & Nagin, D. S. (2011). Prisons Do Not Reduce Recidivism: The High Cost of Ignoring Science. *Prison Journal, 91*(3, Suppl.), S48–S65.

DaGrossa, J. A. (2018). *The Incapacitation and Specific Deterrent Effects of Responses to Technical Non-Compliance of Offenders under Supervision: Analysis from a Sample of Federal Judicial Districts* [Unpublished doctoral dissertation]. Temple University.

Davies, G. (2006). *Crime, Neighborhood and Public Housing.* LFB Scholarly Publishing.

Day, P. J. (1977). The Scarlet W: Public Welfare as Sexual Stigma for Women. *Journal of Sociology & Social Welfare, 4*, 872–881.

DeLisi, M. (2001a). Extreme Career Criminals. *American Journal of Criminal Justice, 25*(2), 239–252.

DeLisi, M. (2001b). Scaling Archetypal Criminals. *American Journal of Criminal Justice, 26*(1), 77–92.

DeLisi, M. (2006). Zeroing In on Early Arrest Onset: Results From a Population of Extreme Career Criminals. *Journal of Criminal Justice, 34*, 17–26.

DeLisi, M. (2010). The Criminal Justice System Works! *Journal of Criminal Justice, 38*(6), 1097–1099.

DeLisi, M., & Gatling, J. (2003). Who Pays for a Life of Crime? Empirical Assessment of the Assorted Victimization Costs Posed by Career Criminals. *Criminal Justice Studies, 16*(4), 283–293.

Desai, M. A. (2002). *The Corporate Profit Base, Tax Sheltering Activity, and the Changing Nature of Employee Compensation* [Working paper no. 8866]. National Bureau of Economic Research.

Desmond, M. (2018, September 16). Why Work Doesn't Work Anymore. *New York Times Magazine,* 36–41, 49.

Ditton, P. M., & Wilson, D. J. (1999). *Truth in Sentencing in State Prisons.* Bureau of Justice Statistics.

Doleac, J. L., & Hansen, B. (2016). *Does "Ban the Box" Help or Hurt Low-Skilled Workers? Statistical Discrimination and Employment Outcomes for Those with and without Criminal Records* [Working paper no. 22469]. National Bureau of Economic Research.

Drake, E. K., Aos, S., & Miller, M. G. (2009). Evidence-Based Public Policy Options to Reduce Crime and Criminal Justice Costs: Implications for Washington State. *Victims and Offenders, 4,* 170–196.

Driessen, G. (2016). *Spending and Tax Expenditures: Distinctions and Major Programs* (No. R44530). Congressional Research Service. https://crsreports.congress.gov/

Duggan, M., & Imberman, S. (2008). Why Are the Disability Rolls Skyrocketing? The Contribution of Population Characteristics, Economic Conditions, and Program Generosity. In D. Cutler & D. Wise (Eds.), *Health at Older Ages: The Causes and Consequences of Declining Disability among the Elderly.* University of Chicago Press.

Duneier, M. (2000). *Sidewalk.* Farrar, Straus, & Giroux.

Durose, M. R., Cooper, A. D., & Snyder, H. N. (2014). *Recidivism of Prisoners Released in 30 States in 2005: Patterns From 2005 to 2010.* Bureau of Justice Statistics, U.S. Department of Justice.

Duwe, G., & Clark, V. (2013). Blessed Be the Social Tie That Binds: The Effect of Prison Visitation on Offender Recidivism. *Criminal Justice Policy Review, 24*(3), 271–296.

Eason, J. (2017). *Big House on the Prairie: Rise of the Rural Ghetto and Prison Proliferation.* University of Chicago Press.

Eberstadt, N. (2016). *Men without Work: America's Invisible Crisis.* Templeton Foundation Press.

Economic Policy Institute. (2020). *Family Budget Calculator.* https://www.epi.org/resources/budget/

Edin, K., & Lein, L. (1997). *Making Ends Meet: How Single Mothers Survive Welfare and Low-Wage Work.* Russell Sage Foundation.

Edin, K., Lein, L., & Nelson, T. (2002). Taking Care of Business: The Economic Survival Strategies of Low-Income, Noncustodial Fathers. In F. Munger (Ed.), *Laboring Below the Line: The New Ethnography of Poverty, Low-Wage Work, and Survival in the Global Economy* (pp. 125–147). Russell Sage Foundation.

Edin, K., & Shaefer, L. (2015). *$2.00 a Day: Living on Almost Nothing in America.* Houghton Mifflin.

Ehrenreich, B. (2009a, August 9). Is It Now a Crime to Be Poor? *New York Times.*

Ehrenreich, B. (2009b, June 14). Too Poor to Make the News. *New York Times,* WK10.

Eissa, N., & Hoynes, H. (2011). Redistribution and Tax Expenditures: The Earned Income Tax Credit. *National Tax Journal, 64*(2 (part 2)), 689–730.

Ellwood, D. T. (1988). *Poor Support: Poverty in the American Family.* Basic Books.

Fader, J. J. (2013). *Falling Back: Incarceration and Transitions to Adulthood among Urban Youth.* Rutgers University Press.

Fagan, J., & Freemen, R. B. (1999). Crime and Work. *Crime and Justice: A Review of Research, 25*, 225–290.

Falk, G. (2017). *The Temporary Assistance for Needy Families (TANF) Block Grant: A Primer on TANF Financing and Federal Requirements* (No. 7–5700). Congressional Research Service.

Falk, G., Sherlock, M. F., Carter, J. A., & Hughes, J. S. (2019). *The Earned Income Tax Credit (EITC) for Childless Workers* (No. IN11134). Congressional Research Service. https://crsreports.congress.gov

Faricy, C., & Ellis, C. (2013). Public Attitudes toward Social Spending in the United States: The Differences between Direct Spending and Tax Expenditures. *Political Behavior, 36*, 53–76.

Farrell, G., Tseloni, A., Mailley, J., & Tilley, N. (2011). The Crime Drop and the Security Hypothesis. *Journal of Research in Crime and Delinquency, 48*(2), 147–175.

Farrington, D. P., Coid, J. W., & Murray, J. (2009). Family Factors in the Intergenerational Transmission of Offending. *Criminal Behaviour & Mental Health, 19*, 109–124.

Farrington, D. P., Gundry, G., & West, D. J. (1975). The Familial Transmission of Criminality. *Medicine, Science & the Law, 15*(3), 177–186.

Feeley, M. M., & Simon, J. (1992). The New Penology: Notes on the Emerging Strategy of Corrections and Its Implications. *Criminology, 30*(4), 449–474.

Fontenot, K., Semega, J., & Kollar, M. (2018). *Income and Poverty in the United States, 2017*. U.S. Census Bureau. https://www.census.gov/library/publications/2018/demo/p60-263.html

Ford, M. (2015). *Rise of the Robots: Technology and the Threat of a Jobless Future*. Basic Books.

Foster, H., & Hagan, J. (2007). Incarceration and Intergenerational Social Exclusion. *Social Problems, 54*(4), 399–433.

Fraser, N. (1989). *Unruly Practices Power, Discourse, and Gender in Contemporary Social Theory*. University of Minnesota Press.

Fraser, N., & Gordon, L. (1994). A Genealogy of Dependency: Tracing a Keyword of the U.S. Welfare State. *Signs, 19*(2), 309–336.

Fremstad, S., & Vallas, R. (2013). *The Facts on Social Security Disability Insurance and Supplemental Security Income for Workers with Disabilities*. Center for American Progress.

Frey, C. B., & Osborne, M. A. (2013). *The Future of Employment: How Susceptible Are Jobs to Computerisation* [Working paper]? Oxford Martin Program on Technology and Employment, University of Oxford.

Funicello, T. (1993). *Tyranny of Kindness: Dismantling the Welfare System to End Poverty in America*. Atlantic Monthly Press.

Gabor, M. (2014). New College Degree in Hand: Now What? *Monthly Labor Review*.

Gans, H. (1972). The Positive Functions of Poverty. *American Journal of Sociology, 78*(2), 275–289.

Garfinkel, H. (1956). Conditions of Successful Degradation Ceremonies. *American Journal of Sociology, 61*(5), 420–424.

Garland, D. (1996). The Limits of the Sovereign State: Strategies of Crime Control in Contemporary Society. *British Journal of Criminology, 36*(4), 445–471.

Garland, D. (Ed.). (2001). *Mass Imprisonment: Social Causes and Consequences*. Sage.

Garland, D. (2002). *The Culture of Control: Crime and Social Order in Contemporary Society*. Oxford University Press.

Gee, L. C., Gardner, M., & Wiehe, M. (2016). *Undocumented Immigrants' State and Local Tax Contributions*. Institute on Taxation and Economic Policy.

Gellar, A., Garfinkel, I., & Western, B. (2011). Paternal Incarceration and Support for Children in Fragile Families. *Demography, 48*, 25–47.

Ghandnoosh, N. (2018). *Can We Wait 75 Years to Cut the Prison Population in Half?* The Sentencing Project.

Gibson, M., Hearty, W., & Craig, P. (2020). The Public Health Effects of Interventions Similar to Basic Income: A Scoping Review. *The Lancet*, *5*(3), E165–E176.

Gilliom, J. (2001). *Overseers of the Poor: Surveillance, Resistance, and the Limits of Privacy*. University of Chicago Press.

Giordano, P. C., Cernkovitch, S. A., & Rudolph, J. L. (2002). Gender, Crime and Desistance: Toward a Theory of Cognitive Transformation. *American Journal of Sociology*, *107*(4), 990–1064.

Gladwell, M. (2006, February 13). Million-Dollar Murray. *The New Yorker*, *81*(46), 96.

Glaze, L. E., & Maruschak, L. M. (2008). *Parents in Prison and Their Minor Children*. Bureau of Justice Statistics.

Golden, L. (2015). *Irregular Work Scheduling and Its Consequences* [Briefing paper no. 384]. Economic Policy Institute.

Goldin, C., & Katz, L. F. (1998). The Origins of Technology-Skill Complementarity. *Quarterly Journal of Economics*, *113*(3), 693–732.

Goldin, C., & Katz, L. F. (2007). *Long-Run Changes in the U.S. Wage Structure: Narrowing, Widening, Polarizing* [Working Paper 13568]. National Bureau of Economic Research.

Goldin, C., & Katz, L. F. (2008). *The Race Between Education and Technology*. Harvard University Press.

Golub, A. L., & Johnson, B. D. (1997). *Crack's Decline: Some Surprises across U.S. Cities*. National Institute of Justice, U.S. Department of Justice.

Goodwin, L. (1972). *Do the Poor Want to Work? A Social-Psychological Study of Work Orientations*. Brookings Institution.

Goos, M., & Manning, A. (2007). Lovely and Lousy Jobs: The Rising Polarization of Work in Britain. *Review of Economics and Statistics*, *89*(1), 118–133.

Goos, M., Manning, A., & Salomons, A. (2009). Job Polarization in Europe. *American Economic Review*, *99*(2), 58–63.

Goos, M., Manning, A., & Salomons, A. (2014). Explaining Job Polarization: Routine-Biased Technological Change and Offshoring. *American Economic Review*, *104*(8), 2509–2526.

Gordon, L. (1994). *Pitied but Not Entitled: Single Mothers and the History of Welfare*. Harvard University Press.

Gordon, L. (2001). Who Deserves Help? Who Must Provide? *Annals of the American Academy of Political and Social Science*, *577*, 12–25.

Goss, S., Wade, A., Skirvin, J. P., Morris, M., Bye, K. M., & Huston, D. (2013). *Effects of Unauthorized Immigration on the Actuarial Status of the Social Security Trust Funds* (Actuarial note #151). Social Security Administration.

Gottfredson, S. D., & Taylor, R. B. (1998). Community Contexts and Criminal Offenders. In T. Hope & M. Shaw (Eds.), *Communities and Crime Prevention* (pp. 62–82). HMSO.

Gottschalk, M. (2016). *Caught: The Prison State and the Lockdown of American Politics*. Princeton University Press.

Gould, E. (2015). *Poor People Work: A Majority of Poor People Who Can Work Do*. Economic Policy Institute.

Gramlich, J. (2019, April 30). *The Gap between the Number of Blacks and Whites in Prison Is Shrinking*. Pew Research Center. https://pewrsr.ch/2J66aNq

Greenberg, G. A., & Rosenheck, R. A. (2008). Jail Incarceration, Homelessness, and Mental Health: A National Study. *Psychiatric Services*, *59*(2), 170–177.

Greene, J. A., & Schiraldi, V. (2016). Better by Half: The New York City Story of Winning Large-Scale Decarceration While Improving Public Safety. *Federal Sentencing Reporter*, *29*(1), 22–38.

Griffith, R., & Miller, H. (2014). Taxable Corporate Profits. *Fiscal Studies*, *35*(4), 535–557.

Grogger, J., & Willis, M. (2000). The Emergence of Crack Cocaine and the Rise in Urban Crime Rates. *The Review of Economics and Statistics, 82*(4), 519–529.

Guendelsberger, E. (2019). *On the Clock: What Low-Wage Work Did to Me and How It Drives America Insane.* Little, Brown.

Hagan, J., & Foster, H. (2012a). Children of the American Prison Generation: Student and School Spillover Effects of Incarcerating Mothers. *Law & Society Review, 46*(1), 37–69.

Hagan, J., & Foster, H. (2012b). Intergenerational Educational Effects of Mass Imprisonment in America. *Sociology of Education, 85*(3), 259–286.

Hagedorn, J. M. (1998). *People and Folks: Gangs, Crime, and the Underclass in a Rustbelt City* (2nd ed.). Lake View Press. https://www.biblio.com/people-and-folks-by-hagedorn-john-m/work/152960

Hale, G., & Hobjin, B. (2011). *The U.S. Content of "Made in China."* Federal Reserve Bank of San Francisco. http://www.frbsf.org/economic-research/publications/economic-letter/2011/august/us-made-in-china/

Halpern-Meekin, S., Edin, K., Tach, L., & Sykes, J. (2015). *It's Not Like I'm Poor: How Working Families Make Ends Meet in a Post-Welfare World.* University of California Press.

Hannan, M. T., & Tuma, N. B. (1990). A Reassessment of the Effect of Income Maintenance on Marital Dissolution in the Seattle-Denver Experiment. *American Journal of Sociology, 95*(5), 1270–1298.

Hannan, M. T., Tuma, N. B., & Groeneveld, L. P. (1977). Income and Marital Events: Evidence From an Income-Maintenance Experiment. *American Journal of Sociology, 82*(6), 1186–1211.

Hannan, M. T., Tuma, N. B., & Groeneveld, L. P. (1978). Income and Independence Effects on Marital Dissolution: Results from the Seattle and Denver Income Maintenance Experiments. *American Journal of Sociology, 84*(3), 611–633.

Hanushek, E. A. (1986). Non-Labor-Supply Responses to the Income Maintenance Experiments. In A. H. Munnell (Ed.), *Lessons from the Income Maintenance Experiments (Conference Proceedings)* (pp. 106–121). Brookings Institution and Federal Reserve Bank of Boston.

Harcourt, B. E. (2008). *Against Prediction: Profiling, Policing, and Punishing in an Actuarial Age.* University of Chicago Press.

Harding, C. S. (2020). *Patterns of Cross-System Involvement and Factors Associated with Frequent Cycling: The Relationship between Emergency Department Visits and Arrest by Police* [Unpublished doctoral dissertation]. Temple University.

Harding, C. S., & Roman, C. G. (2017). Identifying Discrete Subgroups of Chronically Homeless Frequent Utilizers of Jail and Public Mental Health Services. *Criminal Justice and Behavior, 44*(4), 511–530.

Hardyns, W., & Rummens, A. (2018). Predictive Policing as a New Tool for Law Enforcement? Recent Developments and Challenges. *European Journal on Criminal Policy and Research, 24*(3), 201–218.

Harrington, M. (1962). *The Other America: Poverty in the United States.* MacMillan.

Haugen, S. E. (2009). *Measures of Labor Underutilization from the Current Population Survey* [Working paper no. 424]. Bureau of Labor Statistics, U.S. Department of Labor, Office of Employment and Unemployment Statistics.

Heller, D. (2012, December 1). Higher Education: Not What It Used to Be. *The Economist.*

HELP [US Senate Committee on Health, Education, Labor, and Pensions]. (2012). *For-Profit Higher Education: The Failure to Safeguard the Federal Investment and Ensure Student Success.* https://www.help.senate.gov/imo/media/for_profit_report/Contents.pdf

Henrichson, C., & Delaney, R. (2012). *The Price of Prisons: What Incarceration Costs Taxpayers.* Center for Sentencing and Corrections, Vera Institute of Justice.

Higginbotham, E. B. (1993). *Righteous Discontent: The Women's Movement in the Black Baptist Church*. Harvard University Press.

Hipple, S. (2016). Labor Force Participation: What Has Happened Since the Peak? *Monthly Labor Review*.

Holzer, H. J. (2009). The Labor Market and Young Black Men: Updating Moynihan's Perspective. *Annals of the American Academy of Political and Social Science, 62*, 47–69.

Holzer, H. J., Offner, P., & Sorensen, E. (2005). Declining Employment among Young Black Less-Educated Men: The Role of Incarceration and Child Support. *Journal of Policy Analysis and Management, 24*(2), 329–350.

Holzer, H. J., Raphael, S., & Stoll, M. A. (2006). Perceived Criminality, Criminal Background Checks, and the Racial Hiring Practices of Employers. *Journal of Law & Economics, 49*(2), 451–480.

Hotz, V. J., & Scholz, J. K. (2006). *Examining the Effect of the Earned Income Tax Credit on the Labor Market Participation of Families on Welfare* [Working paper no. 11968]. National Bureau of Economic Research.

House Budget Committee. (2014). *The War on Poverty: 50 Years Later*. https://republicans-budget.house.gov/initiatives/war-on-poverty/

Howard, C. (1997). *The Hidden Welfare State: Tax Expenditures and Social Policy in the United States*. Princeton University Press.

Howard, C. (2007). *The Welfare State Nobody Knows: Debunking Myths about U.S. Social Policy*. Princeton University Press.

Huddleston, W., & Marlowe, D. B. (2011). *Painting the Current Picture: A National Report on Drug Courts and Other Problem-Solving Court Programs in the United States*. National Drug Court Institute.

Hughes, T. A., Wilson, D. J., & Beck, A. J. (2001). *Trends in State Parole, 1990–2000*. Bureau of Justice Statistics, U.S. Department of Justice.

Hum, D., & Simpson, W. (1993). Economic Response to a Guaranteed Annual Income: Experience from Canada and the United States. *Journal of Labor Economics, 11*(1), 263–296.

Hutcherson, D. T. (2012). Crime Pays: The Connection between Time in Prison and Future Criminal Earnings. *Prison Journal, 92*(3), 315–335.

Internal Revenue Service. (2020). *Statistics for Tax Returns with EITC*. https://www.eitc.irs.gov/

Irwin, J. (1985). *The Jail: Managing the Underclass in American Society*. University of California Press.

James, D. J., & Glaze, L. E. (2006). *Mental Health Problems of Prison and Jail Inmates*. Bureau of Justice Statistics.

Johnson, D. S., Rogers, J. M., & Tan, L. (2001, May). A Century of Family Budgets in the United States. *Monthly Labor Review*, 29–45.

Johnson, W. R. (1980). The Effect of a Negative Income Tax on Risk-Taking in the Labor Market. *Economic Inquiry, 18*(3), 395–407.

Jones, L., E., & Michelmore, K. (2018). The Impact of the Earned Income Tax Credit on Household Finances. *Journal of Policy Analysis and Management, 37*(3), 521–545.

Jones, M. R., & Ziliak, J. P. (2019). *The Antipoverty Impact of the EITC: New Estimates from Survey and Administrative Tax Records* (CES 19-14). Center for Economic Studies, U.S. Bureau of the Census.

Kajstura, A., Wagner, P., & Wright, B. (2016). *Counting Incarcerated People at Home in the Census*. Prison Policy Initiative. www.prisonpolicy.org

Kang-Brown, J., Montagnet, C., Schattner-Emaleh, E., & Hinds, O. (2020). *People in Prison in 2019*. Vera Institute of Justice.

Katz, J. (1988). *Seductions of Crime: Moral and Sensual Attractions in Doing Evil*. Basic Books.

Katz, L. F., & Autor, D. H. (1999). Changes in the Wage Structure and Earnings Inequality. In O. C. Ashenfelter & D. Card (Eds.), *Handbook of Labor Economics* (Vol. 3, part A, pp. 1463–1555). Elsevier.

Katz, L. F., & Krueger, A. B. (2016). *The Rise and Nature of Alternative Work Arrangements in the United States, 1995–2015* [Working paper no. 22667]. National Bureau of Economic Research.

Katz, M. B. (1989). *The Undeserving Poor: From the War on Poverty to the War on Welfare.* Pantheon Books.

Kaufmann, M., Egbert, S., & Leese, M. (2019). Predictive Policing and the Politics of Patterns. *British Journal of Criminology, 59*(3), 674–692.

Kehrer, B., & Wollin, C. (1979). Impact of Income Maintenance on Low Birth Weight: Evidence from the Gary Experiment. *Journal of Human Resources, 14*(4), 434–462.

Kennedy, D. M. (1997). Pulling Levers: Chronic Offenders, High-Crime Settings, and a Theory of Prevention. *Valparaiso University Law Review, 31*(2), 449–484.

Kneebone, E., & Murray, C. (2017). Mapping Working Family Tax Credits and Their Anti-Poverty Impact. *Brookings Institution, The Avenue.* https://www.brookings.edu/blog/the-avenue/2017/02/21/mapping-working-family-tax-credits/

Krueger, A. B. (2017). Where Have All the Workers Gone? An Inquiry into the Decline of the U.S. Labor Force Participation Rate. *Brookings Papers on Economic Activity,* 1–59.

Kudlyak, M., Lubik, T., & Tompkins, J. (2011). Accounting for the Non-Employment of US Men, 1968–2010. *Economic Quarterly, 97*(4), 359–387.

Kuznets, S. (1961). *Capital in the American Economy: Its Formation and Financing.* Princeton University Press.

Langan, P. A., & Levin, D. J. (2002). *Recidivism of Prisoners Released in 1994.* Bureau of Justice Statistics.

Lange, S., Rehm, J., & Popova, S. (2011). The Effectiveness of Criminal Justice Diversion Initiatives in North America: A Systematic Literature Review. *International Journal of Forensic Mental Health, 10*(3), 200–214.

La Tourette, J. E. (1965). Potential Output and the Capital-Output Ratio in the United States Private Business Sector, 1909–1959. *Kyklos, 18*(2), 316–332.

Lattimore, P., & Visher, C. (2009). *Assessment of the Serious and Violent Offender Reentry Initiative.* Urban Institute.

Laub, J. H., & Sampson, R. J. (2003). *Shared Beginnings, Divergent Lives: Delinquent Boys to Age 70.* Harvard University Press.

Lee, Helena. (2013, June 4). Why Finnish Babies Sleep in Cardboard Boxes. *BBC News.*

Legislative Analyst's Office. (2009). *Achieving Better Outcomes for Adult Probation.* https://lao.ca.gov/2009/crim/Probation/probation_052909.pdf

Leibman, J. B. (2015). Understanding the Increase in Disability Insurance Benefit Receipt in the United States. *Journal of Economic Perspectives, 29*(2), 123–150.

Leigh, A. (2010). Who Benefits From the Earned Income Tax Credit? Incidence Among Recipients, Coworkers and Firms. *B. E. Journal of Economic Analysis and Policy, 10*(1), 1–41.

Levine, R. A., Watts, H., Hollister, R., Williams, W., O'Connor, A., & Wilderquist, K. (2004). *A Retrospective on the Negative Income Tax Experiments: Looking Back at the Most Innovative Field Studies in Social Policy* [Discussion paper]. U.S. Basic Income Guarantee Network. www.usbig.net/papers/086-Levine-et-al-NIT-session.doc

Levitt, S. D. (2004). Understanding Why Crime Fell in the 1990s: Four Factors That Explain the Decline and Six That Do Not. *Journal of Economic Perspectives, 18*(1), 163–190.

Liedka, R. V., Piehl, A. M., & Useem, B. (2006). The Crime-Control Effect of Incarceration: Does Scale Matter? *Criminology & Public Policy, 5*(2), 245–276.

Link, N. W. (2019). Criminal Justice Debt During the Prisoner Reintegration Process: Who Has It and How Much? *Criminal Justice and Behavior, 46*(1), 154–172.

Link, N. W., & Roman, C. G. (2017). Longitudinal Associations among Child Support Debt, Employment, and Recidivism after Prison. *The Sociological Quarterly, 58*(1), 140–160.

Lino, M. (2011). *USDA Food Plans.* Agricultural Outlook Forum, U.S. Department of Agriculture.

Livingston, J. (2011). *Against Thrift: Why Consumer Culture Is Good for the Economy, the Environment, and Your Soul.* Basic Books.

Livingston, J. (2016). *No More Work: Why Full Employment Is a Bad Idea.* University of North Carolina Press.

Lofstrom, M., & Raphael, S. (2013a). Prison Downsizing and Public Safety: Evidence from California. *Criminology & Public Policy, 15*(2), 349–366.

Lofstrom, M., & Raphael, S. (2013b). *Public Safety Realignment and Crime Rates in California.* Public Policy Institute of California.

Looney, A., & Turner, N. (2018). *Work and Opportunity before and after Incarceration.* Brookings Institution.

Loury, G. C. (2008). *Race, Incarceration and American Values.* MIT Press.

Lowery, A. (2018). *Give People Money: How a Universal Basic Income Would End Poverty, Revolutionize Work, and Remake the World.* Random House.

Lowery, W. (2016). *"They Can't Kill Us All": The Story of the Struggle for Black Lives.* Little, Brown.

Lynch, J. P., & Sabol, W. J. (1997). *Did Getting Tough on Crime Pay* [Crime policy report no. 1]? Urban Institute.

Lynch, J. P., & Sabol, W. J. (2004). Assessing the Effects of Mass Incarceration on Informal Social Control in Communities. *Criminology & Public Policy, 3*, 267–294.

Mai, C., & Subramanian, R. (2017). *The Price of Prisons: Examining State Spending Trends, 2010–2015.* Vera Institute of Justice.

Mallik-Kane, K., & Visher, C. (2008). *Health and Prisoner Reentry: How Physical, Mental, and Substance Abuse Conditions Shape the Process of Reintegration.* Urban Institute.

Manheim, L. M., & Minchilla, M. E. (1978). *The Effects of Income Maintenance on School Performance of Children: Results from the Seattle and Denver Experiments.* Mathematica Policy Research.

Martin, W. G. (2016). Decarceration and Justice Disinvestment: Evidence from New York State. *Punishment and Society, 18*(4), 479–504.

Marx, A., & Peeters, H. (2008). An Unconditional Basic Income and Labor Supply: Results from a Pilot Study of Lottery Winners. *Journal of Socio-Economics, 37*, 1636–1659.

Massoglia, M., & Pridemore, W. A. (2015). Incarceration and Health. *Annual Review of Sociology, 41*, 291–320.

Mauer, M., & Chesney-Lind, M. (Eds.). (2002). *Invisible Punishment: The Collateral Consequences of Mass Imprisonment.* New Press.

Mauer, M., & Ghandnoosh, N. (2014). *Fewer Prisoners, Less Crime: A Tale of Three States.* The Sentencing Project.

Mauer, M., & King, R. S. (2007). *A 25-Year Quagmire: The War on Drugs and Its Impact on American Society.* The Sentencing Project.

Maynard, R., & Crawford, D. C. (1977). *School Performance. Rural Income Maintenance Experiment: Final Report.* Mathematica Policy Research.

Maynard, D. C., & Feldman, D. C. (Eds.). (2011). *Underemployment: Psychological, Economic, and Social Challenges.* Springer.

Maynard, R., & Murnane, R. (1979). The Effects of a Negative Income Tax on School Performance: Results of an Experiment. *Journal of Human Resources, 14*(4), 463–476.

McCord, J. (2003). Cures That Harm: Unanticipated Outcomes of Crime Prevention Programs. *Annals of the American Academy of Political and Social Science, 587*(1), 16–30.

McDaniel, A., DiPrete, T. A., Buchmann, C., & Shwed, U. (2011). The Black Gender Gap in Educational Attainment: Historical Trends and Racial Comparisons. *Demography, 48*(3), 889–914.

McDonald, J. F., & Stephenson, S. P. Jr. (1979). The Effect of Income Maintenance on the School Enrollment and Labor-Supply Decisions of Teenagers. *Journal of Human Resources, 14*(4), 488–495.

McGarry, K. (2013). The Safety Net for the Elderly. In S. Danziger & M. J. Bailey (Eds.), *Legacies of the War on Poverty* (pp. 179–205). Russell Sage Foundation.

McNeill, F. (2018). Mass Supervision, Misrecognition, and the "Malopticon." *Punishment & Society, 21*(2), 207–230.

Men Adrift: Manhood. (2015a). *The Economist, 415*(8940), 21–26.

Mendenhall, R., Edin, K., Crowley, S., Sykes, J., Tach, L., Kriz, K., & Kling, J. R. (2012). The Role of the Earned Income Tax Credit in the Budgets of Low-Income Households. *Social Services Review, 86*(3), 367–400.

Merton, R. K. (1938). Social Structure and Anomie. *American Sociological Review, 3*(5), 672–682.

Merton, R. K. (1957). *Social Theory and Social Structure.* Free Press.

Messner, S. F., Galea, S., Tardiff, K., Tracy, M., Bucciarelli, A., Piper, T. M., Frye, V., & Vlahov, D. (2007). Policing, Drugs, and the Homicide Decline in New York City in the 1990s. *Criminology, 45*(2), 385–414.

Miller, R. J., & Stuart, F. (2017). Carceral Citizenship: Race, Rights, and Responsibility in the Age of Mass Supervision. *Theoretical Criminology, 21*(4), 532–548.

Mishel, L., Bivens, J., Gould, E., & Schierholz, H. (2012). *The State of Working America* (12th ed.). Cornell University Press.

Moffitt, R. A. (2015). The Deserving Poor, the Family, and the U.S. Welfare System. *Demography, 52*, 729–749.

Moffitt, R. A., Phelan, B. J., & Winkler, A. E. (2017). *Welfare Rules, Incentives, and Family Structure* [Working paper no. 21257]. National Bureau of Economic Research.

Moffitt, T. E. (1993). Adolescence-Limited and Life-Course- Persistent Antisocial Behavior: A Developmental Taxonomy. *Psychological Review, 100*(4), 674–701.

Morris, W. (2016). *Useful Work Versus Useless Toil: How We Live and How We Might Live.* LM Publishers.

Mueller-Smith, M. (2015). *The Criminal and Labor Market Impacts of Incarceration* [Working paper]. Department of Economics, University of Michigan. http://sites.lsa.umich.edu/mgms /wp-content/uploads/sites/283/2015/09/incar.pdf

Mullainathan, S., & Shafir, E. (2013). *Scarcity: The New Science of Having Less and How It Defines Our Lives.* Picador.

Mumola, C. C., & Karberg, J. C. (2006). *Drug Use and Dependence, State and Federal Prisoners, 2004.* Bureau of Justice Statistics.

Murphey, D., & Cooper, P. M. (2015). *Parents Behind Bars: What Happens to Their Children?* Child Trends. childrends.org

Murray, C. (1984). *Losing Ground: American Social Policy 1950–1980.* Basic Books.

Nagin, D. S., Cullen, F. T., & Jonson, C. L. (2009). Imprisonment and Reoffending. *Crime and Justice: A Review of Research, 38*(1), 115–200.

National Association of Drug Court Professionals (NADCP). (2012). *Position Statement on Marijuana.* Professionals. https://web.archive.org/web/20180903014841/https://www.nadcp .org/sites/default/files/nadcp/NADCP%20Board%20Position%20Statement%20-%20 Marijuana.pdf

National Center for Education Statistics. (2017). *The Condition of Education 2017*. US Department of Education.

National Conference of State Legislatures. (2021). *Earned Income Tax Credit Overview*. https://www.ncsl.org/research/labor-and-employment/earned-income-tax-credits-for-working-families.aspx

National Institute of Justice. (2006). *Drug Courts: The Second Decade*. https://nij.ojp.gov/library/publications/drug-courts-second-decade

National Institute of Justice. (2013). *Overview of Offender Reentry*. https://nij.ojp.gov/topics/articles/overview-offender-reentry

National Institute of Justice. (2020). *Drug Courts*. https://nij.ojp.gov/library/publications/drug-courts

Newman, K. S. (2000). *No Shame in My Game: The Working Poor in the Inner City*. Vintage and Russell Sage Foundation.

New York State Corrections and Community Supervision. (2016). *Under Custody Report: Profile of Under Custody Population as of January 1, 2016*. www.doccs.ny.gov

Norris, D. R. (2016). *Job Loss, Identity, and Mental Health*. Rutgers University Press.

O'Connor, B. (2004). *A Political History of the American Welfare System: When Ideas Have Consequences*. Rowman & Littlefield.

O'Connor, J. F., & Madden, J. P. (1979). The Negative Income Tax and the Quality of Dietary Intake. *Journal of Human Resources*, 14(4), 507–517.

Office of Family Assistance. (2018). *Temporary Assistance for Needy Families: 12th Report to Congress*. U.S. Department of Health and Human Services, Administration for Children and Families.

Office of Family Assistance. (2020). *Caseload Data (AFDC/TANF)*. U.S. Department of Health and Human Services, Administration for Children and Families. https://www.acf.hhs.gov/ofa

Office of Tax Analysis. (2016). *Average Effective Federal Corporate Tax Rates*. U.S. Department of the Treasury.

Olson, P. (2018). Amazon Just Sparked a Race to Bring Robots to Our Doors. *Forbes*. https://www.forbes.com/sites/parmyolson/2018/01/31/amazon-just-sparked-a-race-to-bring-robots-to-our-doors/?sh=feb665c2b3a2

O'Neill, J. A., Bassi, L. J., & Wolf, D. A. (1987). The Duration of Welfare Spells. *Review of Economics and Statistics*, 69(2), 241–248.

Pager, D. (2003). The Mark of a Criminal Record. *American Journal of Sociology*, 108(5), 937–975.

Pager, D. (2007). *Marked: Race, Crime, and Finding Work in an Era of Mass Incarceration*. University of Chicago Press.

Pager, D., & Karafin, D. (2009). Bayesian Bigot? Statistical Discrimination, Stereotypes, and Employer Decision Making. *Annals of the American Academy of Political and Social Science*, 621(1), 70–93.

Pager, D., Western, B., & Bonikowski, B. (2009). Discrimination in a Low-Wage Labor Market: A Field Experiment. *American Sociological Review*, 74(5), 777–799.

Pager, D., Western, B., & Sugie, N. (2009). Sequencing Disadvantage: Barriers to Employment Facing Young Black and White Men with Criminal Records. *Annals of the American Academy of Political and Social Science*, 623(1), 195–213.

Parks, T. B. (2012). The Unfairness of the Fair Sentencing Act of 2010. *University of Memphis Law Review*, 42(4), 1105–1137.

Petersilia, J. (2009). *When Prisoners Come Home: Parole and Prisoner Reentry*. Oxford University Press.

Pettit, B. (2012). *Invisible Men: Mass Incarceration and the Myth of Black Progress*. Russell Sage Foundation.

Pettit, B., & Western, B. (2004). Mass Imprisonment and the Life Course: Race and Class Inequality in U.S. Incarceration. *American Sociological Review, 69*, 151–169.

Pew Center on the States. (2009). *One in 31: The Long Reach of American Corrections*. https://www.pewtrusts.org/en/research-and-analysis/reports/2009/03/02/one-in-31-the-long-reach-of-american-corrections

Pew Center on the States. (2011). *State of Recidivism: The Revolving Door of America's Prisons*. https://www.pewtrusts.org/en/research-and-analysis/reports/0001/01/01/state-of-recidivism

Pew Charitable Trusts. (2010). *Collateral Costs: Incarceration's Effect on Economic Mobility*. https://www.pewtrusts.org/~/media/legacy/uploadedfiles/pcs_assets/2010/collateralcosts1pdf.pdf

Phelps, M. S. (2016). The Paradox of Probation: Community Supervision in the Age of Mass Incarceration. *Federal Sentencing Reporter, 28*(4), 283–289.

Phelps, M. S. (2018). Ending Mass Probation: Sentencing, Supervision, and Revocation. *Future of Children, 28*(1), 125–146.

Piketty, T., & Saez, E. (2003). Income Inequality in the United States, 1913–1998. *Quarterly Journal of Economics, 118*(1), 1–39.

Piketty, T., Saez, E., & Zucman, G. (2018). Distributional National Accounts: Methods and Estimates for the United States. *Quarterly Journal of Economics, 133*(2), 553–609.

Piquero, A. R., West, V., & Fagan, J. (2006). Neighborhood, Race, and the Economic Consequences of Incarceration in New York City, 1985–1996. In R. D. Perterson, L. J. Krivo, & J. Hagan (Eds.), *The Many Colors of Crime: Inequalities of Race, Ethnicity, and Crime in America*. New York University Press.

Piven, F. F., & Cloward, R. (1971). *Regulating the Poor: The Functions of Public Welfare*. Knopf Doubleday.

President's Commission on Combating Drug Addiction and the Opioid Crisis. (2017). *Report: The President's Commission on Combating Drug Addiction and the Opioid Crisis*. White House.

Project on Student Debt. (2017). *Student Debt and the Class of 2016*. Institute for College Access & Success.

Rengert, G. F. (1996). *The Geography of Illegal Drugs*. Westview Press.

Riddell, C., & Riddell, W. C. (2014). The Pitfalls of Work Requirements in Welfare-to-Work Policies: Experimental Evidence on Human Capital Accumulation in the Self-Sufficiency Project. *Journal of Public Economics, 117*, 39–49.

Robins, P. K. (1985). A Comparison of the Labor Supply Findings from the Four Negative Income Tax Experiments. *Journal of Human Resources, 20*(4), 567–582.

Rodriguez, M. N., & Emsellem, M. (2011). *65 Million "Need Not Apply": The Case for Reforming Criminal Background Checks for Employment*. National Employment Law Project. https://www.nelp.org/publication/65-million-need-not-apply-the-case-for-reforming-criminal-background-checks-for-employment/

Roeder, O., Eisen, L. B., & Bowling, J. (2015). *What Caused the Crime Decline?* Brennan Center for Justice.

Rose, D. R., & Clear, T. R. (1998). Incarceration, Social Capital, and Crime: Implications for Social Disorganization Theory. *Criminology, 36*, 441–480.

Rosin, H. (2012). *The End of Men: And the Rise of Women*. Riverhead Books.

Saez, E., & Zucman, G. (2019). *The Triumph of Injustice: How the Rich Dodge Taxes and How to Make Them Pay*. Norton.

Salkind, N. J., & Haskins, R. (1982). Negative Income Tax: The Impact on Children from Low-Income Families. *Journal of Family Issues, 3*(2), 165–180.

Saloner, B., Parish, K., & Ward, J. A. (2020). COVID-19 Cases and Deaths in Federal and State Prisons. *JAMA, 324*(6), 602–603.

Sampson, R. J., & Laub, J. H. (1993). *Crime in the Making: Pathways and Turning Points Through Life.* Harvard University Press.

Schlosser, E. (2001). *Fast Food Nation: The Dark Side of the All-American Meal.* Houghton Mifflin.

Schmieser, M. (2012). Expanding New York State's Earned Income Tax Credit Programme: The Effect on Work, Income, and Poverty. *Applied Economics, 44*(16), 2035–2050.

Scholz, J. K., & Levine, K. (2001). The Evolution of Income Support Policy in Recent Decades. In S. Danziger & R. H. Haveman (Eds.), *Understanding Poverty* (pp. 193–228). Harvard University Press.

Schrantz, D., DeBor, S., & Mauer, M. (2018). *Decarceration Strategies: How 5 States Achieved Substantial Prison Population Reductions.* The Sentencing Project.

Schumpeter, J. A. (1942). *Capitalism, Socialism, and Democracy.* Routledge.

Schwarz, J. E. (1988). *America's Hidden Success: A Reassessment of Public Policy from Kennedy to Reagan* (Rev. ed.). Norton.

Serrato, J. C. S., & Zidar, O. (2018). The Structure of State Corporate Taxation and Its Impact on State Tax Revenues and Economic Activity. *Journal of Public Economics, 167*, 158–176.

Sevigny, E. L., Pollack, H. A., & Reuter, P. (2013). Can Drug Courts Help to Reduce Prison and Jail Populations? *Annals of the American Academy of Political and Social Science, 647*, 190–212.

Shaffer, D. K. (2011). Looking Inside the Black Box of Drug Courts: A Meta-Analytic Review. *Justice Quarterly, 28*(3), 493–521.

Shannon, L. W. (1991). *Changing Patterns of Delinquency and Crime: A Longitudinal Study in Racine.* Westview.

Shaw, M. (2017). Photos Reveal Media's Softer Tone on Opioid Crisis. *Columbia Journalism Review.*

Sherman, L. W., Gartin, P. R., & Buerger, M. E. (1989). Hot Spots of Predatory Crime: Routine Activities and the Criminology of Place. *Criminology, 27*(1), 27–55.

Shipler, D. K. (2005). *The Working Poor: Invisible in America.* Vintage.

Silver, H. (2007). *The Process of Social Exclusion: The Dynamics of an Evolving Concept* [Working paper no. 95]. Chronic Poverty Research Centre.

Snarr, H. W. (2013). Was It the Economy or Reform That Precipitated the Steep Decline in the US Welfare Caseload? *Applied Economics, 45*, 525–540.

Social Security Administration. (2017). *Annual Report on the Social Security Disability Insurance Program, 2017.*

Social Security Administration. (2021). *Disability Evaluation under Social Security, Part 1: General Information.* https://www.ssa.gov/disability/professionals/bluebook/general-info.htm

Solis, M. (2016). *The Trans-Pacific Partnership: The Politics of Openness and Leadership in the Asia-Pacific* (Order from Chaos: Foreign Policy in a Troubled World). Brookings Institution.

Soper, S. (2011, September 18). Inside Amazon's Warehouse. *The Morning Call.* https://www.mcall.com/news/watchdog/mc-allentown-amazon-complaints-20110917-story.html

Spreen, T. L. (2013). Recent College Graduates in the U.S. Labor Force: Data from the Current Population Survey. *Monthly Labor Review, 136*(2), 3–13.

Standing, G. (2011). *The Precariat: The New Dangerous Class.* Bloomsbury.

Stansfield, R., Mowen, T. J., O'Connor, T., & Boman, J. H. (2017). The Role of Religious Support in Reentry: Evidence From the SVORI Data. *Journal of Research in Crime and Delinquency, 54*(1), 111–145.

Steadman, H. J., Osher, F. C., Robbins, P. C., Case, B., & Samuels, S. (2009). Prevalence of Serious Mental Illness Among Jail Inmates. *Psychiatric Services*, 60(6), 761–765.

Steensland, B. (2008). *The Failed Welfare Revolution: America's Struggle Over Guaranteed Income Policy*. Princeton University Press.

Stemen, D. (2017). *The Prison Paradox: More Incarceration Will Not Make Us Safer*. Vera Institute of Justice.

Sterk, C. E. (1999). *Fast Lives: Women Who Use Crack Cocaine*. Temple University Press.

Storey, J. (1973). Systems Analysis and Welfare Reform: A Case Study of the Family Assistance Plan. *Policy Sciences*, 4, 1–11.

Sullivan, M. L. (1989). *Getting Paid: Youth Crime and Work in the Inner City*. Cornell University Press.

Sundt, J., Salisbury, E. J., & Harmon, M. G. (2016). Is Downsizing Prisons Dangerous? The Effect of California's Realignment Act on Public Safety. *Criminology & Public Policy*, 15, 315–341.

Sykes, J., Kriz, K., Edin, K., & Halpern-Meekin, S. (2015). Dignity and Dreams: What the Earned Income Tax Credit (EITC) Means to Low-Income Families. *American Sociological Review*, 80(2), 243–267.

Sykes, B. L., & Pettit, B. (2014). Mass Incarceration, Family Complexity, and the Reproduction of Childhood Disadvantage. *Annals of the American Academy of Political and Social Science*, 654, 127–149.

Taylor, C. J. (2015a). Gendered Pathways: Differential Effects of Family Support by Gender. *Women and Criminal Justice*, 25(3), 169–183.

Taylor, C. J. (2015b). Recent Victimization and Recidivism: The Potential Moderating Effects of Family Support. *Violence and Victims*, 30(2), 342–360.

Taylor, C. J. (2016). The Family's Role in the Reintegration of Formerly Incarcerated Individuals: The Direct Effects of Emotional Support. *Prison Journal*, 96(3), 331–354.

Taylor, C. J., & Auerhahn, K. (2015). Community Justice and Public Safety: Assessing Criminal Justice Policy through the Lens of the Social Contract. *Criminology & Criminal Justice*, 15(3), 300–320.

Teer, P. (2020). *The Coming Age of Imagination: How Universal Basic Income Will Lead to an Explosion of Creativity*. Unbound.

Tirado, L. (2014). *Hand to Mouth: Living in Bootstrap America*. Penguin.

Torry, M. (2013). *Money for Everyone: Why We Need a Citizen's Income*. Policy Press.

Travis, J., Western, B., & Redburn, S. (2014). *The Growth of Incarceration in the United States: Exploring Causes and Consequences of High Rates of Incarceration*. National Academies Press.

Turney, K. (2018). Adverse Childhood Experiences Among Children of Incarcerated Parents. *Children and Youth Services Review*, 89, 218–225.

UCLA Labor Center. (2016). *Get to Work or Go to Jail: Workplace Rights Under Threat*. UCLA Institute for Research on Labor and Unemployment.

Uggen, C., Larson, R., & Shannon, S. (2016). *6 Million Lost Voters: State-Level Estimates of Disenfranchisement, 2016*. The Sentencing Project.

Uggen, C., & Manza, J. (2002). Democratic Contraction? Political Consequences of Felon Disenfranchisement in the United States. *American Sociological Review*, 67(6), 777–803.

U.S. Department of Agriculture. (2021). *Dietary Guidelines for Americans, 2020–2025*. https://www .dietaryguidelines.gov/sites/default/files/2020-12/Dietary_Guidelines_for_Americans _2020-2025.pdf

Valentine, B. (1978). *Hustling and Other Hard Work: Lifestyles in the Ghetto*. Free Press.

Vaughn, M. G., DeLisi, M., Gunter, T., Fu, Q., Beaver, K. M., Perron, B. E., & Howard, M. O. (2011). The Severe 5%: A Latent Class Analysis of the Externalizing Behavior Spectrum in the United States. *Journal of Criminal Justice*, 39, 75–80.

Venkatesh, S. A. (2006). *Off the Books: The Underground Economy of the Urban Poor*. Harvard University Press.

Visher, C., & Lattimore, P. (2009). *Assessment of the Serious and Violent Offender Reentry Initiative*. Urban Institute.

Wacquant, L. (2001). Deadly Symbiosis: When Ghetto and Prison Meet and Mesh. *Punishment and Society*, 3(1), 95–133.

Waddan, A. (1998). A Liberal in Wolf's Clothing: Nixon's Family Assistance Plan in the Light of 1990s Welfare Reform. *Journal of American Studies*, 32(2), 203–218.

Wagner, D. (2005). *The Poorhouse: America's Forgotten Institution*. Rowman & Littlefield.

Wakefield, S., & Wildeman, C. (2014). *Children of the Prison Boom: Mass Incarceration and the Future of American Inequality*. Oxford University Press.

Warr, P. B. (1987). *Work, Unemployment, and Mental Health*. Oxford University Press.

Watts, H. W., & Rees, A. (1977). *The New Jersey Income Maintenance Experiment: Labor-Supply Reponses* (Vol. 2). Institute for Research on Poverty.

The Weaker Sex: Social Change. (2015b). *The Economist*, 415(8940), 11.

Weaver, V. M., Hacker, J. S., & Wildeman, C. (2014). Detaining Democracy: Criminal Justice and American Civic Life. *Annals of the American Academy of Political and Social Science*, 651, 6–21.

Weil, D. (2014). *The Fissured Workplace: Why Work Became So Bad for So Many and What Can Be Done to Improve It*. Harvard University Press.

Weiss, D. B., & MacKenzie, D. L. (2010). A Global Perspective on Incarceration: How an International Focus Can Help the United States Reconsider Its Incarceration Rates. *Victims and Offenders*, 5(3), 268–282.

Welsh, B. C., Loeber, R., Stevens, B. R., Stouthamer-Loeber, M., Cohen, M. A., & Farrington, D. P. (2008). Costs of Juvenile Crime in Urban Areas: A Longitudinal Perspective. *Youth Violence and Juvenile Justice*, 6(1), 3–27.

West, C., & Zimmerman, D. H. (1987). Doing Gender. *Gender & Society*, 1(2), 125–151.

Western, B., & Beckett, K. (1999). How Unregulated Is the U.S. Labor Market? The Penal System as a Labor Market Institution. *American Journal of Sociology*, 104(4), 1030–1060.

Western, B., Braga, A. A., Davis, J., & Sirois, C. (2015). Stress and Hardship after Prison. *American Journal of Sociology*, 120(5), 1512–1547.

Western, B., & Muller, C. (2013). Mass Incarceration, Macrosociology, and the Poor. *Annals of the American Academy of Political and Social Science*, 647, 166–189.

Western, B., & Pettit, B. (2010). Incarceration and Social Inequality. *Daedalus*, 139(3), 8–19.

Western, B., & Wildeman, C. (2009). The Black Family and Mass Incarceration. *Annals of the American Academy of Political and Social Science*, 621(1), 221–242.

Wiener, R. L., & Brank, E. M. (2013). *Problem Solving Courts: Social Science and Legal Perspectives*. Springer.

Wildeman, C. (2010). Paternal Incarceration and Children's Physically Aggressive Behaviors: Evidence from the Fragile Families and Child Wellbeing Study. *Social Forces*, 89(1), 285–309.

Wildeman, C., & Wakefield, S. (2014). The Long Arm of the Law: The Concentration of Incarceration in Families in the Era of Mass Incarceration. *Journal of Gender, Race, and Justice*, 17(2), 367–389.

Wilkinson, R. G., & Pickett, K. (2009). *The Spirit Level: Why Greater Equality Makes Societies Stronger* (US ed.). Bloomsbury Publishing.

Wilson, D. B., Mitchell, O., & MacKenzie, D. L. (2006). A Systematic Review of Drug Court Effects on Recidivism. *Journal of Experimental Criminology*, 2(4), 459–487.

Wilson, W. J. (1987). *The Truly Disadvantaged: The Inner City, the Underclass, and Public Policy*. University of Chicago Press.

Wilson, W. J. (1997). *When Work Disappears: The World of the New Urban Poor.* Knopf Doubleday.

Wilson, W. J. (2009). *More Than Just Race: Being Black and Poor in the Inner City.* W. W. Norton & Company.

Witte, A. D., & Tauchen, H. (1994). *Work and Crime: An Exploration Using Panel Data* [Working paper no. 4794]. National Bureau of Economic Research.

Wolfgang, M. E., Figlio, R. M., & Sellin, T. (1972). *Delinquency in a Birth Cohort.* University of Chicago Press.

Wright, J. D., & Rossi, P. H. (1986). *Armed and Considered Dangerous: A Survey of Felons and Their Firearms.* Aldine de Gruyter.

Zarkin, G. A., Cowell, A. J., Hicks, K. A., Mills, M. J., Belenko, S., Dunlap, L. J., & Keyes, V. (2012). Lifetime Benefits and Costs of Diverting Substance-Abusing Offenders from State Prison. *Crime and Delinquency, 61*(6), 829–850.

Zatz, N., Koonse, T., Zhen, T., Herrera, L., Lu, H., Shafer, S., & Valenta, B. (2016). *Get to Work or Go to Jail.* UCLA Labor Center.

Zelenev, A. (2011). *Analyzing and Measuring Social Exclusion in the United States* [Unpublished doctoral dissertation]. Yale University.

Zimring, F. E. (2007). Little Changes, Big Results. *New York Times,* CY9.

# INDEX